Queer Livability

Social History, Popular Culture, and Politics in Germany
Kathleen Canning, Series Editor

For a complete list of titles, please see www.press.umich.edu

Queer Livability

German Sexual Sciences and Life Writing

INA LINGE

UNIVERSITY OF MICHIGAN PRESS
Ann Arbor

Published in the United States of America by the
University of Michigan Press
Printed and bound by CPI Group (UK) Ltd, Croydon, CR0 4YY

First published May 2023

A CIP catalog record for this book is available from the British Library.

Library of Congress Cataloging-in-Publication data has been applied for.

ISBN 978-0-472-13306-2 (hardcover : alk. paper)
ISBN 978-0-472-03931-9 (paper : alk. paper)
ISBN 978-0-472-90266-8 (open access ebook)

DOI: https://doi.org/10.3998/mpub.11464019
This work was supported by the Arts and Humanities Research Council and the Cambridge Home and EU Scholarship Scheme (2012–15), the Modern Humanities Research Association (2016-2017) and the Wellcome Trust (2017–2020).

The University of Michigan Press's open access publishing program is made possible thanks to additional funding from the University of Michigan Office of the Provost and the generous support of contributing libraries.

Contents

Digital materials related to this title can be found on the Fulcrum platform via the following citable URL https://doi.org/10.3998/mpub.11464019

Acknowledgments

I am immensely grateful to everyone who has supported me in writing this book. At the University of Michigan Press, my thanks go to my anonymous reviewers, who offered constructive, critical, kind, and uplifting feedback. It has been a pleasure to be in conversation with such brilliant and generous minds, and I hope that my book will meet many more readers like you. My thanks go to Christopher Dreyer and Anna Pohlod at the University of Michigan Press for supporting the project since its beginning. Marcia LaBrenz has been a fantastic production editor and my thanks go to Richard Isomaki for his outstanding copyediting.

Research for this book was partially supported by the Arts and Humanities Research Council and the Cambridge Home and EU Scholarship Scheme (2012–15). I would like to extend my heartfelt thanks to Andrew J. Webber, who shaped my work and took me seriously as a researcher and scholar. Thanks to those who were directly and indirectly involved in the progress of this book during my PhD years at the University of Cambridge: Lucia Ruprecht, David Midgley, Sarah Colvin, Godela Weiss-Sussex, and Heike Bauer. I further developed this work with the help of a Research Scholarship in the Modern European Languages, awarded by the Modern Humanities Research Association (2016-17) and a postdoctoral fellowship on the "Rethinking Sexology" project at the University of Exeter, which was funded by the Wellcome Trust (2017–20). I am grateful to the entire Rethinking Sexology team: Kate Fisher, Jana Funke, Sarah Jones, Jen Grove, and Kazuki Yamada. I could not have asked for a better team of scholars to think (and rethink) with.

For a book that is concerned with readership and reader responses, I am extremely grateful to all those who have read and responded to my writing and drafts over the years. In addition to those mentioned above, I thank Luna Dolezal, Marie Kolkenbrock, Annie Ring, Arthur Rose, Nina Schmidt, Tom

Smith, and Katie Sutton for their kind and constructive feedback. As visiting fellow at the Friedrich Schlegel Graduiertenschule für literaturwissenschaftliche Studien I was able to have conversations with many scholars based in or passing through Berlin, and I am grateful for their generous time and feedback. Over the years, I have presented the research that forms part of this book at the History of Sexuality seminar series at the Institute of Historical Research (January 2016), the History of Medicine seminar series at the University of Exeter (November 2015), the conference "Grenzen der Trans_Konzepte (Limits of Trans_Concepts)" at the University of Tübingen (April 2015), the Queer Cultures Graduate Symposium at Cambridge (February 2015), the German Studies Association conference seminar "Theories of/on Sexual Pathology since 1800" (September 2014), the Department of Germanic Studies at the University of Chicago (June 2014), the interdisciplinary conference "This Is My Body" at Addenbrooke's Hospital/Centre for Research in the Arts, Social Sciences and Humanities (November 2013), the "Crimes of Passion" conference at the University of Münster (July 2013). I am grateful for comments and feedback received at these events.

Both as a postdoctoral fellow at the University of Exeter and in my permanent role as Lecturer in German since 2020 I have had fantastic colleagues whose expertise, research, and support have enriched my work. Thank you to colleagues in the Department of Languages, Cultures and Visual Studies, the Department of English, the Sexual Knowledge Unit, the Centre for Medical History, and the Wellcome Centre for Cultures and Environments of Health. I started my current job during a pandemic lockdown in the UK and I am grateful to the German section at Exeter for making me feel a part of the team during this challenging time.

Writing and research is hard, and I would not have been able to persevere and thrive without the support and encouragement of my *Doktorschwestern* and other kin: Marie Kolkenbrock, Polly Dickson, Annja Neumann, Melisa Trujillo, Denise Henschel, Lizzie Stewart, Katharina Karcher, Annie Ring, Katrina Zaat. Many thanks to Leon Rocha for asking, hey have you heard of this book by N. O. Body? You might find it interesting. I did. My thanks to Juliet Mitchell for giving me work when I desperately needed it. I want to thank Doug Cowie and Kristen Kreider for writing just so many references for me over the years, when they had much more important things to write.

Thank you to my parents who supported me during my studies, even though I did a terrible job of explaining what it is that I do. Thank you, Robin, for everything.

Some sections of this book were first published in different form in the following articles and book chapters: "Gender and Agency between *Sexualwissenschaft* and Autobiography: The Case of N. O. Body's *Aus eines Mannes Mädchenjahren*," *German Life and Letters* 68, no. 3 (2015): 387–405; "Körper, Name, Geschlecht: 'Trans-Investitur' in Erich Amborns *Und dennoch Ja zum Leben*," *Grenzen der Überschreitung: Kontroversen um Transkultur, Transgender und Transspecies*, ed. Stephanie Lavorano, Carolin Mehnert, and Ariane Rau (Bielefeld: transcript, 2016), 93–108; "'Mal etwas Anderes': Narrative Representations of Queer Performance and Commodified Bodies on the Early Twentieth-Century Shop Floor," *Tales of Commerce and Imagination: Department Stores and Modernity in Film and Literature*, ed. Godela Weiss-Sussex and Ulrike Zitzlsperger (Oxford: Peter Lang, 2015), 107–23; "Hospitable Reading: An Approach to Life Writings of Gender and Sexual 'Deviants,'" *Crimes of Passion: Repräsentationen der Sexualpathologie im frühen 20. Jahrhundert*, ed. Japhet Johnstone and Oliver Böni (Berlin: de Gruyter, 2015), 74–92.

List of Abbreviations

Full bibliographical references to these texts are listed in the Bibliography at the end of this book.

DMB *Diary of a Male Bride (Tagebuch einer männlichen Braut)*. All translations of this text are my own. Page numbers refer to the 2010 edition, unless otherwise noted.

LN *Life Nonetheless (Und dennoch Ja zum Leben)*. All translations of this text are my own.

MGY *A Man's Girlhood Years (Aus eines Mannes Mädchenjahren)*. All translations of this text are my own, unless otherwise noted. Page numbers refer to the 1993 edition, unless otherwise noted.

MNI *Memoirs of My Nervous Illness (Denkwürdigkeiten eines Nervenkranken)*. I cite from the following translation throughout: Daniel Paul Schreber, *Memoirs of My Nervous Illness*, trans. and ed. Ida MacAlpine and Richard A. Hunter (New York: New York Review Books, 2000).

List of Abbreviations

Introduction

German Sexual Sciences and Life Writing

I was born as a boy, raised as a girl. The fabric of my life was made of tangled threads until suddenly and with great force the inner nature of my masculinity tore through the veils and half-truths that my education, habits, and the desperate circumstances of my life had spun tightly around me.
    —N. O. Body, *A Man's Girlhood Years*

And so Martin became a part of this world of abnormality and yet secretly yearned to be part of a normal world.
    —Erich Amborn, *Life Nonetheless*

Since then, I have, with full consciousness, written the cultivation of femininity onto my banner and will continue to do so, as far as respect for my surroundings permits; other people . . . may think of me as they wish.
    —Daniel Paul Schreber, *Memoirs of My Nervous Illness*

My father thought there was no reason at all why Anna should not wear boy's clothes to the party. Mademoiselle, on the other hand, contended that it was not seemly for "une jeune fille comme il faut."
    — "The Memoirs of the Wolf-Man," in Muriel Gardiner,
       The Wolf-Man by the Wolf-Man

If you believe that it might be useful to those who are my fellow sufferers if you publish these notes as a whole or parts of it, you can do so.
    —Walter Homann, *Diary of a Male Bride*

A Man's Girlhood Years (*Aus eines Mannes Mädchenjahren*), published in 1907 under the pseudonym N. O. Body, tells the story of Norbert Body (Karl Baer), who was raised as a girl, but grew up to live and be legally recognized as a man. Accompanied by an afterword by sexologist Magnus Hirschfeld, Body's narrative is presented as a truthful account that serves as an educational and cautionary tale about the necessity to speak openly about matters of sex and sexuality. In *Diary of a Male Bride* (*Tagebuch einer männlichen Braut*), the protagonist, Dori, is raised as a boy but later lives and works as a woman. Whereas Body legally transitions, Dori experiences social prejudice and unlivable encounters with medical professionals. *Life Nonetheless* (*Und dennoch ja zum Leben*) narrates the life of Martin/Toni, who was raised as a girl but spends his early adulthood in the 1920s living and working as a man at the Institute of Sexology in Berlin. Daniel Paul Schreber's *Memoirs of My Nervous Illness* (*Denkwürdigkeiten eines Nervenkranken*) tells a complex narrative that outlines the experiences of Judge Schreber with mental illness and their perception of becoming a woman during certain periods. Schreber never met Sigmund Freud, but in 1911 the latter published an article discussing Schreber's memoirs, outlining a case of repressed homosexual desires during adolescence. Finally, the Wolf Man archive goes beyond Freud's analysis of the Wolf Man and spans published and unpublished documents from the 1910s to the 1970s. For Freud, the Wolf Man case was key to the development of his theory of sexuality, but I argue that the longer Wolf Man archive also reveals a trans narrative of the most tentative kind.

These texts and textual archives form the central focus of *Queer Livability: German Sexual Sciences and Life Writing*. Together, they represent the shared characteristics as well as the diversity within sexual-scientific life writing, which engages with developments in early twentieth-century sexual sciences—here considered to include both sexology and psychoanalysis—where modern concepts of sex, gender, and sexuality emerged. Out of this archive, queer and trans voices emerge.[1] This study provides a conceptual framework for analyzing these voices. It argues for the importance of life writing in the formation of sexual subjectivity in the early twentieth century in Germany.

This introduction begins with the voices of sexual-scientific life writers because these autobiographical and semi-autobiographical encounters with sexual-scientific knowledge are the central focus of this book. One of the book's major aims is to approach historical sexual sciences from the point of view of sexual-scientific life writers in order to analyze how normative constraints impact the construction of sexual subjectivity. In doing so, this book contributes to the study of what Benjamin Kahan has called (borrowing a term

---

1. I write about "queer and trans" voices not to imply that these two categories cannot overlap, but to emphasis the presence of trans voices in this archive. I use both transgender and trans interchangeably, which is in line with current scholarly practice. See for example Susan Stryker, *Transgender History* (Berkeley: Seal Press, 2008). Laurie Marhoefer, *Racism and the Making of Gay Rights: A Sexologist, His Student, and the Empire of Queer Love* (London: University of Toronto Press, 2022).

from Stephanie Foote) "vernacular sexology," where life writers write with and against sexual-scientific knowledge to create a sense of sexual subjectivity.[2] *Queer Livability* asks: How do these narratives contain and construct subjectivity with and beyond sexology and psychoanalysis? What does it mean to write autobiographically when one's very identity is at stake? How can we read them on their own terms? By this I mean to suggest that, rather than bracketing out the function, importance, and framing structure of sexology and psychoanalysis, I see as the end point of my analysis not how sexological and psychoanalytic theories and practices develop, but how narratives of gender identity manage to survive and thrive. I argue that these texts not only highlight the contribution of life writing to sexual-scientific knowledge production, but that they also give insight into how queer and trans life writers make sense of themselves through agential self-reflection and creation. In doing so, this book goes beyond the dominant voices of modernism and instead pays attention to the subaltern literary voices of sexological and psychoanalytic patients or interlocutors as literary agents who significantly shaped the emergence of modern sexual and transgender rights politics in Germany.

The driving question of this book is to ask how sexological and psychoanalytic life writings explore the possibilities and impossibilities of a livable life, or a life worth living, even during moments of crisis. In order to answer this question, the five chapters of this study investigate how livability is negotiated via a series of textual strategies, including textual accounts of masking and clothing, an address to a readership, and textual enactments of legal change that were impossible in "real" life, in order to create the possibilities—both real and imagined—of a life worth living. In doing so, the book makes a contribution to a number of disciplines and fields: it introduces little-known textual examples of sexual-scientific life writing to the German studies corpus and curriculum. Consequently, my book also contributes to research in the history of sexuality by showing how the analysis of sexual-scientific life writing can give scholars a deeper insight into the construction of sexual subjectivity during this important period of modern German history. My book furthermore contributes to the medical humanities by arguing that sexual knowledge is established in entangled networks of medico-

---

2. Benjamin Kahan, *The Book of Minor Perverts: Sexology, Etiology, and the Emergences of Sexuality* (Chicago: University of Chicago Press, 2019), 2–3; Stephanie Foote, "Afterword: Ann Aldrich and Lesbian Writing in the Fifties," in Ann Aldrich, *We Walk Alone*, ed. Marijane Meaker (New York: First Feminist Press, 2006), 158. On doing the history of medicine from below, see Roy Porter, "The Patient's View: Doing the History of Medicine from Below," *Theory and Society* 14, no. 2 (1985): 175–98.

scientific discourses and literary writing and thereby evidences the importance of written narrative and autobiography in the construction and critique
of sexual knowledge. Finally, each chapter investigates a textual strategy
employed by sexual-scientific life writing in order to achieve a livable life.
As a result, the book builds a theoretical framework for thinking queer livability in the context of autobiographical writing and thereby contributes to
research in gender and sexuality studies.

This introduction outlines how this study draws on, and intervenes in, current scholarship on the history of sexual sciences, including sexology and psychoanalysis, the case study in history and literature, and the applications of
queer theory to the history of sexuality. It also specifies the broader contributions of this book to investigating the importance of sexual sciences in shaping
sexual subjectivity and a reassessment of the literary accounts of patients or
individuals subjected to sexual-scientific discourses. I argue that listening to
these voices is not only an ethical duty for those interested in LGBTQ+ literature, autobiography, and history, but also enriches scholarly knowledge of the
construction of sexual subjectivity in the first decades of the twentieth century.

1. Queer Livability

Queer Livability: German Sexual Sciences and Life Writing contributes to
research on individual narratives concerned with sexual subjectivity as well as
the study of historical sexual sciences, but most importantly it opens up a third
way to approach these texts: by analyzing the negotiation, achievement, and
failure of a livable life with a focus on the subject in crisis. Although this study
will touch on the agency of the writing self as it influences sexual-scientific
thought in turn, the emphasis is on how sexual-scientific discourses are used
prosthetically to construct a livable life. The central endeavor of this book is to
understand the narrative strategies used by the writing subject to reframe
sexual-scientific discourses in order to achieve a sense of livability. How do
life writings play with fact and fiction to create the possibilities, real or imagined, of a life worth living? It is the ethical impetus underlying this study to
answer this question.

A focus on queer livability as the central methodological framework for
reading sexual-scientific life writing shows the importance of norms in both
constraining and making possible certain forms of living. A concern for livability and an awareness of the threat of an unlivable life runs through the larger
part of Judith Butler's work on gender and its performative nature, as well as

Butler's work on language and violence. The relation of each subject to the norms through which it is shaped and to which it must continue to relate throughout its life is an important one here: "A livable life does require various degrees of stability. In the same way that a life for which no categories of recognition exist is not a livable life, so a life for which those categories constitute unlivable constraint is not an acceptable option."[3] Normative constraints can limit a subject's life to such an extent that life becomes impossible, yet, at the same time, to fall outside any category forecloses the opportunity to be recognized at all. This livability is tangible and real: "Bodies only appear, only endure, only live within the productive constraints of certain highly gendered regulatory schemas."[4] Livability, then, is the result of an embodied positioning with regard to norms that support and protect the subjects they define.

The ability of sexual-scientific life writers to navigate normative constraints is complicated by the fact that norms are far from clear. In their recent study on the role of the norm and normativity in the history of sexuality, *Normality: A Critical Genealogy*, Peter Cryle and Elizabeth Stephens offer a critique of normativity by investigating the "persistent but elusive influence of the normal,"[5] arguing that the normal becomes influential not when its remit is clear, but when it is contested. They intervene in contemporary accounts of the history of the normal, arguing that "often its ubiquity and stringency are taken for granted even as the normal is made an object of critique and identified as a cultural force to be resisted."[6] In line with Cryle's and Stephens's argument, I will show that one of the difficulties for sexual-scientific life writers is that they attempt to use normative accounts of sexual and gendered bodies as a narrative guideline, but that definitions of these powerful norms are not necessarily clear or evident. In this light, livability becomes both more and less contested: more, because it requires compromise, sacrifice, denial; less, because the norm is never obvious or given and is therefore open to change.

Particularly in the case of those who are considered to deviate from the norm, lacking a livable life is a precarious situation to be in. To be unable to find recognition means that one cannot be protected by the law, cannot be loved or grieved, because one's life is no longer recognized as livable. Indeed, for Butler, livability and grievability are often linked to such an extent that the

---

3. Judith Butler, *Undoing Gender* (London: Routledge, 2004), 8.

4. Judith Butler, *Bodies That Matter: On the Discursive Limits of "Sex"* (New York: Routledge, 1993), xi.

5. Peter Cryle and Elizabeth Stephens, *Normality: A Critical Genealogy* (Chicago: University of Chicago Press, 2017), 2.

6. Cryle and Stephens, *Normality*, 6.

words are used interchangeably.[7] Livability thus extends into death, beyond the merely biological fact of life:

> When we ask what makes a life livable, we are asking about certain normative conditions that must be fulfilled for life to become life. And so there are at least two senses of life, the one that refers to the minimum of biological form of living, and another that intervenes at the start, which establishes minimum conditions for a livable life with regard to human life. And this does not imply that we can disregard the merely living in favour of the livable life, but that we must ask . . . what humans require in order to maintain and reproduce the conditions of their own livability. And what are our politics such that we are, in whatever way is possible, both conceptualizing the possibility of the livable life, and arranging for its institutional support? . . . [T]o live is to live a life politically, in relation to power, in relation to others, in the act of assuming responsibility for a collective future.[8]

Butler here points out the close link between livability and its institutional recognition and support, an aspect of livability that will prove to be particularly important in this study. Any negotiation of livability must take note of the existing political and institutional power relations that make life legal, legible, recognizable, and grievable. But livability, here, is precisely not the same as the biological fact of being alive. Accordingly, livability is a potent tool to examine the narrative form of life writing as a life extending beyond death. The difference between the merely living and the livable life lies in the collective nature of livability expressed in a collective responsibility to maintain the possibilities for a livable life. In this study, such collectivity is acknowledged with regard to both the subject studied and the studying subject. The primary sources come together as a community of life writers, but this community passes on responsibilities to the reader, who is called upon to participate in the recognition of queer lives as livable lives. In this sense, this book is as much about the texts as it is about its readers. Via my proposed methodology of hospitable reading, which I develop in Chapter One, I investigate how we might understand these texts today. What critical tools do we have available to read them? What are they asking of us? What action do they require? And what response?

---

7. Judith Butler, *Frames of War: When Is Life Grievable?* (London: Verso, 2009), viii, 180, 184.

8. Butler, *Undoing Gender*, 39.

If queer livability is an embodied as well as epistemological positioning in relation to norms and normative constraints, what happens to the antinormative and transgressive potential that the term "queer" entails? Especially in its linguistic appropriation by German academic discourse, "queer" has had potent results. Although used as a loan word that remains untranslated, it is often also pronounced as a homophone of *quer*, meaning crosswise, or to cut across, which quite aptly describe the queer project and its potential subversion, whether intended or perceived as such.[9] Yet Teresa de Lauretis, credited with coining the term "queer theory" in 1991, soon abandoned the term "queer," arguing that its radical tone had been undermined by having been too easily assimilated by the institutions it was meant to resist. It had become "a vacuous creature of the publishing industry."[10] The works of other influential queer theorists, including Michael Warner, David Halperin, and Leo Bersani, further insist that antinormativity should remain the driving force of queer theory.

The expectation to be radically antinormative or transgressive, however, cannot be met by the sexological and psychoanalytic life writings discussed in this study. For the queer life writers discussed in this book, transgression and subversion of norms are less essential than safety, knowability, and livability. An adequate reading of sexual-scientific life writing requires a queer theoretical approach that focuses on the function of norms and the queer subject's ability to navigate them. Tackling the question of what might become of queer theory if its links to antinormativity were less secure, Robyn Wiegman and Elizabeth A. Wilson explore alternative models for queering normativity. They suggest that "norms are more dynamic and more politically engaging than queer critique has usually allowed," and that we might "encounter normativity on something other than oppositional terms."[11] Heather Love addresses this need for a methodological shift in queer studies by investigating the "queer ordinary," which reveals queer life to be quite as ordinarily attached to social

---

9. For studies that pioneered the discussion of queer theory in German-language academia, see Andreas Kraß, ed., *Queer denken: Gegen die Ordnung der Sexualität* (Frankfurt am Main: Suhrkamp, 2003); Andreas Kraß, ed., *Queer Studies in Deutschland: Interdisziplinäre Beiträge zur kritischen Heteronormativitätsforschung* (Berlin: Frankfurter Kulturwissenschaftliche Beiträge, 2009); AG Queer Studies, ed., *Verqueerte Verhältnisse: Intersektionale, ökonomiekritische und strategische Interventionen* (Berlin: Männerschwarm Verlag, 2009).

10. Teresa de Lauretis, "Habit Changes: Response," in *Feminism Meets Queer Theory*, ed. Elizabeth Weed and Naomi Schor (Bloomington: Indiana University Press, 1997), 316.

11. Robyn Wiegman and Elizabeth A. Wilson, "Introduction: Antinormativity's Queer Conventions," *differences* 26, no. 1 (May 2015): 2.

recognition and a place in the social world as life across the human spectrum.[12] The ordinariness of queer lives described by Love, which is not tied to expectations of radical breaks or disruptions, rejects the trope of queerness as inevitably transgressive. In a similarly critical take on queer transgression, Biddy Martin also warns that normativity might not have been the defining issue for homosexual women around 1900, who were more urgently concerned with the need to access work and education to create new private and public spaces.[13]

Similarly, Emma Heaney unpacks expectations of transfeminine narratives as a "story of a treacherous crossing."[14] Heaney argues that the transgressive narrative of "a woman trapped in a man's body" became the definition of trans femininity during the modernist period despite the fact that many trans women did not in fact identify with this: "Instead of metaphors of being trapped in the wrong body or expression of yearning to change that body, subjects often narrate an understanding of their bodies as female."[15] In my study I remain alert to such externally imposed expectations of queer and trans narratives. I also explore how the particular narrative of transgression, already evident in the epigraphs at the beginning of this chapter, is utilized and repurposed by sexual-scientific life writers themselves in order to achieve a livable life. Accordingly, this study is concerned with the textual performance of queer identity and its role in contributing to livability, the recognition of queer lives as livable lives, and the various ways in which queer practices can thereby be performatively invested with a power that is ordinarily reserved for normative forms and modes of identifications.

2. Queering the Modernist Self

Sexual-scientific life writings are products of a modernist moment that introduced broader social and cultural developments such as individualization, emancipation, an increasing interest in personal identities, and the psychologization of Western society. At the turn of the twentieth century, the nature of writing about the gendered and sexual self went through several significant

---

12. Heather Love, "Doing Being Deviant: Deviance Studies, Description, and the Queer Ordinary," *differences* 26, no. 1 (May 2015): 74–95.

13. Biddy Martin, "Extraordinary Homosexuals and the Fear of Being Ordinary," *differences* 6, nos. 2–3 (Summer–Fall 1994): 100–125.

14. Emma Heaney, *The New Woman: Literary Modernism, Queer Theory, and the Trans Feminine Allegory* (Evanston, IL: Northwestern University Press, 2017), 6.

15. Heaney, *The New Woman*, 155.

changes. Daniel Pick argues that during the late nineteenth century, scientists, writers, and artists became interested in those aspects of life that were hidden from—or rather hidden in—plain sight. The mind was no longer considered as simply organic matter, but expanded into the realm of the unconscious. Conceptualizations of perception expanded to consider one's inner life in the context of broader scientific inquiry into the body and its organic matter.[16] At the same time, Steven Connor argues that, in the early decades of the twentieth century, an understanding of the self as a singular point of view, distinct from the external world, made way for a more fluid model, where "observer-observed duality and distinctions between separated points and planes dissolve."[17] Connor writes that "modernity is identified both with the making and the unmaking of the self,"[18] and so the quintessentially modernist self is open to the world, not alienated from it, but is also now under threat of disintegration. The self has to will itself into being, again and again, in a performative act of self-construction. Connor calls this "the epistemized self which takes itself as an object of self-knowledge."[19] Increasing suspicion of perceptual capabilities means that this knowledge about the self is not self-evident or straightforward. Knowing the self requires a sustained investigation. One form this investigation can take is the form of life writing. As this book will show, sexual-scientific life writing intensively engages in such self-investigation.

Writing during this period offers "a literary site where the complexities of self-experience and the problems of their expression are activated and engaged."[20] As Dennis Brown notes, "It is clear that such literary exploration did not take place in a vacuum: a variety of factors are involved in the phenomenon—most obviously, the general diffusion of social alienation, the rise of the psychoanalytic movement, the disorientation brought about by the shock of the Great War and the increasing experimentalism of almost all the contemporary artistic movements."[21] In this book, I argue that the development of sexual sciences is another major influence on the way in which self-experience and expression changed during the early decades on the twentieth century, with profound consequences for the late twentieth and early twenty-

16. Daniel Pick, "Stories of the Eye," in *Rewriting the Self: Histories from the Renaissance to the Present*, ed. Roy Porter (London: Routledge, 1997), 199.

17. Steven Connor, "The Modern Auditory I," in Porter, *Rewriting the Self*, 207ff.

18. Connor, "The Modern Auditory I," 203.

19. Connor, "The Modern Auditory I," 203.

20. Dennis Brown, *The Modernist Self in Twentieth-Century English Literature: A Study in Self-Fragmentation* (London: Palgrave Macmillan, 1989), 1.

21. Brown, *Modernist Self*, 1.

first centuries. This shifting sense of self-perception was explored in literature as well as the sciences. Scientific, scholarly, and literary explorations of sex, gender, and sexuality developed an interest in a sexual and gendered self that is open to the world of external influences.[22] From Gustav von Aschenbach's queer disintegration in Thomas Mann's *Death in Venice* (1912) to the psychological demise of Else in Arthur Schnitzler's *Fräulein Else* (1924), the crisis of subjectivity experienced by the modernist self is profoundly tied up with experiences of sex, gender, and sexuality. Sexuality and modernity are intricately linked.[23]

Sexology and psychoanalysis, in particular, register this shifting sense of self and bring it into dialogue with new investigations into gender and sexuality. They provide what Nikolas Rose elsewhere calls "experts of experience" that are intricately linked with the way we understand ourselves.[24] Focusing on the psy-sciences, Rose argues that this creates "psychological selves," or what in this study I want to consider as sexual-scientific selves.[25] Like Connor, Rose makes the case that understanding the modernist self as an exercise in individuation has to be supplemented by an understanding of the modernist self as assemblage, where interiority is constructed through its relationship with discursive structures and practices.[26] Sexual-scientific theories of gender and sexuality profoundly shaped a sense of sexual and gender subjectivity, but they also shaped a modern sense of the self.[27] Sexuality is understood to be definitional of the human experience, not a moment in life, but a sustained experience that is framed differently and variously through medico-scientific discourses.

---

22. Benjamin Kahan argues that congenital models of homosexuality were not the dominant representative of sexological thought during the late nineteenth and early twentieth centuries, but that models of homosexuality as acquired were also important during this period and were the subject of serious sexological consideration. See Kahan, *Book of Minor Perverts*.

23. On the relationship between sexuality and modernity, see Benjamin Kahan, "What Is Sexual Modernity?," Print Plus platform of *Modernism/Modernity* 1, no. 3 (October 2016); Harry Oosterhuis, "Sexual Modernity in the Works of Richard von Krafft-Ebing and Albert Moll," *Medical History* 56, no. 2 (2012): 133–55.

24. Nikolas Rose, "Assembling the Modern Self," in Porter, *Rewriting the Self*, 224.

25. Rose, "Assembling the Modern Self," 225.

26. Rose, "Assembling the Modern Self," 225.

27. Katie Sutton makes a similar argument: "Encounters between sexologists and psychoanalysts throughout the first half of the twentieth century had a crucial impact not only on modern understandings of human sexuality, but on modern understandings of the self." Katie Sutton, *Sex between Body and Mind: Psychoanalysis and Sexology in the German-Speaking World, 1890s–1930s* (Ann Arbor: University of Michigan Press, 2019), 2.

Fragmentation and self-fragmentation are crucial aspects of modernist representations of the self.[28] For Brown, selfhood in modernist writing is "pluralist, heterogeneous and discontinuous. . . . Writers represent fragmentary selves, and such representations constitute selfhood as inherently fragmentary . . . 'fragmenting' is used here to express not a fixed conceptualization but an active, exploratory process."[29] Together with Peter Gay's definition of artistic modernism as a preoccupation with the "lure of heresy" and the "commitment to a principled self-scrutiny,"[30] and the influence of sexual sciences on sexual subjectivity, we might understand sexual literary modernism as a form of self-scrutiny and reflection that actively fragments and rebuilds the self in ways that are contrary to orthodox or normative expectations and beliefs.

Self-fragmentation, however, is not necessarily a livable option for all sexual-scientific life writers, whose lives are often already fragmented and thereby made unlivable through exclusion, harassment, or persecution. Instead of using self-fragmentation as a tool for self-exploration, sexual-scientific subjects in crisis might seek to rebuild the self without further fragmentation. At the same time, such fragmented selves can be overlooked by scholarly exploration. Commenting on research in sexuality studies, Benjamin Kahan argues:

> In its methodological focus on fully formed subjects, sexuality studies as a field has not adequately examined the discourses that forged sexual personhood. . . . This has meant both the exclusion of racialized subjects as not fully human, as not people, but also the exclusion of acquired sexual practices and minor perversions that have not crystallized into varieties of personhood or come to be understood as congenital and biologized.[31]

Reading sexual-scientific life writing through the lens of modernism allows us to see subjects who are not, or not yet, "fully formed." Some of the subjects I discuss are subjects in the making, homing in on a particular identity without ever fully inhabiting it. By focusing only on fully formed subjects with a clear sense of a recognized (if pathologized) sexual or gender identity, we run the risk of neglecting documents that deal with identities that do not clearly map onto contemporary identity categories or, importantly, fixed narratives of how sexual or gender subjectivity comes to be recognized by a subject. Similarly,

---

28. Brown, *Modernist Self*, 1.
29. Brown, *Modernist Self*, 1ff.
30. Peter Gay, *Modernism: The Lure of Heresy* (London: Norton, 2008), 3ff.
31. Kahan, *Book of Minor Perverts*, 7ff.

Love detects what she calls an "affirmative bias" in writing about the queer past, which neglects those aspects of queer pasts that are unsavory, unsuccessful, and unhappy in favor of affirmative success stories.[32] If we take the texts discussed in my study seriously as offering an insight into the formation of sexual subjectivity, then these fragmentary life writings are foundational texts of sexual modernity, even—or especially—if they do not present fully formed gender or sexual identities, but focus instead on an emerging sense of subjectivity.

3. Narrating Sexual Subjectivity

Sexual-scientific life writing is a form of writing that emerges out of early twentieth-century scientific discourses about sex, gender, and sexuality. This does not mean that queer and trans individuals did not establish meaningful ways of living and community outside of the medico-scientific context. Subcultures that formed in physical as well as print environments show that community and peer support was of vital importance to queer and trans individuals.[33] Acknowledging the importance of peer support and community over and above the authority of medico-scientific discourse is especially important when thinking, for example, about the complicated role of medical authority in the lives of trans and nonbinary individuals today. However, sexual-scientific knowledge did form a focal point for many queer and trans individuals. Talking specifically about trans people in the early decades of the twentieth century, Sutton argues that sexual-scientific studies were a core part of queer "world-making," where sexual-scientific writing offered a focal point for personal narratives.[34] By focusing on this world-making inherent in life writing and shifting the focus onto narrative strategies for making queer and trans lives livable, this book enriches sexological and psychoanalytic scholarship. Where encounters between sexually and gender-diverse individuals and sexual scientists did

---

32. Heather Love, *Feeling Backward: Loss and the Politics of Queer History* (Cambridge, MA: Harvard University Press, 2007), 4 and 45.

33. See Kirsten Plötz, *Einsame Freundinnen: Lesbisches Leben während der zwanziger Jahre in der Provinz* (Hamburg: MännerschwarmSkript, 1999); Rainer Herrn, *Schnittmuster des Geschlechts: Transvestitismus und Transsexualität in der frühen Sexualwissenschaft* (Gießen: Psychosozial-Verlag, 2005); Katie Sutton, "'We Too Deserve a Place in the Sun': The Politics of Transvestite Identity in Weimar Germany," *German Studies Review* 35, no. 2 (May 2012): 335–54.

34. Sutton, *Sex between Body and Mind*, 179.

take place, sexual-scientific life writing evidences the important work and effort that sexually and gender-diverse writers put into making sexual-scientific discourse work for them. In this context, I analyze how the sexual-scientific life writer can use sexual-scientific encounters to achieve a livable life, despite the difficult, violent, and life-threatening circumstances in which they emerge.

Queer Livability: German Sexual Sciences and Life Writing situates the specificities of sexual-scientific debates in the German-speaking world, where sexual-scientific discourses and life writing come together to co-construct concepts of modern sexual subjectivity. The origin of such sexual-scientific debate can be traced to at least the 1850s, when the discourse around sex shifts away from models of crime toward models of sickness and health. The place of discussions about sex and sexuality is now in forensic medicine, psychiatry, and neurology, disciplines that were developing in the nineteenth century and significantly influenced sexology after 1900, where it drew on endocrinology, genetics, eugenics and venereology. Topics such as health, cure, and the relationship between body and mind continued to form central aspects of sexual-scientific debate. Here sexual knowledge production contributes to the complexity of fin de siècle metropolitan life: it marks advances in medical and scientific thought and also brings a preoccupation with deviance and degeneracy into full view. Rather than a dualistic opposition between scientific Enlightenment and modern cultural decadence, Scott Spector highlights that the sensational and the scientific were intimately tied together in the production of sexual subjectivity.[35]

This particular period in sexual knowledge production encouraged several important shifts in sexual-scientific thought that brought ideas of sex, gender, and sexuality into closer contact with a sense of self and subjectivity. The work of the German-Austrian psychiatrist Richard von Krafft-Ebing is notable here. As Harry Oosterhuis has shown in his study of Krafft-Ebing's *Psychopathia Sexualis*, first published in 1886 and revised many times, Krafft-Ebing "did not consider sexuality to be just a biological instinct; he presented it as something that was inextricably bound up with individual life histories, mediated by experience, and vested with personal meaning. . . . [S]exuality played a core part in the narratives of self and perverse desire was linked to the individual makeup."[36] Krafft-Ebing's study goes beyond understanding sexuality as an instinct tied to

---

35. Scott Spector, *Violent Sensations: Sex, Crime and Utopia in Vienna and Berlin, 1860–1914* (Chicago: University of Chicago Press, 2016).

36. Harry Oosterhuis, *Stepchildren of Nature: Krafft-Ebing, Psychiatry, and the Making of Sexual Identity* (Chicago: University of Chicago Press, 2000), 215.

biological functions of the body and frames sexuality as an all-encompassing sense of self.

This emerging understanding of sexual subjectivity goes hand in hand with Krafft-Ebing's use of the case study as sexological method. *Psychopathia Sexualis* relied on a dialogic exchange between Krafft-Ebing as psychiatrist and the self-accounts of those individuals who recognized themselves in Krafft-Ebing's sexual categories. The use of case studies first emerged in a medical context, where they served to compare symptoms and diseases to reveal patterns in order to improve treatment and diagnosis. For psychiatrists, these case studies also became a currency by which they sought to establish themselves in an emerging field.[37] However, as Oosterhuis persuasively argues, patients or individuals who provided material for case studies in turn influenced the way in which Krafft-Ebing understood and revised his categories in important ways. Whereas Krafft-Ebing began his psychiatric work by considering his patients and case studies as presenting pathologies that deviated from a sexual norm, he progressively altered these views in response to the self-accounts he received. In appearing directly in scientific works, patients' voices were thereby also given a privileged, visible space.[38] Damousi, Lang, and Lewis call this the "narrative turn" in scientific thinking about sex, where an increasing credibility was given to patients' own voices and the writers gained a sense of being an expert on their own sexual and gender identity.[39] As such, nonmedical professionals and patients became "brokers of case knowledge."[40] This scientific "feedback loop" is key to understanding the agency of sexual-scientific life writing and the importance of life writers as contributors to the development of sexual subjectivity.[41]

Arising out of nineteenth-century psychiatry, the new scientific branch of psychology developed into its own distinct medico-scientific discipline that helped to locate sexuality as a foundational aspect of our sense of self. Psychologists understood their discipline as revolutionary, believing that "psy-

---

37. Birgit Lang, Joy Damousi, and Alison Lewis, *A History of the Case Study: Sexology, Psychoanalysis, Literature* (Manchester: Manchester University Press, 2017), 5. See also Ivan Crozier, "Pillow Talk: Credibility, Trust and the Sexological Case History," *History of Science* 46, no. 4 (December 2008): 380.

38. Lang, Damousi, and Lewis, *History of the Case Study*, 5.

39. Lang, Damousi, and Lewis, *History of the Case Study*, 5.

40. Lang, Damousi, and Lewis, *History of the Case Study*, 1.

41. Ian Hacking, "The Looping Effects of Human Kinds," in *Causal Cognition: A Multidisciplinary Debate*, ed. Dan Sperber, David Premack, and Ann James Premack (Oxford: Oxford University Press, 1995).

chology would complete the scientific revolution through applying the scientific method to all aspects of human life. . . . Psychology would replace . . . incomplete and partial knowledges."[42] Arising out of this context of psychology, Sigmund Freud's psychoanalytic method aimed to illuminate the processes of the mind and the absolute importance of sexuality for these processes.[43] For Freud, too, the case study became a primary method. Commenting on Freud's appropriation of the case study, John Forrester describes the case as "combin[ing] two unlikely features: it promotes a new way of telling a life in the 20th century, a new form for the specific and unique facts that make that person's life their life; and at the same time, it attempts to render that way of telling a life public, of making it scientific."[44] The purpose of the case is pulled in two directions; as Andrew Webber notes, "The treatment of cases is always a compromise between the instantiation of general laws and the characteristic singularity that marks them out as exceptional, as lying in part beyond that which they are used to exemplify."[45] The discovery of general laws was certainly important to Freud—Sulloway goes as far as saying that Freud's case studies are guided and shaped to the point of manipulation and distortion, with the aim to prove his psychoanalytic theories.[46] Nonetheless, as Webber points out, they remain as singular stories of a life. Lang and Sutton argue that Freud rethought the case study genre as it was used in earlier sexological thought by shifting the focus from homosexuality as stable, inborn identity to a discussion of desire, repression, universal bisexuality, and uncovering the patient's "more 'authentic' self."[47]

Freud's own self-analysis in *Die Traumdeutung* (*The Interpretation of Dreams*) shows the importance of looking inward and toward the self—as John

---

42. Mikkel Borch-Jacobsen and Sonu Shamdasani, *The Freud Files: An Inquiry into the History of Psychoanalysis* (Cambridge: Cambridge University Press, 2011), 4.

43. Beyond psychology, Freud's psychoanalytic studies were also grounded in evolutionary and developmental biology. Volkmar Sigusch, *Geschichte der Sexualwissenschaft* (Frankfurt am Main: Campus-Verlag, 2008), 60.

44. John Forrester, "If P, Then What? Thinking in Cases," *History of Human Sciences* 9, no. 3 (August 1996): 10.

45. Andrew J. Webber, "The Case Study," in *A Concise Companion to Psychoanalysis, Literature, and Culture*, ed. Laura Marcus and Ankhi Mukherjee, 34–48 (Oxford: Wiley Blackwell, 2014), 43.

46. Frank J. Sulloway, "Reassessing Freud's Case Histories: The Social Construction of Psychoanalysis," *Isis* 82, no. 2 (June 1991): 245–75.

47. Birgit Lang and Katie Sutton, "The Queer Cases of Psychoanalysis: Rethinking the Scientific Study of Homosexuality, 1890s–1920s," *German History* 34, no. 3 (September 2016): 430.

Forrester summarizes, "The founding text of psychoanalysis, its pamphlet and recipe-book all in one, is also an autobiographical document."[48] The psychoanalytic method is based on an exploration of the sexual self through self-reflection and exploration. I am not arguing that Freud's self-conscious self-analysis performs the same function as the case studies that informed sexual-scientific inquiry. But I do want to argue that they both regard an inquiry into the self as an epistemological exercise that can bring forth knowledge. Freud's self-analysis as the origin of the psychoanalytic method shows how autobiographical writing can be foundational and powerful. Furthermore, Freud's *Die Traumdeutung*, despite often being heralded as the first analysis ever completed and conducted by Freud alone, relies on Freud's close colleague, Wilhelm Fliess, as first reader, and, if we follow Forrester's argument, this makes Fliess the analyst of Freud; thus "Freud's readers stand in the position of analysts to Freud."[49] This anticipates the important role that reading and the reception of autobiographical writing holds in the recognition and construction of selfhood, a topic that I will discuss in detail in Chapter 1.

In the preface to the fourth edition (1920) of the *Drei Abhandlungen zur Sexualtheorie (Three Essays on the Theory of Sexuality)*, Freud reminds his readers of "the importance of sexuality in all human achievements."[50] As Stella Sandford argues, "Freud's conception of what he called the *Sexualtrieb* . . . had a role to play in the construction of a general theory of the human being—a philosophical anthropology—that is simply not on his predecessors' intellectual agendas."[51] As Sandford maintains, while Krafft-Ebing conceptualizes sexuality as functional, that is, reproductive and heterosexual, where perversion shows a deviation from this presupposed norm, Freud highlights the diversity of sexual life beyond the strictly reproductive. In his *Three Essays*, he specifically emphasizes that the popular opinion that the *Geschlechtstrieb* is absent in childhood and develops during adolescence with a clear aim of heterosexual reproduction is false.[52] In detaching sexuality from a strict function

---

48. John Forrester, *Dispatches from the Freud Wars: Psychoanalysis and Its Passions* (Cambridge, MA: Harvard University Press, 1997), 140.

49. Forrester, *Dispatches*, 144.

50. Sigmund Freud, *Three Essays on the Theory of Sexuality*, in *The Standard Edition of the Complete Psychological Works of Sigmund Freud*, trans. James Strachey, vol. 7, *1901–1905: A Case of Hysteria, Three Essays on Sexuality and Other Works* (London: Hogarth, 1953), 133.

51. Stella Sandford, "From *Geschlechtstrieb* to *Sexualtrieb*: The Originality of Freud's Conception of Sexuality," in *The Oxford Handbook of Philosophy and Psychoanalysis*, ed. Richard G. T. Gipps and Michael Lacewing (Oxford: Oxford University Press, 2019), 86.

52. Freud, *Three Essays*, 135.

and focusing instead on the development of sexuality and gender identity during infancy, we might say that Freud's psychoanalytic work emphasizes the foundational importance of sex, gender, and sexuality in the development of sexual subjectivity as an important sense of self. As Sandford notes, "Although Freud could not himself be said to have explicitly developed a theory of the subject (the philosophical concept of the subject is quite absent in his writings) readers are at liberty to attempt to construct such a theory as an interpretation of his work."[53] If we cannot speak explicitly of psychoanalysis as proposing a dynamic theory of the subject, we *can* see how such a subject might eventually emerge. Importantly, Freud did not consider sexuality a given, but a developmental process resulting from original bisexuality and a polymorphous perverse disposition and gradually developing into a subject position with a stable object choice.[54] While, as Birgit Lang and Katie Sutton argue, "Freud's early cases . . . refused the singular, conscious narratives of sexual identity typical of sexological case writings,"[55] psychoanalysis was certainly interested in the formation of the psychic self and paved the way for the emergence of the queer subject.

The use of patient testimony as case studies was also central to the work of Magnus Hirschfeld. Hirschfeld was an influential German-Jewish sexologist who wrote prolifically and widely about issues related to gender and sexuality. As sexual rights activist, writer, publisher, and practitioner, Hirschfeld was a prominent public figure in early twentieth-century Germany. In his sexological theories, Hirschfeld attempted to argue for the naturalness of sexual variation. Hirschfeld's lifelong commitment to the legal rights and protection of homosexual men was formalized by the founding of the Wissenschaftlich-humanitäres Komitee (Scientific Humanitarian Committee) in 1897, together with his publisher Max Spohr, the author Franz Joseph von Bülow, and the lawyer Edward Oberg. Although Hirschfeld's approach breaks with nineteenth-century medical discussions of sex in terms of sickness and disease, Hirschfeld's rather different framing of sexual diversity as healthy and natural stems from the late nineteenth-century understanding of sexuality as a form of identity. Case studies were central to highlighting the sexual subjectivity of queer and trans individuals. His approach to the study of sexology was formalized by the foundation of the Institute of Sexology in Berlin (1919-1933), together with colleagues Arthur Kronfeld and Friedrich Wertheim.

---

53. Sandford, "From *Geschlechtstrieb* to *Sexualtrieb*," 99.
54. Freud, *Three Essays*.
55. Lang and Sutton, "Queer Cases of Psychoanalysis," 420.

While concepts of "gender" and "sexuality" were not always separated in turn of the century sexual-scientific discourses, sexologists were increasingly willing to accept such a distinction. New diagnoses of "eonism" and "transvestism" made it possible to move away from older concepts of inversion that combined sexuality and gender, and these diagnoses were taken up by individuals who identified with and shaped such new categories. Psychoanalysts, however, resisted this strict separation. Discussing the case of the Wolf Man (which I discuss in Chapter 5), Freud understands the Wolf Man's neurosis as informed by his latent homosexual attachment to the father. Here, he equates his analysand's "identification with women" with a "homosexual attitude" and thereby conflates the categories of gender and sexuality, implying a link between homosexuality and trans-identification.[56] This separation between gender and sexuality was so contentious that, according to Katie Sutton, "the question of gender identity constituted one of the last significant sites of encounter between sexologists and psychoanalysts in the years following World War I, one that marks an increasingly irreconcilable theoretical and therapeutic divergence between these fields."[57] In spite of these divergences, my book shows that sexual-scientific life writing after 1900, whether it arises out of a psychoanalytic or sexological context, provides materials that show an increasing awareness of trans ways of being, even if expressed only tentatively. Such trans ways of being and writing are not unique to early-twentieth-century Germany, but in this book I show that sexual-scientific life writing provides a particularly articulate and creative engagement with trans subjectivity that allows us to understand the work that goes into making queer and trans life livable at this particular moment in time.

Across different sexological and psychoanalytic approaches, case studies not only bring personal queer and trans narrative into the heart of sexual knowledge production, but also show the importance of narrative and literariness in scientific knowledge production. Sacher-Masoch's *Venus im Pelz* became an important case study in Krafft-Ebing's work, and Freud's psychoanalytic work featured studies of Shakespeare's *Hamlet*, Wilhelm Jensen's *Gradiva*, and the Oedipus myth.[58] This relationship between literary and scientific discourses of

---

56. Sigmund Freud, "From the History of an Infantile Neurosis (1918 [1914])," in *The Standard Edition of the Complete Psychological Works of Sigmund Freud*, trans. James Strachey, vol. 17, *1917–1919: An Infantile Neurosis and Other Works* (London: Hogarth, 1955), 78.

57. Katie Sutton, *Sex between Body and Mind*.

58. Birgit Lang, "The Shifting Case of Masochism: Leopold von Sacher-Masoch's *Venus*

sexuality has been discussed extensively by recent scholarship. Heike Bauer has shown the profound influence both nonprofessional men and women writers had on the development and translation of sexological thinking.[59] Robert Deam Tobin's study *Peripheral Desires* shows that it was literary writings at the periphery of the German-speaking world that brought forth the German discovery of sex.[60] Writing about the journal *Sex and Society* (*Geschlecht und Gesellschaft*, 1905–27), Birgit Lang and Katie Sutton argue that early twentieth-century thinking about sexuality was not solely influenced by scientific and medical discourses, but also by an aesthetic discourse. The authors show that *Sex and Society*, a journal to which both Freud and Hirschfeld contributed, was preoccupied with fine arts and literature. Its canonical content ranged from Renaissance literature to new readings of the Bible in order to promote a progressive reform of sexual ethics.[61]

This whistle-stop tour through the history of sexual sciences and its entanglement with literary and narrative writing not only shows that vibrant debates took place in the German-speaking world, but demonstrates the specificities of these debates. Sexual-scientific inquiries in the German-speaking world eked out a particular understanding of sexuality and gender as central to one's sense of being, not as pathology or crime but as fundamental to a modernist sense of sexual subjectivity. Although many differences exist between sexological and psychoanalytic theories and methods, in this book I want to consider how sexological and psychoanalytic discourses similarly constructed sex, gender, and sexuality as part of a sense of self via sexual-scientific life writing. In her book *Berlin Psychoanalytic*, Veronika Fuechtner goes so far as to describe psychoanalysis and sexology as "twin sciences."[62] Indeed, what she summarizes under

im Pelz (1870)," in Lang, Damousi, and Lewis, *History of the Case Study*. On the connection between Freud's writing with art and literature see, for example, Sander L. Gilman, Jutta Birmele, Jay Geller, and Valerie D. Greenberg, eds., *Reading Freud's Reading* (London: New York University Press, 1994); Sarah Kofman, *Freud and Fiction* (Cambridge: Polity Press, 1991); Graham Frankland, *Freud's Literary Culture* (Cambridge: Cambridge University Press, 2006); Marcus and Mukherjee, *Concise Companion*.

59. Heike Bauer, *English Literary Sexology: Translations of Inversion, 1860–1930* (Basingstoke: Palgrave Macmillan, 2009).

60. Robert Deam Tobin, *Peripheral Desires: The German Discovery of Sex* (Philadelphia: University of Pennsylvania Press, 2015).

61. Birgit Lang and Katie Sutton, "The Aesthetics of Sexual Ethics: *Geschlecht und Gesellschaft* and Middle-Class Sexual Modernity in *Fin-de-Siècle* Germany," *Oxford German Studies* 44, no. 2 (June 2015): 178.

62. Veronika Fuechtner, *Berlin Psychoanalytic: Psychoanalysis and Culture in Weimar Republic Germany and Beyond* (Berkeley: University of California Press, 2011), 8.

the term "Berlin psychoanalytic" is intended to describe "not only 'psycho-analysis' but also a particular interdisciplinary network of intellectuals that included psychoanalysts, psychiatrists, sexual scientists, writers, artists, jour-nalists, and figures who would have described themselves as all of the above—something that was not uncommon in 1920s Berlin."[63] Sigusch describes Freud as a "Pionier der Sexualwissenschaft," a pioneer of sexual science, because he recognized the sexual drive as a definitional human drive.[64] Hirschfeld himself notes: "We can compare the work of psychoanalysts and sexologists to the labor of tunnel workers, who dig their way through a mountain from opposite sides. Provided both dig in the right direction, they will meet one another in the middle."[65] Rather than tracing these tunnels, as other scholars have expertly done, my book acknowledges these subterraneous disciplines as the roots out of which sexual-scientific life writings grow to provide an increasingly com-plex understanding of queer and trans subjectivity.

4. Transgender Life Writing

In this study, I am particularly interested in those life writers who navigate the normative constraints of a gender binary. In order to understand the particular strategies involved in making transgender and nonbinary life in the early twen-tieth century livable, my study specifically draws on and contributes to work in transgender studies. Transgender studies as a field of critical inquiry developed out of or in response to queer theory in the late 1990s, responding to the urgent need to account for the particular positioning and embodiment of transgender or transsexual individuals. Susan Stryker and Paisley Currah elaborate that, in the 1990s, in the infancy of queer theory,

> *Transgender* was press-ganged into service as an avatar of its age: an elas-tic, recategorizable identity; a fluid universal medium with the capacity to absorb and dissolve other categories of personhood, thereby configuring as it flowed new zones of contact that conflicted with more established modes of embodied subjectivization; and a dematerializable and reconsti-tutable embodiment simultaneously everywhere and nowhere at once,

63. Fuechtner, *Berlin Psychoanalytic*, 2.

64. Sigusch, *Geschichte der Sexualwissenschaft*, 59.

65. Magnus Hirschfeld, "Leonardo da Vinci," *Jahrbuch für sexuelle Zwischenstufen* 10 (1909–10): 426.

like the Internet. That was in theory, of course, or perhaps in fantasy, though never in actual practice. Practically speaking, transgender bodies are always somewhere.[66]

Stryker and Currah emphasize that transgender bodies *do* always have a place, a particular body, and are "partial, situated, and concrete."[67] While the body plays a central role in all chapters of this study, it will become evident that the body, here, is not necessarily singular and not necessarily bodily. The Wolf Man experiences various and complicated trans-identifications that can be felt in the body but do not necessarily materialize there. Fantasy and (sexological and psychoanalytic) theory, the very realm to which Stryker and Currah assign transgender as elastic and reconstituted identity, play an important role in placing the trans and nonbinary body in the sexual-scientific life writings selected for this study.

Similar to Stryker and Currah, Jay Prosser, in his study *Second Skins: The Body Narratives of Transsexuality*, draws on gender studies and queer theory, but critically questions why transsexuality continues to be used as an example to illuminate queerness and subversiveness. Instead, Prosser formulates a theory of transsexual embodiment. In an argument as central to his study as it is to my study here, Prosser argues that "transsexuality is always narrative work, a transformation of the body that requires the remolding of the life into a particular narrative shape."[68] With regard to the place of the body, he explains: "My compound 'body narrative' is intended to spin out the broader implications of transsexuality for contemporary theory, to allow transsexuality through its narrative to bring into view the materiality of the body."[69] The body, here, can only become real and become fully comprehended through narrative.

Queer Livability draws on these works in transgender studies, both the broad and inclusive definition of the variety of identifications the term "transgender" might include, and the importance of the body that becomes central to the transgender narrative. Interested as I am in this study in the concealment and masquerade of the body as a productive way to create the body in narrative, I am led to understand the transgender and gender-variant body, as it appears to me in the texts considered here, as a different kind of materiality

---

66. Susan Stryker and Paisley Currah, "General Editors' Introduction," *TSQ* 2, no. 4 (November 2015): 540.

67. Stryker and Currah, "General Editors' Introduction," 540.

68. Jay Prosser, *Second Skins: The Body Narratives of Transsexuality* (New York: Columbia University Press, 1998), 4.

69. Prosser, *Second Skins*, 12.

that is not limited to flesh but nonetheless remains haptic, narrative, discursive, and sartorial.

Transgender studies has also contributed to understanding and challenging the conventions of trans life writing. The special issue "Trans Narratives" in *Auto/biography Studies* discusses trans life writing as a field emerging out of the study of life writing and trans studies. The introduction to the special issue outlines some of the ways in which life writing and transness have come together in intimate but also problematic ways. For example, trans life writing shared a history of problematic intertwinement with medical discourses, the influence of cisgender editors who shift the emphasis on "titillating" details, and the introduction of a legitimizing foreword.[70] These tropes are familiar from early twentieth-century sexual-scientific life writing. However, we have to be careful about considering such recurring narratives as defining features of trans life writing throughout history. As the authors of the special issue show, trans narratives go beyond memoir and engage with other formats, such as performance art. Trans life writing is a complex and varied field, and trans authors are continually challenging its conventions.[71] Accordingly, rather than contemplating how certain narrative patterns constitute a genre of historical trans life writing, this study seeks to show the diversity of textual strategies employed by sexual-scientific life writers in order to create a livable queer life.

Finally, the field of transgender studies is particularly important because it brings up important questions about the archival (in)visibility of transgender identity. In their introduction to the special issue of *Transgender Studies Quarterly* "Archives and Archiving," Stryker and Currah explain the issue as follows:

> *Archive* . . . became a kind of code word cultural scholars could use to signal certain attention to the politics of knowledge production. It meant one was asking meta-level questions pertaining not only to what we can know of the recoverable past but also to how we know it and who can know it, what gaps and elisions the archive might contain, whose lives are deemed worthy of remembrance, and what counts as knowing in the first place.[72]

---

70. Ana Horvat, Orly Lael Netzer, Sarah McRae, and Julie Rak, "Unfixing the Prefix in Life-Writing Studies: Trans, Transmedia, Transnational," *Auto/biography Studies* 34, no. 1 (May 2019): 1–17.

71. Horvat et al., "Unfixing the Prefix," 5.

72. Stryker and Currah, "General Editors' Introduction, 539ff.

It is the central aim of this study to make visible a small but meaningful number of sexological and psychoanalytic life writings that have hitherto only been considered in a fragmentary fashion, without any real dedication to their importance as the documents of gender-variant subjects—that is, to access this partial but significant archive of texts and bestow upon it the academic attention it deserves.

Although I make the case that "queer," "transgender," and "nonbinary" are useful terms of analysis for the study of sexological and psychoanalytic life writing, they are by no means synonyms. Rather, I use these terms to account for the various forms of sexual subjectivity that take place within my textual archive. The life writers I examine would not have understood themselves as "queer," "transgender," and "nonbinary," but might have had access to different terms. For example, two concepts that became increasingly meaningful during the period studied are "cross-dressing" and "transvestism"/ "transvestitism". Both terms are not identical but overlap in usage. To some, "transvestism" denotes a process of transitioning toward a gender perceived to be truer than the one assigned at birth, to others it might refer to the experience of temporary or periodic "cross-dressing." In today's usage, these terms are often considered offensive and hurtful. In this book, I use these terms when the writers discussed make use of them or when they provide a framework through which a piece of life writing can be understood in its historical context. In doing so, I do not mean to claim that the historical term "transvestite" is the equivalent of the contemporary term transgender. By using historical terminology I acknowledge that forms of identity are always historically situated. But by drawing connections between historical and contemporary terminology, it is my intention here to open up these texts to multiple readings and to open up the opportunity to claim these texts as belonging to multiple histories and forms of identification. Anne Linton thoughtfully examines the history of "hermaphroditism" in nineteenth century France through stories of individuals who resisted "true sex" narratives, and shows how both intersex and transgender rights movements today are rooted in this common history.[73] As Laura Doan argues, "What queer teaches us is that no matter how many new words we invent, none will ever adequately capture the commonalities, contradictions, and confusions of sexual subjects; simply put, according to

---

73. Anne E. Linton, *Unmaking Sex: The Gender Outlaws of Nineteenth-Century France* (Cambridge: Cambridge University Press, 2022).

Sedgwick's first axiom, 'people are different from each other.'"[74] As new terms and categories of identity and belonging emerge, new readings of the texts discussed in this book will be welcomed.

In practical terms, however, some clarification on the use of language has to follow. The majority of works were published under a nom de plume or simply by shortening the author's name to initials. This obfuscation of identity complicates the understanding of authorship. These pseudonyms are evidently chosen as a means of concealment or protection, for example from criminal law. The confessional status of life writing can then also be understood in a criminally inflected sense. But the choice of pseudonym that accompanies these narratives and protects the author's identity is often telling. Take, for example, a text called *Urningsliebe* (*Uranian Love*), published in 1930, whose authors calls herself O. Liebetreu.[75] The courtly name "Liebetreu"—literally "faithful love"—for a woman who sacrifices her own freedom to save the woman she loves from imprisonment, ensuring her safe return to husband and child, is a pseudonym loaded with meaning. Not only does the pseudonym protect the author and her married lover from discovery and harm (her lover dies, but her family remains protected from shame), but to associate the term "Uranian love" (*Urningsliebe*) with faithful love also casts a positive light on same-sex love, which, in the case of women, was not punishable by law, but was certainly bound up with social sanctions and pathologization.

This issue of naming also poses another question on the level of method: which names or pronouns do I refer to when speaking about such narratives? The use of gendered pronouns is highly problematic in the context of these narratives, as it inevitably inflicts a certain injustice on the protagonists, whose complex gender identities often defy consistent naming. I will use the pronouns used in the texts by the narrators to describe themselves, if available. In cases where no clear pronoun is given, I use a pronoun that respects the subject's presentation. Where gender identity is more ambivalently expressed or is unclear, I use they/them pronouns. Like Jen Manion in *Female Husbands* and Anne Linton in *Unmaking Sex*, I use gender-neutral pronouns to represent and honor, within the language available to me today, the identity and self-descriptions of historical life writers.[76]

---

74. Laura Doan, *Disturbing Practices: History, Sexuality, and Women's Experience of Modern War* (Chicago: University of Chicago Press, 2013), 51.

75. O. Liebetreu, *Urningsliebe: Aus den Erlebnissen einer gleichgeschlechtlich Liebenden* (Leipzig: Fickers, 1930).

76. Jen Manion, *Female Husbands: A Trans History* (Cambridge: University of Cambridge Press, 2020). Linton, *Unmaking Sex*.

Throughout this study, I will refer to the pseudonyms or initials that sign the narratives, rather than the identities that may have been revealed since publication. This is because, as pointed out in the example of Liebetreu, such pseudonyms can tell us much about the reason for writing, the desired audience, and much more. The decision to refer to pseudonyms is also guided by the ethical demand of these texts and the wish to honor the author's desire for anonymity by refraining from the violence of unmasking. But there is another reason, too: such large, externally imposed revelations distract from the subtle staging of revelatory acts that take place within all of these narratives. This, in turn, poses another question: how is it possible to take a closer look at narratives whose pseudonymous author-figure refuses such closeness or intimacy? What kind of analysis can they bear? This requires a methodological approach that acknowledges pseudonymous or anonymous author-identities as a meaningful second face or mask fashioned by the writing self. This will be developed into a methodology of hospitality in the first chapter of this study. And indeed, the double trope of concealment/revelation or masking/unmasking and the function of the name as carrier of meaning will form a central part of my analysis in all five chapters of this study.

5. The Limits of Sexual-Scientific Life Writing

Comprising a large variety of texts, from diaries, memoirs, letters, conversations, interviews, confessions, biographies, and autobiographies to published or unpublished material written in the first or third person, life writing is not strictly limited to the factual recounting of a life but is attentive to narrative aspects of and influences on the telling of a specific life. In a consideration of the kind of writing at the intersection with medico-scientific discourses about sexuality that this study is concerned with, the term "life writing" is deliberately broad so as to accommodate the various creative and narrative outlets that allow the telling of such a life. Life writing is not quite a genre but rather an evolving collective term that acknowledges the variety of narrative forms, the desires for varying levels of publicity and publication, and the hybrid combinations of fact and fiction necessary to produce life writings. And it acknowledges, too, the emergence of a community of life writers, as different as they may be. Finally, the term "life writing" also acknowledges the double function of these texts as both a documentation of self, and the process of writing this self into existence at the moment of composition. Here life is written into existence.

The selection of these texts is "symptomatic rather than comprehensive."[77] They are not meant to give a comprehensive overview of German-language, sexual-scientific life writing in the first few decades of the twentieth century, but rather symptomatically show the various methods employed by life writers to describe the construction of sexual subjectivity. I am not aiming to uncover general laws of sexual-scientific life writing, but rather I am investigating the particular and situated demands of a selection of sexological and psychoanalytic life writings in order to show the various textual strategies they engage in creating a livable queer life. By including two texts that discuss events that took place during the first three decades of the twentieth century but were published later than that (*Und dennoch Ja zum Leben* and the Wolf Man archive), I make explicit that sexual-scientific discourses had a lasting impact on sexual-scientific life writing across the twentieth century.

Although this corpus covers both sexological and psychoanalytic life writings, there is a marked difference in the scholarly responses to these texts. As Jana Funke notes, "If readings of Freudian case histories tend to come down in favour of literary analysis, the literary dimension of sexological case histories is often ignored."[78] The same holds true for sexological and psychoanalytic life writings. Whereas Schreber's memoirs have become a canonical piece in psychoanalytic scholarship and Freud's analysis with the Wolf Man sparked long-standing discussion in psychoanalytic circles and beyond, the three examples of sexological life writings selected for this study have received much less scholarly attention. Although *Life Nonetheless* and *Diary of a Male Bride* have been noted by historians in the German-speaking world, no attention has been given to them in the study of literature or in English-speaking scholarship.[79] Neither of them has been translated into English. Because these five narratives are juxtaposed in one study, the richness in scholarly discussions of some of these texts can inform my discussion of the lesser-known cases. At the same time, my study offers new readings of the more canonical cases, for example

---

77. Timothy Morton, *Ecology without Nature: Rethinking Environmental Aesthetics* (Cambridge, MA: Harvard University Press, 2007), 5.

78. Jana Funke, "The Case of Karl M.[artha] Baer: Narrating 'Uncertain' Sex," in *Sex, Gender and Time in Fiction and Culture*, ed. Ben Davies and Jana Funke (London: Palgrave Macmillan, 2011), 141.

79. Rainer Herrn and Jens Dobler have done extensive work on Magnus Hirschfeld's Institut für Sexualwissenschaft, his archive, and his sexological thought. Both have also approached sexological life writings from a historical perspective. See, for example, Rainer Herrn, "Ge- und erlebte Vielfalt—Sexuelle Zwischenstufen im Institut für Sexualwissenschaft," *Sexuologie* 20, nos. 1–2 (2013): 6–14; Jens Dobler, afterword to Walter Homann, *Tagebuch einer männlichen Braut* (Hamburg: Männerschwarm, 2010).

by reading the Wolf Man archive as a transgender narrative of the most tentative kind (Chapter 5).

Despite my efforts to focus on sources that go beyond dominant or privileged discourses, my selection of texts reveals crucial blind spots. By focusing on written sources, this book necessarily excludes individuals who did not write autobiographically. Being a writer requires time, ability, and, where texts are published, a publishing industry interested in the writing thus produced. Such a position of privilege and public interest was foreclosed to many, notably on the grounds of class or race. Where individuals who experience marginalization based on these characteristics do write, these characteristics are often obscured in writing to avoid further exclusion. In N. O. Body's memoirs, for example, the protagonist presents himself as French Catholic, but research has shown that the author was Jewish. This narrative veiling of Jewish identity is enacted in direct response to prevalent antisemitic stereotypes, where Jewishness is associated with effeminacy and diminished masculinity, an issue that I will discuss in Chapters 2 and 3. This shows the need to pay attention to absences and gaps in the text, which is difficult and often impossible. It also draws attention to the larger gaps in the archive of sexual-scientific life writing, which excludes other marginalized groups, including writers of color, those living with disabilities, or those on low or no income struggling to stay alive each day.

Despite these inevitable blind spots, *Queer Livability: German Sexual Sciences and Life Writing* brings together a body of texts and textual archives that illuminate the intersection between life writing and sexual knowledge production in the early twentieth century. The scholarly value of these texts is not that they show us how life writing influences sexology and psychoanalysis, but that they give us an insight into how queer and trans subjects in the early twentieth century made sense of themselves in livable ways via the mode of sexual-scientific life writing. It is this life writing that forms the main focus of my study, in which I ask: what are the conditions of writing made possible by sexology and psychoanalysis and what can be said under these conditions to create a livable life, whether real or imagined? The concept of livability will serve as a structuring narrative arc throughout the following five chapters. Rather than following a chronological order, the chapters in this studies are structured by themes and according to the textual strategies employed to express gender and sexual subjectivity. The works I investigate imagine and create conditions for a livable life under difficult circumstances. Strategies such as masking and clothing, ritualistic and performative crossings between genders, and hiding and concealment are central in this part of the investigation.

The first chapter develops an ethical methodological approach to the literary analysis of sexual-scientific life writings. This "hospitable" approach to reading shifts the focus from the reader's authority to the narrative's claim. With this shift from reader to narrative in mind, I analyze the texts' precarious genre ascription, which often falls somewhere between autobiography and fiction. Taking engagements with autobiographical theory into consideration, I ask: What might a text achieve by way of a claim to authenticity? Which literary strategy might be encoded in this generic affiliation? The chapter shows that the primary texts of this study employ a textual performance on the level of genre that expresses an address to a readership that calls for recognition of queer and trans lives as a condition of queer livability.

In the second chapter, I show how agency enters the complicated relationship between life writing and the medico-scientific context in which it arises by studying the exemplary case of N. O. Body's *A Man's Girlhood Years*. I analyze the circulation of the narrative in sexual-scientific publications and the relationship between sexual-scientific knowledge, practice, and technique and Body's narrative, investigating how each might provide prosthetic support for the other, with the aim to investigate the agency of the life writer in navigating narrative and sexual-scientific discourse. Here I borrow the prosthetic metaphor from disability studies and cultural theory, where it has been rethought from passive support of a normative body to the productive but also often painful relationship between body and prosthesis. I suggest that N. O. Body's memoirs process and incorporate sexology's methodological and ideological impact through literary and linguistic crafting that highlights the creative and idiosyncratic agency of the writing self. I conclude that Body's narrative is a documentation of his agency: a literary, strategic positioning that takes those systems that imposed themselves on the individual—social structures, scientific discourse, and legal power—as a prosthetic support that an embodied subject may rely on but can nonetheless engage with critically, creatively, and actively.

The third chapter compares *A Man's Girlhood Years* with *Diary of a Male Bride*. In this chapter, I analyze how visual, haptic, and contextual concealment and masquerade can be considered through the concept of the frame, with reference to Judith Butler. I will ask: how does the frame's focus on and exclusion of certain aspects of queer life contribute to but also complicate how we might understand queer livability in the early twentieth century? In the first section of this chapter, I will analyze how the queer body is framed in the encounter between sexual-scientific practitioner and patient by drawing on research on early twentieth-century medico-scientific photography, which literally as well as epistemologically frames the body. In the second part, I will investigate how contextual framing functions in the specific realm of commerce and commodification in the fashion and department store after 1900. In both contexts, I argue that, by manipulating the narrative frame in such a way that it is grasped, framed, and staged according to normative gender expectations, the writing subject achieves a sense of livability.

The fourth chapter examines Erich Amborn's *Life Nonetheless* and Daniel Paul Schreber's *Memoirs of My Nervous Illness*. The theoretical framework of this chapter builds on Eric Santner's study of "investiture" in the Schreber case, that is, the performative power of social and legal rites and procedures whereby a social status is awarded. I reconsider this concept of investiture to describe the investiture of gender transgression, or what I call *trans*-investiture. This trans-investiture, I reveal, relies on the *Umschreibung* (transcription) of the new gender status in the documents of law and state. Yet difficult and often impossible barriers had to be overcome in order to be granted this *Umschreibung*. Consequently, unlawfully invested trans identities and names could be withdrawn by figures of authority at any time. This chapter, however, argues that the narrative itself forms an *Umschreibung*, a textual performance of trans-investiture. Accordingly, I show that the act of writing allows the queer self to substitute lawful *Umschreibung* with its own account of trans-investiture and thereby create a livable life in narrative form. Tracing this process, the chapter reveals the importance of life writing in pointing out the requirements, but also the limits, of a livable, recognizable life.

The fifth and final chapter examines the textual archive of the Wolf Man, one of Freud's most famous patients. This chapter considers Freud's case alongside newly released archival material in the form of autobiographical interviews with Pankejeff from the Freud Collection at the Library of Congress. I will present three interrelated readings of the Wolf Man archive that unsettle Freud's mastery of the case material by reading the Wolf Man archive as a trans narrative of the most tentative kind. My first reading focuses on images of the veil, caul, and hood in the Wolf Man archive. Whereas Freud understands the veil as separating the Wolf Man from the world, in this chapter I examine the veil as accoutrement of gender experimentation and expression of sexual subjectivity that mediates and regulates the Wolf Man's queer livability. My second reading reveals the importance of the Wolf Man's sister, Anna, as queer figure. My final reading explores the importance of vision, the gaze, and witnessing in the performance of a trans-invested self in the context of the sexual-scientific encounter. By way of rehearsing, again and again, the Wolf

Man's trans-invested performance, the Wolf Man archive ultimately presents a textual performance of the logic of trans-investiture and reveals the requirements, but also the limitations, of achieving a livable queer life. This shows a principle that holds across the corpus of textual testimonies under review in this study: that life writings do not simply transcribe cases, but in fact create the possibilities for a livable life.

CHAPTER I

Hospitable Reading

Autobiography, Readership, and Ethics in Sexual-Scientific Life Writing

This chapter examines the importance of the reader, or an imagined readership, in sexual-scientific life writing. The very process of writing sexual scientific life writing implies a dialogic encounter with sexologists, psychoanalysts, and their theories and practices. Sexual-scientific life writers might be sexological patients or otherwise engage with sexual-scientific discourses, terminology, or theories in a quasi-confessional encounter that Michel Foucault describes as a primary mode for the formation of sexual subjectivity.[1] Foucault acknowledges the importance of a presence or *virtual* presence of a partner who receives this confession:

> The confession is . . . a ritual that unfolds within a power relationship, for one does not confess without the presence (or virtual presence) of a partner who is not simply the interlocutor but the authority who requires the confession, prescribes and appreciates it, and intervenes in order to judge, punish, forgive, console, and reconcile.[2]

This partner to whom a confession is addressed might be overtly disciplining and authoritative by judging and punishing the confessant, but might also offer (no less authoritative) forgiveness, consolation, or reconciliation.

The confessional appeal of sexual-scientific life writing had wider repercussions, beyond the medical realm. Sexual-scientific life writing published in

---

1. Michel Foucault, *The History of Sexuality*, vol. 1, *The Will to Knowledge*, trans. Robert Hurley (London: Penguin, 1998).

2. Foucault, *The Will to Knowledge*, 61–62.

the early decades of the twentieth century also appealed to a wide readership because it claimed to give full and honest accounts of unusual lives and thus implicated its readers as confessors. *A Man's Girlhood Years* and *Diary of a Male Bride*, the two narratives that will form the main focus of this chapter, were reviewed widely in medico-scientific and literary publications and both went through several editions in quick succession.[3] This, and the fact that *A Man's Girlhood Years* inspired two films with almost identical titles in 1912 and 1919, shows the appeal such stories had, not only for a professional audience but also for a popular readership and audience.[4] Sexual-scientific life writing appealed to those with a professional interest in sexual and gender expression, those who identified with the desires, categories, and identification discussed, and finally also a broad readership who saw these memoirs as titillating accounts of unusual lives, as is suggested by the sensationalist title.[5] The self-declaration of such texts as autobiographical and truthful was a determining factor for this complex interest.

With the National Socialists' rise to power, popular autobiographical accounts by sexological or psychoanalytic patients and many sexual-scientific publications were banned as part of a sustained and devastating attack on queer and trans lives.[6] A renewed interest in reading and studying sexual-scientific

3. For the scientific and popular reception of *A Man's Girlhood Years*, see Hermann Simon, "Wer war N. O. Body?," in N. O. Body, *Aus eines Mannes Mädchenjahren* (Berlin: Edition Hentrich, 1993). For *Diary of a Male Bride*, see Jens Dobler, "Nachwort," in Walter Homann, *Tagebuch einer männlichen Braut* [Diary of a Male Bride] (Hamburg: Männerschwarm Verlag, 2010).

4. The 1912 film is called *Aus eines Mannes Mädchenzeit*. A copy of the film is held at the Stiftung Deutsche Kinemathek. The 1919 version is called *Aus eines Mannes Mädchenjahren* and is only loosely based on Body's memoirs. However, the title strongly suggests that the audience of 1919 was also familiar with the 1907 memoirs. At the time of writing, this film is considered lost. See Simon, "Wer war N. O. Body?," 180.

5. Herman Simon mentions several reviews of Body's book that give prominence to Body's gender transformation and focus on titillating details of the queer relationship between Body (before legal recognition as male) and his girlfriend. Hermann Simon, "N. O. Body – Karl M. Baer", in N. O. Body, *Aus eines Mannes Mädchenjahren*, ed. Hermann Simon (Berlin: Hentrich & Hentrich, 2022), 150–54.

6. One list published in 1935 in the journal *Die Bücherei*, the magazine of the Reich Office for Libraries, includes all literature on sex education and sexual enlightenment and names Hirschfeld in particular. See Staatliche Landesfachstelle für Volksbüchereiwesen Sachsen, "Richtlinien für die Bestandsprüfung in den Volksbüchereien Sachsens," *Die Bücherei: Zeitschrift der Reichsstelle für das Volksbüchereiwesen* 2, no. 6 (1935): 279. The same year, the Reich Ministry of Public Enlightenment and Propaganda published its "list of damaging and undesirable writing," which bans all works by Freud and Hirschfeld and some

life writing and a significant rediscovery of historical sexual sciences arose in the 1980s in West Berlin, most notably through the Magnus Hirschfeld Society, where activists, historians, and literary scholars became the new readership for early sexual-scientific life writing. Since this reinvigoration of the study of historical and literary sexology, life writing and its correlatives, namely the case study, autobiography, and patient testimony, have again become the focus of discussion, and examples of historical life writing, including *A Man's Girlhood Years* and *Diary of a Male Bride*, were republished once more. Scholars of historical sexual sciences have investigated the particular relationship between "confessor" and "confessant," by highlighting the potentially abusive relationship that develops, but also, and more frequently, by highlighting the emancipatory potential that emerges in this relationship. Harry Oosterhuis has shown how sexologist Richard von Krafft-Ebing's patients (or confessant) were not simply subjected to sexual-scientific power, but in turn influenced the way in which Krafft-Ebing understood and revised the categories of gender and sexuality in important ways.[7] Similarly, Klaus Müller examines autobiographies of those embracing the sexual-scientific category of the male homosexual. Here Müller discusses sexual-scientific discourses as both repressive and emancipatory.[8] Such readings, although they offer a critique of the disciplining power of the confession, also highlight the transformative potential of having or gaining an audience or readership.

In this chapter, I examine the enduring confessional mode of sexual-scientific life writing as an appeal to a reader, whether real or imagined. I analyze how such a textual address to a readership might implicate later readers and critics. As I will argue in this chapter, this is important because the address and appeal to a readership of sexual-scientific life writing endures across time and thus asks for a response, even if such a response takes place decades or centuries later. Accordingly, this chapter takes Foucault's discussion of confession in the virtual presence of another as a point of departure to investigate how the asynchronous critic and reader of early twentieth-century sexual-scientific life writing is implicated in the text. It thereby examines what

---

of Iwan Bloch's works. This list also includes *Tagebuch einer männlichen Braut*. See Reichsschrifttumskammer, *Liste des schädlichen und unerwünschten Schrifttums* (Berlin: Reichsdruckerei, 1935).

7. Harry Oosterhuis, *Stepchildren of Nature: Krafft-Ebing, Psychiatry, and the Making of Sexual Identity* (Chicago: University of Chicago Press, 2000).

8. Klaus Müller, *Aber in meinem Herzen sprach eine Stimme so laut: Homosexuelle Autobiographien und medizinische Pathographien im neunzehnten Jahrhundert* (Berlin: Rosa Winkel, 1991).

the reader and critic's responsibility, authority, and disciplinary power might be, even over a century later.

If confessional writing constructs a truth that significantly shapes sexual subjectivity through authorship, then what is the role of the person—whether real or imagined—who receives the confession? What ethical ways of listening and responding are implied? I offer a theorization of the confessional address of sexual-scientific life writing that will develop the methodological framework for the chapters that follow. I develop this methodology of reading by discussing, first, how the tension between fact and fiction has been central in critical discussions about autobiography; second, how ethical criticism might be employed to solve this tension; and, finally, how autobiographical theory and ethical criticism can be synthesized into what, with Derrida in mind, I call "hospitable reading," which welcomes the sexual-scientific text with radical openness. In order to analyze how queer livability is established in sexual-scientific life writing, as is the central aim of this study, this first chapter therefore moves at the threshold between reader and text, analyzing the address and call for response presented in sexual-scientific life writing in order to set the terms for the textual analysis conducted across the following four chapters.

1. "Real Experiences and Nothing Was Made Up": The Problem with Autobiography

In 1907, two German-language narratives were published that each told the story of a person who (temporarily or permanently) transitioned away from the gender assigned at birth. *Aus eines Mannes Mädchenjahren* (*A Man's Girlhood Years*), written under the pseudonym N. O. Body, describes the life of Nora Body, who is raised as a girl and transitions to become legally recognized as Norbert Body in early adulthood. *Tagebuch einer männlichen Braut* (*Diary of a Male Bride*) was published anonymously with only the name of the editor, Walter Homann, revealed. It relates the story of Dori, whose appearance, desire and behavior is continually called out as at odds with their ascribed male identity.[9] In what appear to be confessional autobiographies, both first-person nar-

---

9. It is not clear which pronoun is most appropriate for Dori. "He" denies Dori any female identification. "She" never appears in the text as a pronoun used to describe Dori and also risks obscuring how identifications as *Homosexueller* and *Urning* that are mentioned in the text indicate that Dori's account vacillates between gender and sexual identification (DMB 68). Instead, I will use the pronoun "they" throughout. This should not be confused with an understanding of Dori as nonbinary. Here "they" is used to postpone and avoid the assign-

rators recount their experiences of gender and sexual identity that are very different from those of their peers.

In his preface to the original publication of *A Man's Girlhood Years* in 1907, German author Rudolf Presber draws the reader's attention to the fact that this book contains "real experiences and nothing was made up." (MGY 2). Body's text, thus introduced, confirms: "This book is a book of truth" (MGY 8). Similarly, *Diary of a Male Bride* declares in its title the diaristic mode of writing. In the preface, Walter Homann describes the narrative as "a true depiction of life, where nothing has been omitted and nothing has been added" (DMB 7). Both narratives insist that they speak nothing but the truth without adding fictional elements. In both cases, this claim seems to comply with the definition of autobiography used by the French theorist and leading figure of the field of autobiography studies, Philippe Lejeune, which he uses as a starting point for further remarks on autobiographical writing. Here autobiography is understood as a "retrospective prose narrative written by a real person concerning his [*sic*] own existence, where the focus is his [*sic*] individual life, in particular the story of his [*sic*] personality."[10] Lejeune goes on to argue that any autobiography thus written constitutes an "autobiographical pact" between writer and reader, where writers signal truthfulness by using their name as writer, narrator, and protagonist, or by implying truthfulness in the title (e.g., by adding the words "memoir" or "autobiography" to the title).[11] It is under this condition of truth-claiming that autobiography can be distinguished from the autobiographical novel, which does not make such unequivocal claims.[12]

Both *Diary of a Male Bride* and *A Man's Girlhood Years* claim to be truthful accounts. In sexological circles, *Diary* was understood by some as a successful and serious autobiographical account of the life of a homosexual.[13]

---

ment of a clear gender. This is not a perfect solution, but I believe it is more appropriate to leave gender assignment open in this way than to ascribe a male or female gender.

10. Philippe Lejeune, "The Autobiographical Pact," in *On Autobiography*, trans. Katherine Leary, ed. Paul John Eakin (Minneapolis: University of Minnesota Press, 1989), 4. As Carole Allamand emphasizes, this is a dictionary definition of autobiography that Lejeune uses to frame his actual contribution to the study of autobiography, namely the autobiographical pact. Carole Allamand, "The Autobiographical Pact, Forty-Five Years Later," *European Journal of Life Writing* 7 (2018): CP51.

11. Lejeune, "The Autobiographical Pact."

12. In her chapter on N. O. Body's memoirs, Geertje Mak already notes that Body's introductory claim can be understood as an autobiographical pact. See Geertje Mak, *Doubting Sex: Inscriptions, Bodies and Selves in Nineteenth-Century Hermaphrodite Case Histories* (Manchester: Manchester University Press, 2012), 212.

13. Dobler, "Nachwort," 166.

One review echoes the book's introductory statement that nothing had been omitted or falsely added.[14] Others were less convinced and saw the book as part of a fad of autobiographical writing, a mere copy of N. O. Body's commercially successful memoirs.[15] The rather sensationalist reference to the male bride in the title refers to an event from 1906 that was discussed in various German newspapers at the time: Dina Alma de Paradeda, whom Magnus Hirschfeld later called a prime example of homosexual transvestitism, committed suicide out of fear that their fiancé, a male teacher from Breslau, would discover that Paradeda was assigned male at birth. In sensationalist newspaper reports about the tragedy, Paradeda was referred to as "die männliche Braut," the male bride.[16] Hirschfeld claimed to have known Paradeda personally and to have seen her perform at one of Berlin's many *Homosexuellenbälle*.[17] In 1906, the newspaper *Berliner Tageblatt* asked Hirschfeld for his opinion on the case of the male bride. In his response, Hirschfeld characterizes Paradeda as a man who is female in character and is therefore attracted to men and enjoys wearing women's clothing. Hirschfeld distinguishes these from men who enjoy wearing women's clothing as a fetish and are otherwise attracted to women. As Jens Dobler notes, this distinction is the basis for Hirschfeld's monograph *Die Transvestiten: Eine Untersuchung über den erotischen Verkleidungstrieb* (*Transvestites: The Erotic Desire to Cross-Dress*), published four years later in 1910.[18]

Despite sexological readings of *Diary* as autobiographical, the publication history of the text reveals inconsistencies that make the text incompatible with the generic definition of autobiography outlined by Lejeune. In 1907, *Tagebuch einer männlichen Braut: Die Geschichte eines Doppelwesens* (*Diary of a Male Bride: The Story of a Double Creature*) was published with Walter Homann's name appearing as editor.[19] The narrative is framed by various paratexts, that is, elements of a publication that are situated on the threshold of the text and that communicate how a text is to be read.[20] The main narrative is

---

14. Dobler, "Nachwort," 167.
15. Dobler, "Nachwort," 167–68.
16. Dobler, "Nachwort," 154.
17. Dobler, "Nachwort," 170.
18. Dobler, "Nachwort," 171–72.
19. This 1907 version was republished in 2010 by Männerschwarm Verlag (Berlin) under the title *Tagebuch einer männlichen Braut* with Walter Homann listed as author. Throughout this chapter I will make reference to this version.
20. Gérard Genette and Marie Maclean, "Introduction to the Paratext," *New Literary History* 22, no. 2 (Spring 1991): 261. See also Gérard Genette, *Paratexts: Threshold of Interpretation*, trans. Jane E. Lewin (Cambridge: Cambridge University Press, 1997).

introduced by a preface by Walter Homann, followed by a suicide letter signed "Dein blonder Dori" ("Your blond Dori"), and a final commentary on this signed "W. H." All three serve to support the autobiographical claim of Dori's narrative. However, looking at the various republications of the narrative, we find this claim is put into doubt. When *Diary of a Male Bride* was taken up by different publishers, it was republished in varying editions, sometimes anonymously, sometimes with Homann as editor. But a very early version of the text, which is now apparently lost, listed Homann as author, leading Dobler to draw the conclusion that this might have been the original version of *Diary*, then titled *Tagebuch eines Geächteten, von einem der an Liebe starb* (*Diary of an Outlaw, by Someone Who Died of Love*).[21] Dobler shows that several of Homann's other publications – mostly novellas – featured topics of homosexuality and cross-dressing. Homann was also familiar with Berlin's gay clubs and participated in meetings of the Scientific Humanitarian Committee.[22] Homann's profession as writer could support the claim that *Diary of a Male Bride* is a fictionalized account of what he saw in Berlin. On the other hand, the addition of a letter signed by Homann to Dori's account could be understood as a distancing device employed by Homann to avoid any assumption that Dori might indeed be a fictionalized account of his own experiences, fears and hopes (as presented, for example, in Dori's suicide and Homann-as-editor's call for compassion). In any case, the changing attribution of authorship, from Homann to an anonymous author and back to Homann, puts the autobiographical pact between reader and writer into serious doubt.

Despite this paratextual ambiguity, it would be too simple to dismiss the narrative as a "fake" autobiography. Writing about the appeal of fake memoir, Leigh Gilmore writes that "drawing a bright line between fiction and nonfiction and placing memoir firmly on the side of nonfiction fails to address the ongoing appeal of certain kinds of stories and the identificatory desire they elicit."[23] The existence of multiple reviews of the text, as mentioned above, shows that Paradeda's fate is likely to have provided one such story that appealed to a diverse readership of heterosexual and cisgendered readers as well as queer and trans readers. Dori's narrative shows a certain openness to multiple forms of gender and sexual identification by making use of various categories of gender and sexuality, from "Uranian" to "homosexual" and mem-

---

21. Dobler, "Nachwort," 165.

22. Dobler, "Nachwort," 162.

23. Leigh Gilmore, "Learning from Fakes: Memoir, Confessional Ethics, and the Limits of Genre," in *Contemporary Trauma Narratives: Liminality and the Ethics of Form*, ed. Susana Onega and Jean-Michel Ganteau (Abingdon: Routledge, 2014), 23.

ber of the "third sex" (DMB 58, 68, 7). Homann himself, if he is to be considered an author figure of some kind, might have filtered his own personal experiences through Paradeda's story.

The 2010 edition adds an additional paratextual frame: following the narrative is a summary of the text's divergence from previous editions, as well as an afterword by Dobler. The 2010 version depicts on the cover a photograph of Dina Alma de Paradeda and announces Homann once more as author, not editor. Dobler's epilogue includes a historical overview of the various publications of the text and Homann's life. This most recent publication of Dori's narrative, then, cannot be classified straightforwardly as either a novel or an autobiography: although it puts Homann back on the cover as author, it also depicts Dina Alma de Paradeda, merging ideas of Homann as the author of a fictitious text and Paradeda as autobiographer in spirit, coauthor, or collaborator. This paratextual information reveals the reader's desire for an author figure, here answered and visualized in the form of a photograph of Paradeda. Both the question of the text's genre status and the question of authorship—ultimately unresolved—thus construct other forms of the "double creature" suggested by the 1907 subtitle. Its publication history and the marketing strategies employed merge autobiography and novel, Paradeda and Homann, into a hybrid narrative, or performance of sorts, that certainly complicates Lejeune's autobiographical definition (to which I will return).

N. O. Body's *A Man's Girlhood Years* is similarly ambiguous in its identification of author and genre. First published in 1907, the narrative is framed by various paratexts: an original editorial preface, written by Rudolf Presber, and an afterword, written by Hirschfeld. Presber, Hirschfeld, and Body all assure their readers that the text is an autobiography that contains nothing but the truth. In 1993, the text was republished. Here an additional paratextual frame is added, namely a brief editorial preface and a longer afterword, both by historian Hermann Simon. In the afterword, Simon acts as literary detective to reveal the "real" Norbert Body to be Martha, later Karl, Baer. Uncovering Baer's social and cultural milieu and political engagement, Simon's work furnishes the narrative with a historical backdrop, but also highlights the divergence of certain details in the book from actual events; Baer, for example, was not French Catholic, as claimed in the narrative, but of Jewish origin.[24]

In his very brief introduction, Simon foreshadows his findings and promises that he can "reveal the secret," thus suggesting that he believes his bio-

---

24. Simon, "Wer war N. O. Body?," 180.

graphical outline to complete the otherwise unfinished autobiography and, in a way similar to *Diary of a Male Bride*, positing the narrative somewhere between fact and fiction.[25] Simon's disclosure of Body's private life shows Body to be in breach of Lejeune's autobiographical pact. Similarly, Sander Gilman's introduction to the English translation of Body's memoirs states that "'N. O. Body' is a most appropriate pseudonym for Karl M. Baer . . . [f]or being 'nobody' was his way of seeing his body. . . . But it is 'nobody' that Odysseus tricks the Cyclops into answering when asked who has harmed him. . . . In his autobiography, Baer is simultaneously the clever trickster but also the damaged giant."[26] If we follow Simon's and Gilman's analyses, it seems that Body's narrative breaks the autobiographical pact.

In the most recent republication of the text, the name Karl M. Baer is now attributed to the main narrative and the text is introduced by an additional foreword by Christina von Braun, which situates the text in gender and Jewish studies.[27] It is followed by an updated historical essay by Hermann Simon, in which he justifies that unlike the early twentieth century, we no longer have inhibitions to speak about sex and that the revelation of further biographical data about Body can help us tell fact from fiction. His call to investigate Body's medical history is answered in the following essay by Marion Hulverscheidt, who traces medico-scientific discussions of Baer to understand if the "minor surgery" claimed to have taken place in the narrative did indeed take place and in what form. A short but thorough essay by Konstanze Plett then analyses the historical legal context of Baer's amended birth certificate. All three essays seek to extend and contextualize Body's narrative, wavering between taking seriously the text's claims and feeling called upon to supplement and correct its veiled claims.

How, then, can we take seriously the repeated autobiographical claims of both texts if they appear to enter into an autobiographical pact with their readers, but also fail to meet expectations one would bring to autobiographical writing? Lejeune's autobiographical pact appears at first glance as a formalist description of autobiography as genre. However, Carole Allamand argues that Lejeune continually reviewed his understanding of the autobiographical pact, which sought to complicate his initial thought on autobiography as concerned

---

25. Hermann Simon, preface to *Mädchenjahren*, no continuous pagination.

26. Sander Gilman, "Whose Body Is It, Anyway? Hermaphrodites, Gays, and Jews in N. O. Body's Germany," in N. O. Body, *A Man's Maiden Years*, trans. Deborah Simon (Philadelphia: University of Pennsylvania Press, 2006), vii.

27. N. O. Body, *Aus eines Mannes Mädchenjahren*, ed. Hermann Simon (Berlin: Hentrich & Hentrich, 2022).

with identity, proper name, and the contractual relationship between reader and writer. Identity became a particular talking point as Lejeune developed his theories at a time when social-constructivist ideas around identity emerged: is identity expressed in autobiography, or is autobiographical writing the means by which identity is being shaped in the first place? Allamand suggests that Lejeune's later thoughts on the autobiographical pact do not in fact imply "a hypothetical subjective unity."[28]

As a closely related point, Allamand argues that Lejeune's radical contribution to the study of autobiography was to treat "reference as a question of reading, not writing," shifting the focus from truth-value of the narrative to the ways in which a reader may understand such autobiographical claims.[29] Lejeune writes:

> *Textually*, I begin from the position of reader: it is not a question of starting from within the mind of the author, which indeed poses a problem, nor is it one of establishing the canons of a literary genre. By taking as the starting point the position of the reader, (which is mine, the only one I know well), I have the chance to understand more clearly how the texts function (the differences in how they function) since they were written for us, readers, and in reading them, it is we who make them function.[30]

He furthermore notes that "the problematic of autobiography proposed here is thus not grounded on a relationship, established from the outside, between the extratextual and the text . . . but upon analysis, on the global level of *publication* of the implicit or explicit contract proposed by the *author* to the *reader*."[31] Lejeune thereby shifts the emphasis away from extratextual information and away from the author's mind, intention, or identity, to a "reader-based poetics of autobiography" by emphasizing the relationship that is established between autobiographical writing and the reader.[32] Allamand traces how Lejeune remains critical of his pact, which he replaces with the less contractual idea of an autobiographical commitment. Here the contractual nature of the pact is replaced with a performative act, where self-presentation and self-conception are not just verifiable facts of autobiographical writing, but are performatively established.[33]

---

28. Allamand, "Forty-Five Years Later," 52.
29. Allamand, "Forty-Five Years Later," 52.
30. Lejeune, "The Autobiographical Pact," 4.
31. Lejeune, "The Autobiographical Pact," 29.
32. Paul John Eakin, Foreword to Lejeune, *On Autobiography*, ix.
33. Allamand, "Forty-Five Years Later," 52.

These issues of subjectivity and author-reader commitment are particularly important in the context of sexual-scientific life writing. *Diary of a Male Bride* and *A Man's Girlhood Years* clearly ask their readers to understand each text as autobiographical. Such a reading of narrative as autobiography has implications for the livability of the life presented in the narrative. If our reading of these texts is to take this appeal to livability seriously, then it is important to shift the emphasis of textual analysis toward author-reader commitment and an understanding of how such a commitment might relate to the production and maintenance of queer livability.

The issues at stake in the generic description of autobiographical writing become clear when tracing the criticism levied at Lejeune's initial work on the autobiographical pact. In his 1979 essay "Autobiography as De-facement," literary theorist Paul de Man raises two points of criticism against the theory of autobiography, singling out Lejeune's work especially. The first point he raises is that autobiographical theory makes the mistake of considering autobiography as a literary genre comparable with others. Compared to other genres, de Man argues, "Autobiography always looks slightly disreputable and self-indulgent in a way that may be symptomatic of its incompatibility with the monumental *dignity* of aesthetic values."[34] Autobiography, de Man argues, is assumed to be of lower aesthetic value because it is assumed to be less crafted and requiring less literary skill to write.

As discussed above with regard to the reviews of *Diary of a Male Bride*, sexual-scientific life writing is often accused of being derivative, while at the same time the introduction of fictional elements is used to portray the writer as hiding a secret, as was the case with *A Man's Girlhood Years*. Here, sexual-scientific life writing is treated in a way similar to other forms of life writing that discuss the experiences and identities of minority writers, texts that are often accused of literary inferiority. Nina Schmidt examines life writing that discusses illness, disability, and death and points out that literary reviews often dismiss such texts as unaspiring and sensationalist tabloid matter.[35] Similarly, Sarah Colvin, examining the textual self-representation of terrorists and prisoners, notes that the response to these texts assumes that they are aesthetically worthless, drawing a comparison with responses to Holocaust testimony and women's writing.[36] Sexual-scientific life writing, similar to such other forms of

---

34. Paul de Man, "Autobiography as De-facement," *MLN* 94, no. 5 (December 1979): 919. Emphasis added.

35. Nina Schmidt, *The Wounded Self: Writing Illness in Twenty-First-Century German Literature* (Rochester, NY: Camden House, 2018), 24–31.

36. Sarah Colvin, "Leaning In: Why and How I Still Study the German," *German Life and*

marginalized writing, is seen to entail disappointment either as unliterary, that is, "lowbrow" autobiography, or as failing to meet the generic requirements of autobiography by not fulfilling the autobiographical pact, that is, by only posing as autobiography, but being in fact a fictionalized work of art. The question, then, of how to read narratives that describe themselves as autobiographies but may fail to fit into the traditional definition of autobiography is particularly important when considering the way in which the status of the often pseudonymous life writings discussed here have been cast into doubt.

In addition to this criticism of generic attribution, de Man questions the assumed distinction between fact and fiction in autobiography:

> Autobiography seems to depend on actual and potentially verifiable events in a less ambivalent way than fiction does. It seems to belong to a simpler mode of referentiality, of representation, and of diegesis. It may contain lots of phantasms and dreams, but these deviations from reality remain rooted in a single subject whose identity is defined by the uncontested readability of his [sic] proper name.[37]

As a result, he argues, in Lejeune's thinking, "The reader becomes the judge, the policing power in charge of verifying the authenticity of the signature and the consistency of the signer's behavior, the extent to which he [sic] respects or fails to honor the contractual agreement he [sic] has signed."[38] Allamand argues that de Man's criticism fails to understand the radical contribution of Lejeune's intervention: as outlined above, Lejeune prioritizes a reader's response to autobiographical writing over any factual identity between author, narrator, and character.[39] The tension between these very different understandings of Lejeune's reader, understanding them as judge or policing power (de Man) and credence (Allamand), shows the important but ambivalent role of the reader of autobiographical writing and a need to bring an ethics of reading into conversation with classic autobiographical theory.

Finally, de Man tackles the question of the subject in autobiographical writing, which he understands to be inadequately addressed in Lejeune's account.

Letters, 69, no. 1 (January 2016): 136.
37. De Man, "Autobiography as De-facement," 920.
38. De Man, "Autobiography as De-facement," 923.
39. Allamand, "Forty-Five Years Later," 52.

We assume that life *produces* the autobiography as an act produces its consequences, but can we not suggest, with equal justice, that the autobiographical project may itself produce and determine the life and that whatever the writer does is in fact governed by the technical demands of self-portraiture and thus determined, in all its aspects, by the resources of his [*sic*] medium?[40]

According to de Man, autobiographies do not document life, but in fact produce and frame life through the process and conventions of writing. This framing and production of life depends on the relationship between textual subject and reader, which requires dignity (not being compared to and therefore considered less aesthetically valuable than other forms of literary production) and lack of judgment or policing. He concludes:

Autobiography, then, is not a genre or a mode, but a figure of reading or of understanding that occurs, to some degree, in all texts. The autobiographical moment happens as an alignment between the two subjects involved in the process of reading in which they determine each other by mutual reflexive substitution.[41]

Both writer and reader make the autobiographical mode possible.

De Man's approach is reminiscent of Michel Foucault's discussion of confessional writing in *The Will to Knowledge*. Here, Foucault rejects the "repressive hypothesis" that claims intrinsic desires urge a person to confess that which is already within, only hidden and repressed.[42] Confessional writing, Foucault argues, does not liberate the self from an oppressive regime of power, but is thoroughly immersed in the circuit of power that generates such discourses. The subject that confesses to bodily or psychological characteristics that are perceived to deviate from the norm, for example, can do so only by adopting the terms provided by the medico-scientific discourses that categorize and give language to such characteristics. The more the subject talks, the more it becomes discursively entangled in this system of power. Yet Foucault also adopts a more positive view of the constitutive power of self-narration. In "About the Beginnings of the Hermeneutics of the Self," he offers an understanding of confessional discourse that asserts that "the self has . . . not to be discovered but to be

---

40. De Man, "Autobiography as De-facement," 920.
41. De Man, "Autobiography as De-facement," 921.
42. Foucault, *The Will to Knowledge*, 17–49.

constituted, to be constituted through the force of truth."[43] Truth, here, is "not defined by a correspondence to reality but as a force inherent to principles and which has to be developed in a discourse."[44] Therefore, the self speaks truth when it gives a confession that rings true in relation to its social principles, the norms and language that frame it. To give a truthful account of oneself, then, is not a documentary process that aligns a written account with lived experience in a passive way, but an active, constitutive practice.

This dynamic understanding of the confessional encounter also questions the evidential nature of experience. As Joan Scott has argued:

> When experience is taken as the origin of knowledge . . . [q]uestions about the constructed nature of experience, about how subjects are constituted as different in the first place, about how one's vision is structured—about language (or discourse) and history—are left aside. The evidence of experience then becomes evidence for the fact of difference, rather than a way of exploring how difference is established.[45]

Investigating experience as a result of dynamically structured subjecthood can help us understand how difference is established. The process of writing autobiographically, then, is an active process of truth-making that coincides with the dynamic constitution of experience.

Literary scholars have further theorized how autobiographical theory can be productively reframed to account for writing as an active process of truth-making. In her writing on autobiography and the broad category of life writing and autofiction, Martina Wagner-Egelhaaf describes autobiography in a way that resembles Foucault's thesis, arguing that "autobiography does not mean a life that is de-scribed (*be-schriebe[n]*), but one that is trans-scribed (*ge-schriebe[n]*)."[46] In the 1970s, the French critical theorist Serge Doubrovsky coined the term "autofiction" to describe texts that combine two seemingly paradoxical modes of literary production, that of autobiography and fiction. In recent years, the term has again gained currency in the German-speaking world through the work of Wagner-Egelhaaf, among others. For her, the term "auto-

---

43. Foucault, "About the Beginnings of the Hermeneutics of the Self: Two Lectures at Dartmouth," *Political Theory* 21, no. 2 (May 1993): 210.

44. Foucault, "About the Beginnings," 209.

45. Joan Scott, "The Evidence of Experience," *Critical Inquiry* 17, no. 4 (Summer 1991): 777.

46. Martina Wagner-Egelhaaf, *Autobiographie* (Stuttgart: Metzler, 2000), 16. Translations of this text are my own.

fiction" again breaks open the dyad of fiction and autobiography by emphasizing the constructive power of the autofictional mode: "The auto-fictional text performatively exposes the author as that authority which brings forth the texts at the same time as it offers the author a platform on which to perform the role of author."[47] As expressed in the title of Wagner-Egelhaaf's edited volume, *Auto(r)fiktion*, the author here becomes visible as the one who fictionalizes accounts of one's life and thereby one's own authorial identity.

The preceding discussion has shown that autobiographical theory is deeply concerned with the question of how autobiographical claims may be expressed and validated. The ability to recognize a text as autobiographical is shifted to the reader, who enters an autobiographical pact with the text (Lejeune). The importance of the reader or confessor is significant, because autobiographical writing does not merely document life, but in fact narrative constitutes the process of creating and shaping life. In this way, the complex and precarious autobiographical positionings of *Diary of a Male Bride* and *A Man's Girlhood Years* that I described in the first section of this chapter exemplify how sexual-scientific life writing produces the narrative truth of a subject (both real and fictional) as it is being formed in its encounter with a readership. The reader, here, is central to this process of becoming.

Assuming such an intimate relationship between text and reader necessarily opens up the text to the possibility of violence. The disclosure of extratextual biographical detail, for example, violently transgresses textual claims. Furthermore, rejecting sexual-scientific life writing as inauthentic implies a rejection of the life that is being constructed in the writing. This potential for violence at the hand of the reader calls for an ethical obligation to take any autobiographical claim seriously as constitutive of the life that is being written about. The following section considers how autobiographical theory can be brought into conversation with an ethics of reading.

2. Literature, Ethics, and Hospitality

Can literary analysis take place within an ethical framework? In *Love's Knowledge*, philosopher Martha Nussbaum asks for "a future in which literary theory (while not forgetting its many other pursuits) will also join with ethical theory

---

47. Martina Wagner-Egelhaaf, "Einleitung: Was Ist Auto(r)fiktion?," in *Auto(r)fiktion: Literarische Verfahren der Selbstkonstruktion*, ed. Martina Wagner-Egelhaaf (Bielefeld: Aisthesis, 2013), 14. Translations of this text are my own.

in pursuit of the question, 'How should one live?'"[48] Nussbaum's "ethical criticism" project makes possible an important (re)introduction of ethics into the critical discussion of literature. Her suggestion to look toward literature for ethical guidance, thus crediting it with the power to inspire ethical readers, is, in part, a response to purely aesthetic readings of text and a precursor to the "Ethical Criticism Symposium," which took place in two subsequent issues of the journal *Philosophy and Literature* in 1997 and 1998. Here, Nussbaum responds to claims by legal theorist and economist Richard Posner, who, in his article "Against Ethical Criticism," rejects what he understands to be ethical criticism's central claim, arguing that "literature does not make us better citizens or better people."[49] In response to this, Nussbaum defends a critical approach to literature that allows for an ethical framework: "Literary art can be ethical, and . . . responsible criticism of literary artworks can legitimately invoke ethical categories."[50] Ethical conduct might arise from within the literary text, but also expands outwards toward the reader: "[The artist's] conduct is ethical conduct because it strives to come to terms with reality in a world that shrinks from reality. When we follow him [*sic*] as attentive readers, we ourselves engage in ethical conduct, and our readings themselves are assessible ethical acts."[51]

Nussbaum and Posner's exchange reveals the tension between ethics and aesthetics: should the critical reader bring an ethical framework to reading by looking for ethical guidance within the text, or maintain an affective distance from the code of ethics a work of art might present? Posner argues that "any critic who brings ethical categories to the reading of works of art is thus bound to neglect the real aesthetic values the work contains and to impose on the text an alien set of concerns."[52] In her defense of ethics, Nussbaum traces how the moral conduct presented in a text can cultivate ethical behavior in the reader. Ethics, as such, must be found within the text to be analyzed in order to inform the process of critical analysis itself. The impetus for ethical conduct remains within the text. Not only is this a response to Posner, but it is also a way of reading that arises from the particular status of Nussbaum's corpus. Her close

---

48. Martha Nussbaum, *Love's Knowledge: Essays on Philosophy and Literature* (Oxford: Oxford University Press, 1990), 168.

49. Richard A. Posner, "Against Ethical Criticism," *Philosophy and Literature* 21, no. 1 (April 1997): 2.

50. Martha Nussbaum, "Exactly and Responsibly: A Defense of Ethical Criticism," *Philosophy and Literature*, 22, no. 2 (October 1998): 344.

51. Nussbaum, "Exactly and Responsibly," 344.

52. Nussbaum, "Exactly and Responsibly," 344.

readings focus on nineteenth- and early twentieth-century realist novels, such as the works of Henry James, canonical works whose aesthetic value is rarely doubted. The corpus of marginalized writing that is at stake in this study, however, is unlike Nussbaum's objects of analysis: as sexual-scientific life writings, they risk being viewed as incompatible with what de Man calls the dignity of aesthetic value. This is not to say that life writing does not have aesthetic value, but that the recognition of both aesthetics and ethics enables a critical reading that does not let an evaluation of aesthetic value overshadow other literary components pertinent to critical analysis.

Whereas Nussbaum's ethical criticism may be of immense value to a critical analysis that combines ethics and aesthetics in a reading of her specific corpus, it seems that for her the question of whether ethics does or does not have a place in literary criticism exhausts any discussion of *where* ethics might be placed within the process of critical analysis; what role exactly it plays in the dynamic relationship between reader and text. While Nussbaum says little about how the process of close reading itself might be ethically informed, in this chapter I want to propose an ethical reading that develops a method of critical analysis that locates ethics not as the object of analysis, but as a model for critical analysis itself with which to respond to the precariousness of sexual-scientific life writing. In this sense, it is less important to evaluate whether a work is ethical than it is to evaluate how the reader can approach the work from an ethical stance.

Nussbaum's discussion of literature at large cannot pay attention to this ethical relation between narrative and reader that responds to the particular requirements of life writing. Other critics have focused on ethics and literature within the context of autobiographical writing, a discussion that is more relevant to the texts discussed here. In an essay on ethics and autobiography, Richard Freadman regards autobiography and the autobiographer as ethical or ethicist, and so, much like Nussbaum, defines ethics as driven by the narrative or writer.[53] Wayne Booth, who alongside Nussbaum contributed to the "Ethical Criticism Symposium," emphasizes that ethical thinking depends on the *encounter* between narrative and reader and thereby introduces the importance of the reader's participation in generating ethical attitudes, but nonetheless considers the ability to inspire ethical thinking as an adequate criterion to eval-

---

53. Richard Freadman, "Ethics, Autobiography and the Will: Stephen Spender's *World within World*," in *The Ethics in Literature*, ed. Andrew Hadfield, Dominic Rainsford, and Tim Woods (London: Macmillan, 1999).

uate and judge the value of a narrative.[54] Ethical work is modeled by the literary text and finds, in its readers, a capable audience to mirror this ethical behavior.

In "Close but Not Deep: Literary Ethics and the Descriptive Turn," Heather Love criticizes the assumption of the "ethical exemplarity of the interpreter or messenger"[55] put forward by literary criticism. Love develops a "flat reading" (as opposed to close reading) of literature modeled on social science methods that are based on observation in order to "suggest an alternate model of reading that does not depend on the ethical exemplarity of the interpreter or messenger."[56] Her aim is to reject a literary criticism that orients itself around exclusionary humanist ideals. Here Love criticizes Ian Hunter, who argues that literary criticism is part of a new pedagogy that replaces explicit moral education and instead situates ethical value in literature and the critic's reading of it.[57] She points out that poststructuralism and politically informed criticism maintain a link to a universal morality that is imposed by the critic, a moral high ground that she, as critic, rejects. Love's critique both counters the kind of ethical criticism proposed by Nussbaum, who understands literature as moral education, and rejects the critic as judge of a text's ethical potential. Instead, she suggests a descriptive rather than interpretive critical approach to literary texts that she calls "flat reading," one that opens up "the possibility of an alternative ethics, one grounded in documentation and description rather than empathy and witness."[58] Love makes an important contribution to the theory of literary criticism that can aid the development of a specific kind of reading of sexual-scientific life writing. She reminds her readers to be wary of finding ethics only in the moral sovereignty of the critic. Beyond this, I argue that a more dynamic ethics of reading is required to meet sexual-scientific life writing with respect. As will be outlined in what follows, documenting the events described in sexual-scientific life writing is a form of witness that is directly demanded by each text. Therefore, a critical approach to sexual-scientific life writing cannot separate documentation and description from empathy and witness and must think both together.

In order to develop a relational ethics of reading, I want to propose that

---

54. Wayne Booth, *The Company We Keep: An Ethics of Fiction* (Berkeley: University of California Press, 1988).

55. Heather Love, "Close but Not Deep: Literary Ethics and the Descriptive Turn," *New Literary History* 41, no. 2 (Spring 2010): 375.

56. Love, "Close but Not Deep," 375.

57. Love, "Close but Not Deep," 372.

58. Love, "Close but Not Deep," 375.

Jacques Derrida's discussion of hospitality as an ethical relation between guest and host can inform a more suitable approach to sexual-scientific life writing. In *Of Hospitality*, Derrida responds to psychoanalyst and philosopher Anne Dufourmantelle's invitation to present his understanding of hospitality. He makes a distinction between hospitality in its absolute form, or the *Law* of hospitality, and the *laws* of hospitality. The Law of hospitality goes beyond the mere offering of a place to rest to a guest:

> Absolute hospitality requires that I open up my home and that I give not only to the foreigner (provided with a family name, with the social status of being a foreigner, etc.), but to the absolute, unknown, anonymous other, and that I *give place* to them, that I let them come, that I let them arrive, and take place in the place I offer them, without asking of them either reciprocity (entering into a pact) or even their names. The law of absolute hospitality commands a break with hospitality by right, with law or justice as rights.[59]

Derrida's Law of hospitality has absolutely no conditions attached and demands that hosts, or critics, give without expecting anything in return, and give without worrying about compromising their own subject position, losing their home, or being invaded by the unknown guest.[60] In contrast to this, the laws of hospitality are the juridico-political conditions that attach themselves to organized hospitality and that tell us what rights and obligations we have as host or guest.

The laws and the Law of hospitality are incommensurable: the always and necessarily conditional set against the unconditional. Yet it is in the tension between these two understandings of hospitality that Derrida sees its ethical potential: "the two regimes of a law of hospitality: the unconditional or hyperbolical on the one hand, and the conditional and juridico-political, even the ethical, on the other: ethics in fact straddling the two."[61] An ethical relation between host and guest arises from this tension between, on the one hand, giving without holding back, giving everything, including oneself, and, on the

---

59. Jacques Derrida, *Of Hospitality: Anne Dufourmantelle Invites Jacques Derrida to Respond*, trans. Rachel Bowlby (Stanford: Stanford University Press, 2000), 25.

60. Joseph Hillis Miller's discussion of the relationship between deconstructive reading and the text to be read as a relation similar to that of host and parasite is helpful here, too. Due to the negative connotations of "parasite," which Miller aptly refutes in his essay, I prefer to refer to this relation as one of host and *guest*. Joseph Hillis Miller, "The Critic as Host," in *Deconstruction and Criticism* (London: Continuum, 1979).

61. Derrida, *Of Hospitality*, 136.

other, constructing boundaries that structure this relation between guest and host, ensuring it becomes an exchange.

Out of this tension, between laws and Law, ethical questions arise: "Is it more just and more loving to question or not to question? to call by the name or without the name? . . . Does one give hospitality to a subject? . . . to a legal subject?"[62] As host, the ethical reader can remain open to the text, to consider a response that is just and loving, that is ethical because it does not give answers in advance but invites the text to declare itself: "the question *of* the foreigner as question *come from* abroad. And thus of response or responsibility. How should one respond to all these questions? How be responsible for them? How answer for oneself when faced with them?"[63] An ethical reading is a hospitable reading that responds sensitively to a text and that finds in this ethical response its responsibility and response-*ability*, a term I borrow from the work of Donna Haraway. As Haraway's work shows, such response-ability is never just a responsibility to respond to something that already exists in the world, but a process of becoming-together that establishes a "collective knowing and doing."[64] A response-able reader is not only open to the text but understands that they will change in the process of becoming a reader.

The otherness of text and the difference between reader and narrative is then not a hindrance, but a prerequisite for hospitable reading. Indeed for Emmanuel Levinas, the insurmountable alterity of the other is foundational to the ethical and hospitable encounter.[65] This is profoundly different from Nussbaum's analysis, in which critic and text share the same intellectual reality. As Judith Still describes it, "Hospitality is by definition a structure that regulates relations between inside and outside . . . it does not make sense to suggest that a spouse offers hospitality to his/her spouse in the home they share."[66] In her study of empathy in literary reception, Maria Scott not only shows that empathetic reading leads to emotional and affective proximity between reader and literary work, but that fiction importantly "highlights the limits of our ability to

---

62. Derrida, *Of Hospitality*, 29.

63. Derrida, *Of Hospitality*, 131.

64. See Donna Haraway, *Staying with the Trouble: Making Kin in the Chthulucene* (Durham, NC: Duke University Press, 2016), 34.

65. Emmanuel Levinas, *Entre Nous: Thinking-of-the-Other*, trans. Michael B. Smith and Barbara Harshav (New York: Columbia University Press, 1998), 147.

66. Judith Still, *Derrida and Hospitality: Theory and Practice* (Edinburgh: Edinburgh University Press, 2010), 11.

know other people."[67] In this openness to the alterity of the other that Levinas and others describe, the "fictional stranger," who is other to myself and whose otherness I am aware of, becomes, not a marginal figure, but the central focus of reading. The hospitable reading I outline in this chapter is especially appropriate when looking at first-person writing of individuals who experience a contested queer or trans identity, who are positioned at the limits of categories that jar, who are rejected or unwanted. Hospitable reading is a valuable way to respond to such texts and the lives described, which may or may not differ from my own as reader.

Such hospitable reading does not require that a narrative's call for recognition temporally coincide with the reader's response. In *Haunted Subjects*, Colin Davis responds to Emmanuel Levinas's statement that "death is the *without-response*," by arguing that "the absence of the other's response does not curtail all relation and return me to an identity unaffected by the other's existence."[68] An ethical relation, then, can exist even with a guest (i.e., writer) who cannot respond, the dead guest of the narrative. The most extreme version of hospitality that a reader can offer is to take in the guest who cannot respond to the host's hospitality. Yet this does not foreclose any relation with the Other or the text to which the reader can offer hospitality even posthumously. "Maintaining a dialogue with the dead," Davis argues in his chapter about Derrida's haunted subjects, "means keeping their texts alive, which entails preserving them from premature closure. The texts of the dead are still unread in the sense that their full resources have not yet been brought to light, their capacity to generate fresh insight is not yet exhausted."[69] Accordingly, our response as readers and critics today is still crucial to the ethical treatment of historical texts, and, importantly, our continued reading of such texts contributes to the livability of the sexual-scientific subject.

To aim to do justice to a text means to offer a productive reading that does not fear to encounter noncoherence and contradiction as a dead end of meaning, but one that respects internal oppositions (normal or abnormal, man or woman, pathological or healthy, concealment or revelation). As ethical readers, we attribute an ethical imperative, not to the text, but to the ethical treatment of

---

67. Maria C. Scott, *Empathy and the Strangeness of Fiction: Readings in French Realism* (Edinburgh: Edinburgh University Press, 2020), 8.

68. Colin Davis, "Speaking with the Dead: De Man, Levinas, Agamben," in *Haunted Subjects: Deconstruction, Psychoanalysis and the Return of the Dead* (Basingstoke: Palgrave Macmillan, 2007), 117.

69. Colin Davis, "Derrida's Haunted Subjects," in *Haunted Subjects*, 139.

text by the critic herself.[70] This hospitable reading is not a set method for literary analysis of all texts, but an approach to reading texts that avoids establishing a hierarchical relation between narrative and reader that posits the reader as judge, but not initiator, of a literary ethics, thus leaving her protected from harm and without responsibility.[71] Its main endeavor is to avoid an inhospitable reading: one that imposes a hierarchy of genre, one that prioritizes a reading of extratextual information over and above the textual address, one that does not understand the reader as radically implicated in this address.

Elaborating on the status of literature as an astonishing aesthetic and ethical resource, Sarah Colvin examines how one might understand the encounter between reader and text.[72] Colvin endorses an untidy approach to literature that is attentive to a polyphony of voices, allows for the simultaneity of several truths, permits itself to let go of control, and refrains from imposing itself on the text. The methodological approach to queer life writings I develop in this chapter similarly aspires to be untidy in this way. It regards literary criticism's search for ethics in the autobiographical text or any piece of literature as a worthwhile contribution to literary analysis, but wants to add another dimension to such an analysis: viewed through the lens of Derridean hospitality, ethical responsibility becomes more mobile and can shift from narrative to the more dynamic relationship between narrative and reader. Ethics is situated in the encounter between the two. When we read queer and trans autobiographies that actively seek to explore livable ways of

---

70. Feminist critics have scrutinized philosophical accounts of hospitality because they often uncritically link hospitality to femininity and domesticity. However, others have rethought the metaphor of hospitality to conceptualize new ways of thinking embodiment. For example, philosopher Luna Dolezal utilizes feminist understandings of "embodied hospitality" to reframe debates around commercial surrogacy. Luna Dolezal, "The Metaphors of Commercial Surrogacy: Rethinking the Materiality of Hospitality through Pregnant Embodiment," in *New Feminist Perspectives on Embodiment*, ed. Clara Fischer and Luna Dolezal (London: Palgrave Macmillan, 2018).

71. Derrida scholar Derek Attridge has noted that Derrida's "writings on literary works don't . . . offer themselves as models to literary critics . . . ; they are singular responses to the singularity of the works on which he is commenting." However, I want to propose that hospitable reading can be understood, perhaps not as method, but certainly as an attitude toward a singular text that can be replicated and repeated. Derek Attridge, *Reading and Responsibility: Deconstruction's Traces* (Edinburgh: Edinburgh University Press, 2010), 5.

72. Colvin, "Leaning In." Colvin takes the term "tidy thinking" from Jane Adamson, who understands literature as working against tidiness. See Jane Adamson, "Against Tidiness: Literature and/versus Moral Philosophy," in *Renegotiating Ethics in Literature, Philosophy and Theory*, ed. Jane Adamson, Richard Freadman, and David Parker (Cambridge: Cambridge University Press, 1998).

being in the world, it is of critical importance to acknowledge that there is an ethics involved that is found, not (just) on the side of the text, but on that of the reader, an ethical imperative that asks for active participation in an ethical, attentive, and hospitable way of reading.

Viewing sexual-scientific life writings through the lens of such a hospitable reading makes it possible to do justice to their self-description as truthful autobiographies. As a consequence, classic autobiographical theory might indeed be responsive to the hospitable reading that I propose. Returning to the generic description of autobiography as a "retrospective prose narrative written by a real person concerning his [*sic*] own existence, where the focus is his [*sic*] individual life, in particular the story of his [*sic*] personality"[73] we might ask: Who speaks these words? Is it the reader of autobiography, who demands of the text that it should concur with this definition? Or is it the narrative voice itself, asking to be read in this way, a plea that the reader can then respond to hospitably? Through the lens of hospitable reading, I want to argue that it is the latter, echoing words familiar from sexual-scientific life writing: they remind us of N. O. Body's *A Man's Girlhood Years*, which the narrator describes as "a book of truth," or a truthful account (MGY 8, 158). This approach situates Lejeune's definition in a dynamic relationship between text and reader: it is not a one-directional definition, where the reader or critic makes the demands on the text. It is the narrated self that makes these demands of its imagined reader, asking to be read—welcomed—in a certain way. It is the autobiographical voice that speaks: this is what I am, this is the way in which I ask to be understood. The importance of reader response and recognition is shown to be crucial here.

According to Lejeune, the relation between autobiographical narrator and reader is one of need and dependence, where the narrator needs the reader: "He [*sic*] needs me: it is in my expression that he [*sic*] looks for proof of existence, certificate of worth, response of love."[74] Lejeune's statement is ambiguous: on the one hand the reader appears as an authoritative figure superior to the narrative, which they must verify, a kind of sovereign power imbued with juridical agency. On the other hand, Lejeune's affirmation could be understood to propose a symbiotic relationship between text and reader, for if there is a need on the part of the narrative that addresses itself to a reader whose expression or response holds hope, the reader might be seen as holding the responsibility to respond and to find a sense of fulfillment in the role of reader in this response.

---

73. Lejeune, "The Autobiographical Pact," 4.
74. Lejeune, "The Autobiographical Pact," 233.

In such an understanding, we can also reverse the guest-host relationship of hospitable reading: not only is the critic the host, who welcomes the narrative unconditionally, but the critic is also the guest, who is invited in by the narrative. However, as critic, I can only be invited to respond to a text if I am open to such a response. Hospitality is foundational to the reader-text relationship.

Understood in this way, Lejeune's definition can be taken as an acknowledgment of what the text asks its implied, ideal reader to *believe* in. Lejeune himself acknowledges the role of belief when it comes to reading autobiographies:

> Yes, I have been fooled. I believe that we can promise to tell the truth; I believe in the transparency of language, and in the existence of a complete subject who expresses himself [*sic*] through it; I believe that my proper name guarantees my autonomy and my singularity . . . ; I believe that when I say "I," it is I who am speaking: I believe in the Holy Ghost of the first person. And who doesn't believe in it? But of course it also happens that I believe the contrary, or at least claim to believe it.[75]

His absolute faith in autobiography as a true account of a complete self is presented here, and it is described, on the one hand, as foolish and naive and, on the other hand, as a belief that competes with another. This competing belief is mentioned in the paragraph immediately before: "Telling the truth about the self, constituting the self as complete subject—it is a fantasy."[76] He believes that autobiography is both truth *and* fantasy, yet the casual way in which Lejeune admits to apparently incommensurable beliefs suggests that the two are not that different. Lejeune depicts the predicament of writing the self, of making a demand on the implied reader to believe the narrative in question but, at the same time, displaying an awareness that no narrative will ever be an adequate transcript of life. "In spite of the fact that autobiography is impossible," Lejeune summarizes, "this in no way prevents it from existing."[77]

A hospitable way of reading sexual-scientific life writing pays attention to the ways in which the texts communicate their autobiographical nature and what may thereby be asked of the reader who is implicated in such an autobiographical address. The autobiographical pact, then, is not exactly an agreement entered into by author and reader, but a demand of the narrative

---

75. Lejeune, "The Autobiographical Pact," 131.
76. Lejeune, "The Autobiographical Pact," 131.
77. Lejeune, "The Autobiographical Pact," 131–32.

addressed to the implied reader. Understood in this way, it facilitates an investigation into the mechanics of self-narration, how truth-claims are evoked within the narrative and what might be gained from such claims. In keeping with Derrida's concept of hospitality, to read autobiographies thus is to offer a response to the call of the narrative and to recognize in this response my responsibility as reader, one readers and critics must act upon if they want to do justice to the text.

3. Being Addressed and Offering a Response

What are the implications of such a hospitable reading practice for the discussion of sexual-scientific life writings? Reading *Diary of a Male Bride* and *A Man's Girlhood Years* in a way that pays attention to self-description rather than how well they do (or do not) fit into predetermined categories reveals a complex address. *Diary of a Male Bride* opens with a peritextual suicide letter addressed to an unknown addressee, which, we are led to believe, is Walter Homann.[78] Directly below this letter is a comment signed with the initials "W. H." (supposedly Walter Homann), in which he states that he received the letter from the police several days after it had been written. The suicide letter functions to elaborate on the nature of the narrative that follows but simultaneously addresses Homann, who is asked to react in a certain way:

> This letter contains a dossier of pages written in a tangled and confused manner—pages of a diary. See if you can make sense of them. You, who were always able to understand me, will read in these pages how hard I fought and how I lost. If you believe that it might be useful to those who are my fellow sufferers if you publish these notes as a whole or parts of it, you can do so. I leave this decision to you and you alone. (DMB 9)

Importantly, although the following comment suggests that the letter was addressed to Walter Homann, the lack of a direct address in the suicide letter and the plea addressed to a general second-person singular "du" addresses the reader, offering an intimate relationship with the letter writer. This passage communicates how the narrative is to be understood—as a diary—and that it may be opened to a wider readership if "you" decide that these words are useful to the writer's "fellow sufferers."

---

78. Genette and Maclean, "Introduction to the Paratext," 263–64.

This effort to create communities through written work anticipates the community-forming magazine culture of the Weimar period, which Katie Sutton describes thus: "The Weimar transvestite media thus worked to establish an 'imagined community' of transvestite-identifying individuals, complementing the grassroots political activities of the Berlin-based organizations, which included hosting meetings and organizing public lectures."[79] In these imagined communities Sutton sees a parallel to Michael Warner's "counterpublics": "an entity that comes into being through 'an address to indefinite strangers,' but where the 'strangers' addressed are 'not just anybody'; rather they are 'socially marked by their participation in this kind of discourse.'"[80] Dori's appeal to fellow sufferers is anticipated by very similar words in one of Krafft-Ebing's case studies, where an anonymous person addresses an "autobiography of a Uranian" to Krafft-Ebing in the following way: "I am addressing these lines to you in the interest of future fellow sufferers (*Leidensgefährten*)."[81] This also shows the importance of an address to a medico-scientific professional, which I will discuss in more detail in the following chapters.

Although Dori suggests that the reading of their text might be beneficial for fellow sufferers, the address remains somewhat ambivalent: can suffering be helped if others who suffer like Dori read these words, or if others unlike Dori begin to understand the nature of this suffering? The *Nutzen* or usefulness of such a shared experience of suffering remains unclear, too: will communal suffering alleviate, even eradicate that suffering? Dori neither confirms nor denies this, but the disregard of this question and yet the drawing of attention to suffering as communal, indeed asking for this suffering to be shared, indicates that community or a collective of suffering may alter the intensity of such suffering.

Noticeably, the nature of Dori's suffering remains unexplained in this first section of the narrative. In this way, the text tentatively invites a reading on the premise that one can only determine whether one is indeed a fellow sufferer by reading on. However, having read and thus responded to the call of the narrative, the ambiguous address to fellow sufferers and other readers

---

79. Katie Sutton, "Sexological Cases and the Prehistory of Transgender Identity Politics in Interwar Germany," in *Case Studies and the Dissemination of Knowledge*, ed. Joy Damousi, Birgit Lang, and Katie Sutton (London: Routledge, 2015), 54.

80. Sutton, "Sexological Cases," 94, citing Michael Warner, "Publics and Counterpublics," *Public Culture* 14, no. 1 (Winter 2002): 49–90.

81. Richard von Krafft-Ebing, *Psychopathia Sexualis: Mit besonderer Berücksichtigung der conträren Sexualempfindung: Eine klinisch-forensische Studie*, 5th ed. (Stuttgart: Verlag von Ferdinand Enke, 1890), 164.

also ambivalently assigns one to both groups. If, upon reading, I remain unsure which position is my own, and if Dori's invitation endorses this ambivalence, then the call for community might be understood not only as referring to a collective of sufferers, but an offering of response and compassion that enters one into a community of *recognition*, not necessarily identification (but going beyond that).

However, Dori does not only invite a reading of the narrative but rather passes on the option to judge the worth of the words to a "you" (we are led to believe this is Homann) and therefore invites a readership only by proxy. The suicide letter in which Dori issues an invitation to a communal act of recognition is framed by a preface signed by Walter Homann, who introduces the text as records left behind by an *Unglücklicher*, a wretched person, who committed suicide because they were unable to live under the pressures of a difference brought on by nature and the resulting prejudice that led to their marginalization. In his preface, Homann redefines the purpose and potential value of the narrative:

> The topic might cause offense in some circles, but some insightful (*einsichtsvolle*) readers may change their judgment of these wretched people. . . . Should the written words of the deceased . . . contribute to a better understanding of the inner life of such a double creature (*Doppelwesen*), then the purpose of this publication will have been achieved. (DMB, no continuous pagination)

Just like Dori's address to fellow sufferers, Homann's address to an "insightful" public is ambiguous, because I cannot know whether I have insight until I have accepted the invitation to read on, much as I cannot know whether I am a fellow sufferer in advance of reading. Dori's original hope that the text might help others has been supplemented by the desire of Homann as editor to inspire other readers like him—after all, his inviting preface shows that he is an example of an "insightful reader." As Frauke Bode argues, paratexts (such as a preface) function as an authorizing method that can claim (or refute) and stabilize (or destabilize) referential authenticity.[82] In this instance, Homann's preface underlines the narrative's claim to authenticity by performing how one might inhabit the role of insightful reader. At the same time, as Gérard Genette argues, "The addressee of the preface is the reader of the text—the reader, and not

---

82. Frauke Bode, "Paratext," in *Handbook of Autobiography/Autofiction*, vol. 1, *Theory and Concepts*, ed. Martina Wagner-Egelhaaf (Berlin: de Gruyter, 2018), 365.

simply a member of the public."[83] This is because "the preface, in its very message, postulates that its reader is poised for an imminent reading of the text."[84] Accordingly, Homann's preface both performs what an insightful reading might look like and also directly invites the reader to do the same.

If Homann as editor is indeed a reader of Dori's text in the sense that Dori intended and has, as such, entered the narrative, then he has joined a collective of suffering. He does so not necessarily through identification, because he only ambivalently enters himself into the address and does not determine whether he reads as fellow sufferer or as an ally. Rather, Homann begins to establish a community of recognition by recognizing how Dori suffers. By this process Dori's address and tentative invitation has been passed to Homann, who, in his turn, passes on the implied desire for a community of recognition to readers by inviting them to read, too. Here Homann also offers contemporary readers, who may not be fellow sufferers but who might be scandalized by the topic, a safe position in which they do not feel threatened in their own identity and are addressed as members of a compassionate Christian public. From this position, readers, in turn, must now attempt to answer to the hesitant call of the text in their own way, to reciprocate the invitation that was offered to them. Homann—here taking on the role of a second narrator—and his reading practice as self-described editor exemplify a response to Dori's call and act as placeholder for other readers. If this is a position that others may take up, then any reader is hesitantly addressed and asked to be responsible for the text in order to establish or continue a communal recognition of suffering. This aim to incite a certain kind of response and thereby attract a caring and understanding readership and create a community can be understood as the driving force of the narrative.

N. O. Body's *A Man's Girlhood Years* similarly invites a certain kind of reader response. To return once more to the opening sentence of the narrative, a sentence that is repeated in the last paragraph of the text, Body's story proposes that "this book is a book of truth" (MGY 8–9, 158). As the opening sentence of the narrative, this proposition is followed with the words, "Dieses Leben will geglaubt werden, so fremd es auch ist" ("This life wants to be believed, no matter how strange it is") (MGY 8). Here, what it might mean for a book to speak the truth is explained: its truth lies in the acknowledgment that, despite its unusual nature, it can be *believed* as a true life. Body's memoirs demonstrate the constitutive power of self-narration discussed earlier in this

---

83. Genette, *Paratexts*, 194.

84. Genette, *Paratexts*, 194.

chapter, where truth is established in the encounter between narrative and reader. To make the story of this life believable as truthful, it has to be justified and declared to a readership. Like Dori's narrative, its generic self-description as an autobiographical text is thus intimately bound up with an address to a readership, a call for a certain kind of response.

This initial call for a readership to believe the narrative is complemented by another call for action found near the very end of the book: "I didn't want to write this book, but others finally made me aware that I owe it to mankind as a contribution to the psychology of our times and in the interest of science and truth" (MGY 159). Body offers the book to a readership because he feels indebted to do so. It is difficult to see how a life that has been described as so difficult to live throughout, one that has been marginalized and othered, owes anything to a public that might have been involved in perpetuating such difficulty, and it seems difficult to see what favor this debt is meant to repay. Yet this debt is affirmed by the earlier occurrence of the proposition: if the narrator asks for a readership to believe his life and therefore validate his truth-claims, then the story of his life is the price he pays to receive, in return, the reader's belief. Thus, the reader enters into a relation of exchange: if, as reader, I offer the belief that the text speaks the truth, I will, in turn, be able to receive the narrative. In a way similar to Dori's account, I cannot know in advance if I will be able to believe the words that I am about to read, but once I have read them, I am asked to be bound by the introductory words, as I am told that the narrator has now paid his dues.

The foreword to Body's narrative, written by Rudolf Presber, adds another dimension to the narrative's complex address. Presber claims to have written the preface "because I am the indirect reason the book has been written at all" (MGY 2). Presber asserts that he advised Body on the threefold benefits of writing an autobiography: to reduce "heimliche[s] Menschenleid" ("secret suffering") (MGY 2), to educate "those who might be responsible for severe errors in parenting and education" (MGY 4), and finally to function as therapeutic measure for Body himself: "If you want to start a new life, account to yourself and others for all that has happened in your life . . . And with each honest line that you write, a rusted fetter will fall from you, a fetter that has cut into your flesh, a sad piece of the past that weighs you down." (MGY 5). Presber's foreword makes explicit both sides of the exchange between reader and narrator, but also draws attention to a departure from the past. The cathartic exercise of writing that Presber encourages Body to engage in aims to free him from the life that is thus written. As one narrative begins, another one can be let go of, as Nora, now Norbert Body, visits his mother and says: "My mother told me about my birth" (MGY 151). Norbert's mother thus tells the story of the origins of his life anew and helps put to rest the narrative of Nora that Norbert no longer requires. The reader honors the credit of having been trusted with Body's story, by recognizing it to be true, and, through the act of believing the life, helps to sever the life told from the narrator, who is now no longer held back by it. This act of recognition is particularly relevant to the self-ascribed confessional and autobiographical appeal of the narrative: when Body's future life and the narrative of his past are separated, the narrative no longer represents Body's actual life, but a story of girlhood years that now appears distant and fictional. Yet this fiction is achieved only because the narrative is understood, in the first instance, as autobiographical.

My analysis of *Diary of a Male Bride* and *A Man's Girlhood Years* has presented two important aspects of sexual-scientific life writing. It has shown the important role that the autobiographical claim to authenticity plays in the construction of sexual subjectivity in both narratives. Furthermore, it has demonstrated how such an autobiographical claim is addressed to a readership through a call for recognition. This, in turn, reveals the important role of the reader or critic: to respond hospitably to the narrative's autobiographical call for recognition.

Conclusion

In this chapter, I explored how the confessional mode of sexual-scientific life writing calls upon the reader and critic of historical confession to offer a response to the call of the narrative. When discussing the importance of the confessional encounter in the formation of sexual subjectivity, Foucault highlights the importance of a partner or confessor. Confession, Foucault makes clear, cannot happen without the (virtual) presence of this partner, whose response can inflict pain through judgment and punishment, or consolation and reconciliation.[85] This shows the important but ambivalent role of the reader of confessional and autobiographical writing and a need to bring an ethics of reading into conversation with classic autobiographical theory. In this chapter, I attended to this need by proposing what I call hospitable reading as an approach to sexual-scientific life writing.

Such hospitable reading is attentive to the ways in which sexual-scientific

---

85. Foucault, *The Will to Knowledge*, 61–62.

life writing addresses the reader by asking for recognition. Both narratives discussed in this chapter address their readers in a peculiar way, invite them to read intimate details about two lives but also to offer a response to the narrative by believing it. In this address to their readers, the reader's *recognition* of suffering, in Dori's case, and the reader's *recognition* of a life as true, in Body's case, contribute to a sense of livability henceforward. In *Undoing Gender*, Butler argues that the desire for recognition is a condition of every subject's ability to perceive life as livable, that is, in the very least as bearable.[86] If normative constraints urge every subject to ask, "What, given the contemporary order of being, can I be?"[87] there remains for certain subjects a serious threat that the answer might be: nothing. That this is the case in Body's and Dori's lives (at least temporarily) is clear: Dori's narrative ends in suicide, based on the fear of rejection from their fiancé if he finds out about Dori's assigned gender at birth. Body's life is unbearable until he achieves legal recognition and has his legal sex changed. By asking for recognition of marginalized forms of life and appearances of embodiment, Dori's and Body's narratives ask their readers to recognize their lives as fully human, that is, livable and grievable. Importantly, as Butler argues in *Precarious Life*, such recognition does not refer to the acknowledgment of an original, or fully formed self:

> To ask for recognition, or to offer it, is precisely not to ask for recognition for what one already is. It is to solicit a becoming, to instigate a transformation, to petition the future always in relation to the Other. It is also to stake one's own being, and one's own persistence in one's own being, in the struggle for recognition.[88]

Rather than a mere form of observation, recognition is a powerful, participatory, and active interaction with the text that recognizes and thereby collaboratively constructs the livability of the writing subject.

As I have argued in this chapter, it is important to understand that such a call for recognition, as expressed in the two examples of sexual-scientific life writing in this chapter, endures across time. The preservation of such texts from premature closure is all the more urgent if we return to the conditions under which the narratives at the heart of my study arose and survived. The banning of these texts through Nazi agencies and their public defamation and

---

86. Judith Butler, *Undoing Gender* (London: Routledge, 2004), 8.
87. Butler, *Undoing Gender*, 58.
88. Judith Butler, *Precarious Life* (London: Verso, 2000), 44.

literal destruction in book burnings in 1933 effected a violent closure. By responding to the narrative in an ethical and hospitable way that acknowledges the narrative's call for recognition, the reader enters into a community of recognition that Dori's text expresses such a longing for. This recognition is central to an understanding of all narratives of otherness and central to the commemoration of the difficulties of those at the margins of society past and present who go (or have gone) unrecognized. Importantly, this reader response is fundamental to the formation of sexual subjectivity and queer livability expressed in the text. The confessional mode expressed by sexual-scientific life writing, which, as Foucault outlines, takes place in the virtual presence of another, performs the double function of documenting life and the process of creating life by establishing sexual subjectivity through confession. As Foucault recognizes, there are certain limitations to this, as confessional narratives arise under normative constraints, where confessors expose themselves to the potential of violence, judgment, or punishment. The following chapter offers a detailed analysis of one such instance where sexual-scientific life writing constitutes sexual subjectivity by writing with and against the specific framing discourse of sexology.

As this chapter has shown, it is important to pay careful attention to the textual address of sexual-scientific life writing, the relationship between text and reader, and the responsibility and response-ability these texts demand of their readers. In doing so, the enduring relevance not only of sexual-scientific life writing but of a particular kind of reader response to such texts was demonstrated. The hospitable approach to the corpus that I have suggested in this chapter will continue to inform the critical analysis of the following chapters. By understanding autobiographical life writing as neither documentation of facts, nor as fiction, but as a way to construct meaning and identity, as well as an appeal to a readership for recognition, sexual-scientific life writing allows us to understand the narrative construction of queer livability in the early twentieth century. As German historian Dagmar Günther writes about the use of autobiography as a historical source, autobiography is a communicate act, rather than a referential text that can be used to confirm already existing historical narratives.[89] As a consequence, historian Roger Woods writes that autobiography's "significance [is] located not in its closeness to the truth but in the writer's construction of a life at a particular time and in a particular social

---

89. Dagmar Günther, "'And Now for Something Completely Different': Prolegomena zur Autobiographie als Quelle der Geschichtswissenschaft," *Historische Zeitschrift* 272, no. 1 (2001): 25–61.

context."[90] In the following chapters, in addition to a continued awareness of how sexual-scientific life writing positions itself precariously in relation to an imagined and desired readership, I will consider how livable lives are established in the relationship between life writing and the sexual-scientific discourses that frame them, as well as further social, cultural, and legal frameworks for recognition.

---

90. Roger Woods, "Introduction: The Purposes and Problems of German Life Writing in the Twentieth Century," in *German Life Writing in the Twentieth Century*, ed. Birgit Dahlke, Dennis Tate, and Roger Woods (Rochester: Camden House, 2010), 6.

CHAPTER 2

Gender, Agency, and Prosthetic Metaphor

The Case of N. O. Body

Sexual-scientific life writing is characterized by a close relationship between autobiographical narrative and sexual-scientific discourse. This proximity of autobiography to scientific discourses poses important questions about the agency of the writing self. Do sexual-scientific discourses support and foster autobiographical writing? Do they impose limits and restrictions on autobiographical expression? In this chapter, I investigate the relationship between discourse and subject in order to examine various possibilities and expressions of agency. Beyond resistance and rebellion, I investigate how agency can be located in moments of cohesion and coherence between discourse and subject. This agential navigation of sexual-scientific discourse, I argue, leads to the creation of a livable form of sexual subjectivity, where normative frameworks provide possibilities for recognition without foreclosing the possibility for individual expression outside these norms.

N. O. Body's *A Man's Girlhood Years* (1907) offers an exemplary case for examining the role of agency in sexual-scientific life writing.[1] The narrative shows how sexual-scientific discourses, practices, and practitioners influenced the people they sought to study by establishing sexual and gender identity categories that could be taken up by the subject of sexological study.[2] Yet what

---

1. N. O. Body, *Aus eines Mannes Mädchenjahren* [A Man's Girlhood Years] (Berlin: Edition Hentrich, 1993 [1907]).

2. This has been discussed in recent scholarship. See, for example, Klaus Müller, *Aber in meinem Herzen sprach eine Stimme so laut: Homosexuelle Autobiographien und medizinische Pathographien im neunzehnten Jahrhundert* (Berlin: Verlag rosa Winkel, 1991); Harry Oosterhuis, *Stepchildren of Nature: Krafft-Ebing, Psychiatry, and the Making of Sexual Identity* (Chicago: University of Chicago Press, 2000); Geertje Mak, *Doubting Sex: Inscriptions, Bodies and Selves in Nineteenth-Century Hermaphrodite Case Histories* (Manchester: Manchester University Press, 2012).

makes Body's narrative so interesting is not only the fact that the broad link between sexological discourse and gender identity is discernible, but also that the narrative offers an opportunity to examine the very mechanisms of this influence. In the analysis that follows, I show that N. O. Body's memoir directly responds to Magnus Hirschfeld's "psychobiological questionnaire," a series of over one hundred questions that Hirschfeld presented to his patients and later to visitors of the historical Institute of Sexology. In this chapter, I analyze the circulation of the narrative in sexual-scientific publications and the relationship between sexual-scientific knowledge, practice, and technique and Body's narrative, investigating how each might provide prosthetic support for the other, with the aim to investigate the agency of the life writer in navigating narrative and sexual-scientific discourse.

Sociological theory speaks of a tension between structure and agency in establishing social orders.[3] This poses the question: does a subject have agency in navigating dominant social and discursive structures? In order to disrupt and complicate any assumption that subjection to dominant discourses implies a lack of agency, this chapter introduces the metaphor of prosthesis. I borrow this prosthetic metaphor from disability studies and cultural theory more broadly, where it has been rethought from passive support of a normative body to the productive but also often painful relationship between body and prosthesis. As I will show in the discussion that follows, the prosthetic metaphor, which complicates the binary between the "natural" and "artificial" body, can be usefully applied to disrupt the strict separation between structure and agency and thereby allow for a hospitable reading (a concept I introduce in the previous chapter) of sexual subjectivity as expressed in sexual-scientific life writing.

The first part of this chapter traces scholarly discussions of agency in the context of historical sexual sciences and offers the metaphor of prosthesis for thinking through the complex relationship between life writing and sexual-scientific discourse. In the sections that follow, I will use the prosthetic metaphor to investigate three relationships that, together, constitute what I call a prosthetic assemblage: I will consider how Hirschfeld's questionnaire functions as prosthetic support for Body's memoir; how the narrative itself is a prosthetic device that creates the possibility of livability for the life writer; and finally how Body's narrative achieved what I call a prosthetic afterlife in two instances where the autobiography was used in sexual-scientific publications to confirm certain sexual-scientific theories.

---

3. For a detailed overview of the structure-agency debate, see Mike O'Donnell, ed., *Structure and Agency* (London: Sage, 2010).

By making reference to the metaphor of prosthesis, I argue that the relationship between life writing and sexual-scientific discourse can present various opportunities for agency, where narrative writing and sexual-scientific theories are utilized by the life writer to create the possibilities for a livable life. Throughout, I aim to steer clear of idealizing prostheses and remain aware of the very real pain, difficulty, and discrimination experienced by disabled people living with prostheses, which are comparable to (though different from) experiences made by queer and trans individuals whose writing I consider in this study.

1. Gender, Agency, and the Prosthetic Metaphor

In a speech addressed to the Wissenschaftlich-humanitäres Komitee (Scientific Humanitarian Committee) in 1904, the German activist for homosexuals' and women's rights, Anna Rüling, puts forward the thesis that as an *Urninde* (or lesbian), she has advantages over the "normal" woman due to her inherent maleness, which results in a greater sense of assertiveness and rationality. Here Rüling draws on Karl Heinrich Ulrichs's terminology of the *Urninde* as male soul in female body in order to advance a lesbian liberation movement at a time when the *Urninde* was barely recognized as a legitimate political subject. However, by drawing on sexual-scientific theories, Rüling also perpetuates stereotypes that are elsewhere used to pathologize female homosexuality.[4] Kirsten Leng pinpoints the issue with Rüling's speech: "If a subject is constituted in and through discourses of power-knowledge—even as he or she resists them—how can one accurately identify resistance on the part of the subject? . . . And how can or should the historian evaluate forms of resistance that appear to be politically retrograde?"[5] Leng's questions highlight the difficulties of understanding agency within autobiographical expression when that very expression relies on powerful scientific discourses that structure and constrain that which is possible to say.

Leng's chapter is part of a reinvigorated discussion about the emergence of sexuality, which seeks to think with and beyond Foucault about the ways in which powerful discourses structure sexual identity, but also allow for agency

---

4. Kirsten Leng, "Anna Rüling, Michel Foucault, and the 'Tactical Polyvalence' of the Female Homosexual," in *After the History of Sexuality: German Genealogies with and beyond Foucault*, ed. Scott Spector, Helmut Puff, and Dagmar Herzog (Oxford: Berghahn Books, 2012), 97.

5. Leng, "Anna Rüling," 96.

and resistance in navigating such discourses. Describing the disciplinary power of medico-scientific discourse about sex, Foucault maintains that speaking or writing about sexuality subjects the individual to the disciplinary confines of the very language of sexuality. Commenting on the case of Herculine Barbin, whose autobiography Foucault discovered in the French Department of Public Hygiene, he writes that it is only through the encounter with medico-scientific discourse that the category of sex became meaningful—and disciplinary—for Barbin.[6] Once diagnosed as "hermaphrodite," Barbin was subjected to an oppressive regime of power from which no confessional writing could provide liberation.

N. O. Body's memoirs offer a striking parallel to Herculine Barbin's auto-biography (not least because of Hirschfeld's own interest in the category of hermaphroditism, to which I return in the last section of this chapter). In this chapter, I will challenge Foucault's nonagential understanding of confessional writing. In his later writing, Foucault himself explores the role of agency, albeit tentatively, in sexual liberation movements as "movements that start with sexuality, with the apparatus of sexuality in the midst of which we're caught, and which make it function to the limit; but, at the same time, they are in motion relative to it, disengaging themselves and surmounting it."[7] Scholars in sexuality studies have further developed this vague and tentative exploration of agency in fruitful ways. Tracie Matysik calls the relative motion described by Foucault as the "wiggle room that subjects have had in their negotiation of those disciplinary mechanics."[8] This "wiggle room" or relative motion suggests that a subject's room for resistance can be very local, never far from the disciplinary mechanisms that regulate the behavior of individuals in the social body. Yet this relative movement can increase the space of personhood set out for the subject and lead to a troubling of the disciplinary mechanics at its heart.

The process of active self-fashioning in writing and language becomes of focal point of arguments around agency. Véronique Mottier explicates that disciplinary discourses function as "reflexive resources for the active shaping of the sexual self," thereby enabling "active practices of self-fashioning."[9] Harry

---

6. Michel Foucault, *Herculine Barbin: Being the Recently Discovered Memoirs of a Nineteenth Century French Hermaphrodite*, trans. Richard McDougall (New York City: Pantheon, 1980).

7. Michel Foucault, *Politics, Philosophy, Culture: Interviews and Other Writings, 1977–1984*, ed. Lawrence D. Kritzman (New York: Routledge, 1988), 114–15.

8. Tracie Matysik, "Beyond Freedom: A Return to Subjectivity in the History of Sexuality," in Spector, Puff, and Herzog, *After the History of Sexuality*, 185.

9. Véronique Mottier, "Sexuality and Sexology: Michel Foucault," in *Politics of Sexuality:*

Oosterhuis had already made a similar argument with regard to Krafft-Ebing's collection of case studies, proposing that those individuals who reported to Krafft-Ebing about their sexuality actively rethought sexological frameworks depending on their individual circumstances.[10] Writing about sexological narratives of homosexuality, Philippe Weber follows an explicitly Foucauldian and poststructuralist understanding of language as an expression of historically situated practice, considering language and narrative as the constitutive site of sexual-pathological homosexuality.[11] As a consequence, we must assume that sexual-scientific discourses not only put discursive constraints on subjects talking about themselves, but subjects are here also given the language to think and write critically about themselves and, in writing, create the possibilities for a different, more livable life.

All of these approaches highlight that transgression of norms is not the only, and perhaps not even the most powerful, way of achieving agency in the negotiation of one's gender and sexual identity. Instead, the creative agency of subjects can also be found in the way they accommodate, reject, or negotiate otherness in the realm of self-fashioning.[12] Accepting the important role that norms play in the construction of sexual subjectivity offers a more hospitable approach to sexual-scientific life writing. Building on these conceptions of agency through self-fashioning that actively engages with, rather than (or as well as) resists, normative frameworks, I offer the metaphor of prosthesis as a fruitful way to reorient thinking about agency in sexual-scientific life writing. This prosthetic metaphor, which I adopt from disability studies and cultural theory, disrupts the binary between the "natural" and "artificial" body. Examining the relation between homosexual autobiographies and medical theories of homosexuality in the nineteenth century, Klaus Müller considers how the medically informed identity category of "the homosexual" functioned as a "biographical prosthesis" for the autobiographic self.[13] With the help of this biographical prosthesis, a self-image emerges that is intelligible to a wider

---

Identity, Gender, Citizenship, ed. Terrell Carver and Véronique Mottier (London: Routledge, 1998), 122.

10. Oosterhuis, *Stepchildren of Nature*, 12.

11. Philippe Weber, *Der Trieb zum Erzählen: Sexualpathologie und Homosexualität, 1852–1914* (Bielefeld: Transcript, 2008), 25.

12. See also Lois McNay, *Gender and Agency: Reconfiguring the Subject in Feminist and Social Theory* (Cambridge: Polity Press, 2000).

13. Müller, *Aber in meinem Herzen*, 332. Müller's use of the term *biographische Prothese* takes inspiration (but differs) from the work of the Belgian prison anthropologist Jean-Pierre de Waele.

audience, as well as ringing true with the autobiographic writer. It is, as Müller describes it, a construction and fiction, but one that "works."[14] In Müller's account, the narrative thus becomes a prosthetic device that ensures the livability of the life of the author. Indeed, the words Müller uses to describe this are prescient of Butler's concept of livability when he argues that "the analyzed historical autobiographies aimed at a *possible* (*machbare*), *livable* (*lebbare*) *identity* and knowingly or unknowingly ignored experiences that could not be integrated into this identity."[15] The narrative makes use of biographical prostheses on which the writing self relies in order to communicate a possible, recognizable, and livable life.

In philosophy, cultural theory, and posthuman discourse, the prosthetic metaphor has undergone a shift in meaning. Rather than an artificial tool that props up a body in need of support, prosthetics has taken on new meaning as enhancing and augmenting a cyborg body, where the cyborg connotes a human body that overcomes its "natural" limitations.[16] In this context, the prosthetic metaphor is intimately tied to the figure of the cyborg. Although the term "cyborg" is anachronistic to the topic of sexual-scientific life writing, its application shows various productive uses. In her "Cyborg Manifesto," Donna Haraway describes the cyborg as "a cybernetic organism, a hybrid of machine and organism, a creature of social reality as well as a creature of fiction."[17] This collapse of the opposition between social reality and fiction is a foundational characteristic of sexual-scientific life writing (see Chapter 1). In addition to this, Haraway's cyborg disrupts the opposition between the "natural" body and the "artificial" prosthesis, as well as the closely related binary of "normal" versus "pathological" bodies. Similarly, sexual-scientific discourses are profoundly tied up in binaries of normal/abnormal and natural/unnatural, and sexually and gender-diverse life writers have to situate their self-narratives in relation to these categories. Applying the term "cyborg," my analysis can approach sexual-scientific life writing with the critical understanding that the

---

14. Müller, *Aber in meinem Herzen*, 328. My own translation.

15. Müller, *Aber in meinem Herzen*, 333. Müller takes the concept *machbare Identität* from Jean-Pierre de Waele.

16. Luna Dolezal, "Disability as Malleability: The Prosthetic Metaphor, Merleau-Ponty and the Case of Aimee Mullins," in *Medial Bodies between Fiction and Faction: Reinventing Corporeality*, ed. Denise Butnaru (Bielefeld: Transcript, 2020), 125.

17. Donna Haraway, "A Cyborg Manifesto: Science, Technology, and Socialist-Feminism in the Late 20th Century," in *The International Handbook of Virtual Learning Environments*, ed. Joel Weiss, Jason Nolan, Jeremy Hunsinger, and Peter Trifonas (New York: Springer, 2006), 117.

opposition between "natural" and "artificial" (and "fact" and "fiction") is necessarily constructed.

Philosopher Luna Dolezal explains how the body and prosthetic technology come together in the cyborg through reference to Maurice Merleau-Ponty's phenomenological account of the body schema. Merleau-Ponty offers the example of a blind man using a stick to navigate the world. Here the man's body schema has incorporated the stick, which enables the man to experience the external world through an extended bodily experience that now includes the stick.[18] According to Merleau-Ponty, this is not an interaction between discrete objects. Rather, technologies can be acquired to make possible new capabilities of the body.[19] Merleau-Ponty's example illustrates the figure of the cyborg, who collapses the distinction between "natural" body and "artificial" prosthesis and instead highlights new capabilities that arise at the intersection of body and technology.

Just as prosthetics do not define the body to which they belong, they do not simply prop up a body that gladly, uncritically, and uncreatively receives the support. Haraway argues that the link between nonbiological (or here nonbiographical) material and the body need not be a hierarchical imposition of science and technology on the human body. Rather, corporeality can be understood as being on equal terms with scientific technologies without fearing a loss of a supposed primary innocence or independence. Prosthesis, Haraway writes in her essay on science and feminist objectivity, is "a fundamental category for understanding our most intimate selves. Prosthesis is semiosis, the making of meanings and bodies, not for transcendence, but for power-charged communication."[20] Haraway uses the figure of the cyborg "as a fiction mapping our social and bodily reality and as an imaginative resource suggesting some very fruitful couplings."[21] As such, her "cyborg myth is about transgressed boundaries, potent fusions, and dangerous possibilities."[22] As Haraway writes, "For us, in imagination and in other practice, machines can be prosthetic devices, intimate components, friendly selves."[23] From within the mythical world of the cyborg, all parts of the self are machine or machinations. In *Undoing Gender*, Judith Butler similarly notes that "we would be foolish to

---

18. Dolezal, "Disability as Malleability," 131.

19. Dolezal, "Disability as Malleability," 130.

20. Donna Haraway, "Situated Knowledges: The Science Question in Feminism and the Privilege of Partial Perspective," *Feminist Studies* 14, no. 3 (Fall 1988): 598 n. 7.

21. Haraway, "A Cyborg Manifesto," 118.

22. Haraway, "A Cyborg Manifesto," 121.

23. Haraway, "A Cyborg Manifesto," 144.

think that life is fully possible without a dependence on technology, which suggests that the human . . . is dependent on technology, to live. In this sense, we are thinking within the frame of the cyborg."[24] Accordingly, within the world of the cyborg, the inclusion of machinations or technologies—here, sexual-scientific discourse as narrative technology, for example—in the self does not forsake any ability to have agency. As Merleau-Ponty's example of the blind man with the stick exemplifies, agency is introduced by the very fact of making creative use of prosthetic devices.

The figure of the cyborg and its use of prosthetics can be productively applied to the relationship between the writing self and sexual-scientific discourses. When we investigate sexual-scientific life writing, subjective agency cannot be considered separate from sexual-scientific discourse and structure; rather, such writing brings forth new capabilities and possibilities for queer livability. This accounts for the dynamic ways in which life writing irrevocably merges life and sexual-scientific discourse to construct sexual subjectivity. Here I remain careful not to conflate the prosthetic metaphor with a triumphant account of a porous and malleable body. Dolezal notes that the trope of the augmenting, posthuman prosthetic metaphor relies on a liberal humanist ideal of self-determination and individuality and thereby invokes prosthesis as an overcoming of the limitations of biology and disability.[25] As Vivian Sobchack, who describes her own experiences with an above-the-knee amputation, shows, while the prosthetic metaphor has created new possibilities for the lived experience of people living with prostheses, it has also been fetishized and, in doing so, has excluded the reality of prosthetic use.[26]

When I use the prosthetic metaphor as a critical tool to investigate sexual-scientific life writing, I do so because I recognize the shared experiences of marginalization and othering that sexual-scientific life writers as well as disabled people making use of prostheses are exposed to, in particular similar (but not identical) marginalization based on bodily difference. Just like disabled people, queer and trans people in the early twentieth century were considered as outside of the physical or psychological norm. Sobchack writes that her prosthetic leg is not as seductive or observational as it is for her academic colleagues who "make theory" with prostheses, but requires exhaustible energy in

---

24. Judith Butler, *Undoing Gender* (London: Routledge, 2004), 12.
25. Dolezal, "Disability as Malleability," 27.
26. Vivian Sobchack, "A Leg to Stand On: Prosthetics, Metaphor, and Materiality," in *The Prosthetic Impulse: From a Posthuman Present to a Biocultural Future*, ed. Marquard Smith and Joanne Morra (Cambridge, MA: MIT Press, 2006).

use.[27] This is comparable (but not identical) to the very real effort and energy that sexual-scientific life writers have to invest in making sexual-scientific discourses (as technologies) work for them. Although the outcome might be a livable life (similar to Sobchack's ability to move through the world), it is not one free from suffering. Making use of prostheses is not easy or painless work, but precisely by focusing on the work that is required when using prostheses, I hope to return the focus of my discussion to the issue of agency.

Previously I suggested that the prosthetic assemblage can disrupt and complicate any assumption that subjection to dominant discourses implies a lack of agency. Rather than arguing that we are determined by either structure or agency, the prosthetic metaphor shows that they are co-constitutive and therefore intricately and inseparably linked. In the following analysis, I want to consider the meaning of prosthesis as creative and enabling, yet complex and potentially uncomfortable in three ways that, together, constitute a prosthetic assemblage. In the first instance, I consider how Hirschfeld's questionnaire functions as prosthetic support for Body's memoir. The following section considers how the narrative itself is a prosthetic device that creates the possibility of livability for the life writer.[28] This builds on Müller's argument that autobiographies functioned as biographical prosthesis for the lived lives of homosexuals in the nineteenth century, but my analysis further complicates the strict separation between life and life writing. The final section examines the prosthetic afterlife of Body's narrative by investigating two cases where the autobiography was used in sexual-scientific publications to confirm certain sexual-scientific theories. My analysis in these three sections will show that, just as the relationship between body and prosthesis can be rethought as constitutive, creative, and productive, the active and agential co-constitution of life writing and sexual-scientific discourse creates the possibilities for a livable life.

---

27. Sobchack, "Leg to Stand On," 18.

28. My use of this term here is not to be confused with the concept of "narrative prosthesis" developed by David T. Mitchell and Sharon L. Snyder, which summarizes the dependency of literature on disability as an opportunistic metaphor to lend idiosyncrasy to characters, where disability becomes a "crutch upon which literary narratives lean for their representational power, disruptive potentiality, and analytical insight." David Mitchell and Sharon Snyder, "Narrative Prosthesis," in *The Disability Studies Reader*, 4th ed., ed. Lennard J. Davis (London: Routledge, 2013), 224. See also David T. Mitchell and Sharon L. Snyder, *Narrative Prosthesis: Disability and the Dependencies of Discourse* (Ann Arbor: University of Michigan Press, 2000).

2. Sexual-Scientific Method as Biographical Prosthesis

Sexual knowledge production is by no means a one-directional transfer of knowledge from practitioner to patient. Christopher Looby and Benjamin Kahan both point out the important role of literature in shaping how we understand sexuality and sexual interiority.[29] Anna Katharina Schaffner argues that it is in the mutual exchange between literary writers, sexual scientists, and patients that sexual knowledge production takes place.[30] Ian Hacking describes this process as a scientific feedback loop, where categories or "human kinds" are continually revised through the identification of the individual, which then feeds back into the understanding of human kinds in a circular movement.[31] In the following section, I analyze one moment within this larger feedback loop by investigating how N. O. Body made use of a questionnaire developed by Magnus Hirschfeld as prosthetic support for his autobiography. Body's use of Hirschfeld's questionnaire thereby forms a part in a much longer history of exchange between patients and practitioners during which certain topics and scripts around childhood experiences, misguidances, and eventual discovery of a true self crystallized and became dominant.[32] As Geertje Mak argues, navigating these scripts "required methods of self-reflection, professional psychiatric or psychological skills and knowledge, narrative scripts, and not in the least an 'urge to know.'"[33] This reveals a certain level of literacy and agency in navigating dominant discourses and scripts.

In the late 1890s, Magnus Hirschfeld pioneered a questionnaire that sought to collect data on gender and sexual diversity on a large scale. The questionnaire

---

29. Christopher Looby, "The Literariness of Sexuality: Or, How to Do the (Literary) History of (American) Sexuality," *American Literary History* 25, no. 4 (Winter 2013): 841; Benjamin Kahan, *The Book of Minor Perverts: Sexology, Etiology, and the Emergences of Sexuality* (Chicago: University of Chicago Press, 2019), 20.

30. Anna Katharina Schaffner, *Modernism and Perversion: Sexual Deviance in Sexology and Literature, 1850–1930* (Basingstoke: Palgrave Macmillan, 2012), 23.

31. Ian Hacking, "The Looping Effects of Human Kinds," in *Causal Cognition: A Multidisciplinary Debate*, ed. Dan Sperber, David Premack, and Ann James Premack (Oxford: Oxford University Press, 1995). A number of recent publications in the history of sexuality rely on Hacking's feedback loop. See, for example, Schaffner, *Modernism and Perversion*; Peter Cryle and Elizabeth Stephens, *Normality: A Critical Genealogy* (Chicago: University of Chicago Press, 2017); Birgit Lang, Joy Damousi, and Alison Lewis, eds., *A History of the Case Study: Sexology, Psychoanalysis, Literature* (Manchester: Manchester University Press, 2017); Looby, "The Literariness of Sexuality."

32. See Oosterhuis, *Stepchildren of Nature*, 216–17; Mak, *Doubting Sex*, 202.

33. Mak, *Doubting Sex*, 209.

grew out of an interest in collecting the personal stories of individual patients as case studies that could then be used for a broader scientific study. The case generates descriptions of patients that can be analyzed in medical terms while enabling them to remain individual accounts. However, compiling case studies was a cumbersome task that required lengthy analysis in order to provide generalizable data that could evidence the very real prevalence of a variety of human sexual expressions. Hirschfeld's solution to the challenge of collecting sexological data that was both detailed and generalizable was to develop a new methodology that would require much less time on the part of the practitioner and yield a much larger number of responses without compromising their length and detail.[34] Hirschfeld first used the questionnaire in either 1898 or 1899.[35] In 1908, he published a new version of the questionnaire, entitled "psychoanalytic questionnaire," in the *Zeitschrift für Sexualwissenschaft* (*Journal of Sexual Sciences*).[36] This new psychoanalytic questionnaire was reworked with the help of eleven other practitioners: psychoanalyst Karl Abraham, dermatologist and sexologist Iwan Bloch, psychiatrist Otto Juliusburger, psychoanalyst Heinrich Koerber, writer and politician Carl Friedrich Jordan, as well as James Fraenkel, Max Tischler, Georg Tobias, F. Stein, L. S. A. Roemer-Helder, and Paul Bürger-Diether (684).[37] Although exact numbers cannot be stated for certain, Hirschfeld is said to have collected over forty thousand completed questionnaires.[38] Hirschfeld notes that the questionnaire was not for general distribution but was devised as a tool to help the sexological practitioner assess patients (684).

---

34. Douglas Pretsell, "The Evolution of the Questionnaire in German Sexual Science: A Methodological Narrative," *History of Science* 58, no. 3 (2020): 326–49.

35. In "Zur Methodik der Sexualwissenschaft," published in 1908, Hirschfeld writes that he first developed the questionnaire ten years earlier, suggesting it was first used in 1898. In *Die Homosexualität des Mannes und des Weibes*, published in 1914 but, as the foreword suggests, written a year earlier, Hirschfeld claims that he first used it fourteen years ago, suggesting the year 1899. See Magnus Hirschfeld, "Zur Methodik der Sexualwissenschaft," *Zeitschrift für Sexualwissenschaft* 1 (1908): 684; Magnus Hirschfeld, *Die Homosexualität des Mannes und des Weibes* (Berlin: Louis Marcus Verlagsbuchhandlung, 1914), 239–40.

36. Hirschfeld, "Zur Methodik der Sexualwissenschaft." All subsequent references to this article are given in the text.

37. Ivan Crozier shows that Havelock Ellis and John Addington Symonds also discuss the use of a questionnaire, but Crozier has not been able to locate any copies of such a questionnaire. See Ivan Crozier, "Pillow Talk: Credibility, Trust and the Sexological Case History," *History of Science* 46, no. 4 (December 2008): 382; Ivan Crozier, "Introduction: Havelock Ellis, John Addington Symonds and the Construction of Sexual Inversion," in *Sexual Inversion: A Critical Edition*, ed. Ivan Crozier (Basingstoke: Palgrave Macmillan, 2008), 50.

38. Erwin J. Haeberle, introduction to Magnus Hirschfeld, *Die Homosexualität des Mannes und des Weibes* (Berlin: de Gruyter, 1984), v–xxxi.

The original description of the questionnaire as "psychoanalytic" highlights that the initial methodological inspiration was drawn from psychoanalysis. As Elena Mancini points out in her biography of Hirschfeld, Carl Gustav Jung, in his correspondence with Freud about Hirschfeld, criticized Hirschfeld's use of the term "psychoanalytic" for his questionnaire, and Freud himself agreed that the questionnaire was not of direct psychoanalytic relevance.[39] By 1914, Hirschfeld had changed the name of the questionnaire to "psychobiological."[40] A version issued by the Institute of Sexology in 1930 is also called "psychobiological questionnaire."[41] This marked once more sexology's break from psychoanalysis and toward a discovery of a biological understanding of sexual diversity. After Hirschfeld's death in exile and the end of World War II, the questionnaire was reclaimed by psychoanalyst and Berlin Psychoanalytic Institute member Werner Becker, who issued a psychobiological questionnaire, supposedly coauthored by himself and Hirschfeld, in 1949.[42] Becker published pseudonymous articles in Dutch homosexual magazines and used Hirschfeld's questionnaire in his dissertation on the biological nature of homosexuality. He also attempted to revive the Scientific Humanitarian Committee in Berlin Spandau.[43]

In my analysis to follow, I argue that there is reason to assume that N. O. Body filled in Hirschfeld's questionnaire and based his memoirs on the questions posed within it. However, if N. O. Body did indeed fill in Hirschfeld's questionnaire, this document is most likely lost today. Hirschfeld published questionnaires completed by patients.[44] When Hirschfeld's Institute of Sexology was ransacked by members of the Nazi-sanctioned Deutsche Studentenschaft (German Student Union) in May 1933, the questionnaires were left behind and, unlike many of the books and manuscripts held by the institute's library and archive, not destroyed in the book burnings on Berlin's Opernplatz. Sexologist and author of Hirschfeld's first biography, Charlotte

39. Elena Mancini, *Magnus Hirschfeld and the Quest for Sexual Freedom: A History of the First International Sexual Freedom Movement* (New York: Palgrave Macmillan, 2010), 72.

40. Hirschfeld, *Die Homosexualität des Mannes* (1984), 240.

41. Magnus Hirschfeld, *Psychobiologischer Fragebogen: Herausgegeben mit seinen Mitarbeitern*, Magnus Hirschfeld Collection (n.p.: Kinsey Institute for Research in Sex, Gender, and Reproduction, 1930).

42. Magnus Hirschfeld, *Psychobiologischer Fragebogen*, Magnus Hirschfeld Collection (n.p.: Kinsey Institute for Research in Sex, Gender, and Reproduction, 1949).

43. Andreas Pretzel, *NS-Opfer unter Vorbehalt: Homosexuelle Männer in Berlin nach 1945* (Münster: LIT Verlag, 2002), 301.

44. Hirschfeld, *Die Homosexualität des Mannes* (1984), 237–63.

Wolff, argues that the questionnaires were deliberately left behind so they could be used as evidence against homosexual visitors to the institute.[45] However, Heike Bauer argues that the questionnaires were spared for rather mundane, practical reasons: as loose paper they were simply too cumbersome to transport.[46] Some questionnaires were taken out of the country and later reappeared in archives abroad.[47] The fate of the remaining collection of questionnaires remains unknown.

Despite this lack of historical documentation, it is clear that Hirschfeld's particular methodology provides a number of biographical prostheses for Body's autobiographical writing. Various items from Hirschfeld's questionnaire are answered or referred to in Body's autobiography. Out of the questionnaire's 127 questions, over half are answered explicitly in the narrative, while most others can be inferred from the text. A very limited number of questions are not referred to in the autobiography, predominantly those concerning the respondent's engagement in sexual behavior that could have been considered nonheterosexual. This, however, is not surprising: §175 of the German Criminal Code criminalized sexual contact between men, but created a wider fear of nonheterosexual desire. Additionally, according to §184 of the code, the circulation of obscene writing was punishable with imprisonment for up to one year. For this reason, any mention of sexual contact deemed improper in the context of art and literature was prohibited. Hirschfeld himself faced legal prosecution as a result of his statistical research. In December 1903, he surveyed three thousand male students of the Technische Hochschule Berlin to inquire after their sexual orientation. His initial inquiry yielded the fact, so Hirschfeld claimed, that homosexuals made up more than 2 percent of the population, and he used this fact to remind his readership that homosexuality was not a negligible exception to the norm, but a scientifically detectable fact.[48] At a student rally, Hirschfeld was accused of impudence, molestation, and seduction, among other things. The incident was covered in the papers to cause further

45. Charlotte Wolff, *Magnus Hirschfeld: A Portrait of a Pioneer in Sexology* (London: Quartet Books, 1986), 376.

46. Heike Bauer, *The Hirschfeld Archives: Violence, Death, and Modern Queer Culture* (Philadelphia: Temple University Press, 2017), 169.

47. See, for example, Rainer Herrn, Michael Thomas Taylor, and Annette F. Timm, "Magnus Hirschfeld's Institute for Sexual Science: A Visual Sourcebook," in *Not Straight from Germany: Sexual Publics and Sexual Citizenship since Magnus Hirschfeld*, ed. Michael Thomas Taylor, Annette F. Timm, and Rainer Herrn (Ann Arbor: University of Michigan Press, 2017), 64.

48. Magnus Hirschfeld, "Das Ergebnis der statistischen Untersuchungen über den Prozentsatz der Homosexuellen," *Jahrbuch für sexuelle Zwischenstufen* 6 (1904): 170.

outrage. Five students subsequently sued Hirschfeld, who was convicted and required to pay a large fine in retribution for offense caused by the question-naire.[49] Hence, to mention any sexual relations between individuals considered to be of the same sex would have rendered it impossible for the autobiography to comply with censorship laws.

The correlation between some of the information provided in Body's autobiography and corresponding items from the questionnaire could at times certainly be coincidental: indeed, many autobiographies might speak of the number of siblings or physical descriptors such as the color of one's eyes, as both the autobiography and the questionnaire do. Other details, however, are clearly medically informed. Items 2 and 3 of the questionnaire, for example, require the respondent to confirm any cases of incestuous relations in the near family history: "Are your parents or grandparents related by blood (if so, in what way; cousins, uncle or niece etc.)?" (684). Body's text strikingly echoes questions taken from the questionnaire: "She [the grandmother] was one of his cousins, and because some next-of-kin marriages had taken place in the family in previous years, both parents refused to consent" (MGY 18). Such questions, which evidently form part of a patient's medical history, exemplify the close relation between autobiography and questionnaire.

In some instances, the repetition of words and terms from the question-naire in the narrative is telling. Consider the following question from the questionnaire: "Did you prefer to play with boys or girls? Did you prefer boys' games, such as throwing snowballs, scuffling, hobbyhorses, soldiers, etc., or did you prefer feminine child play, such as dolls, cooking, crocheting, knitting?" (686–87). In Body's narrative, particular reference is made to several of these activities. The narrator relates an incident that happened on Body's fifth birthday: "What I found was a doll. . . . I almost cried, when I noticed a hobbyhorse that my aunt, who had guessed my disposition (*Neigung*), had added to the lot" (MGY 27). The reference to both doll and hob-byhorse might be seen as merely generic, rather than necessarily exemplify-ing the influence of the questionnaire on the text. But the narrative also repeats other lexical choices from the questionnaire here: the questionnaire uses the word *Neigung* to inquire about a person's sexual preference, and uses it as a synonym for *Trieb* (sexual drive, item 122), *Empfindung* (sensa-tion, item 127), and *sexuelle Abweichung* (sexual deviance, item 121). Thus, by talking about a preference for boyish toys while using vocabulary that

49. Adolf Thiele, "Kann Homosexualität strafbar sein?," *Sozialistisches Monatsheft* 24 (December 1909): 1566.

links such preference to sexual interests, Body's narrative associates boyish play with masculine sexuality and uses this as a biographical prosthesis to argue that his true identity was always already male.

Handiwork, too, is echoed in the memoirs; the narrator claims: "When it came to knitting, my awkward hands could not hold the needle" (MGY 41). This awkwardness is qualified within the same paragraph. Body claims that his teacher complains: "[Nora] really [is] as awkward in such things as a boy" (MGY 41). The inability to knit is introduced as a masculine trait. Yet his boyishness goes beyond simple comparison: shortly after Body's failed attempts at knitting, he is rejected by his girlfriends with the words "Go away, you foul boy. . . . You are a real boy, and we know it" (MGY 42). Similarly, one of the first few scenes related in the narrative is Body's memory of how other children often called him names, shouting, "Boy, boy, nasty boy!" (MGY 10). Both passages correspond to Hirschfeld's questionnaire, which asks: "Were there comments like . . . 'She is a complete boy'?" (687).

The autobiography continues to emphasize Body's physical maleness and sexual attraction to women. From birth onward, the child's sex is indeterminable and continues to be so throughout childhood and adolescence. As such, question 61 of the questionnaire—"Do abnormalities occur in the genital area or on the genitals?" (689)—is answered in the affirmative in the autobiography: bathing the young child, the maid laughs (MGY 35), and Body's own mother cries at the sight of his body (MGY 12). The reader discovers the reason for this when Body's friends behold his naked body and exclaim: "Look how different Nora is" (MGY 24). When swimming with his male friends, however, they do not find Body's naked body strange or different (MGY 48). Thus, in response to the questionnaire, the narrative clarifies that Body's physical appearance does indeed differ significantly from that of his female friends, yet seems to attract no attention from his male friends. This implies that physically, as well as behaviorally, Body passes as a boy.

The memoir continues to describe Body's physical changes in response to the questionnaire. Prompted by question 36—"When did you develop other signs of pubescence? If you are female, did you notice a lowering of the voice or the development of a soft beard?" (688)—the narrative states both the sudden hoarseness of Body's voice just before his twelfth birthday (MGY 57) as well as the development of a light beard (MGY 71). It therefore seems that Body's hitherto ambiguous body finally shows its true nature as puberty approaches. By now, Body's dreams also confirm his otherwise male, heterosexual identity. While still at school, he experiences erotic visions: "I was lying in bed and beautiful women with brown hair and dark eyes bowed down above me. They were naked, and all obeyed me" (MGY 79). As a student, he dreamed of "possess[ing]" his classmate, Harriet (MGY 112). In the light of question 26 of the questionnaire, which inquires about any recurring dreams (687), both passages from the autobiography indicate that Body is sexually aroused by women, not as equals, but as sexual partners to be possessed, thereby fulfilling the requirements of heterosexual masculinity.

Writing about the emergence of sexuality and the formation of concepts that define what kind of person one can or cannot be at any given moment, historian of philosophy and Foucault scholar Arnold Davidson states that personhood often depends on who we are not but could be.[50] An accepted personhood thereby also gains meaning in relation to those that are rejected. This is exemplified in Body's narrative on several occasions. While questions 12 to 18 of the questionnaire ask the respondent to describe any cases of mental or bodily dysfunction in the family history (e.g., item 12, "Did close relatives suffer from nervous or mental disruptions?" or item 18, "Are you aware of any cases of abnormal sexual tendencies among your close relatives?"), the narrator of *A Man's Girlhood Years* responds as follows:

> I know very little of my mother's family that could have influenced my personal history. They were all healthy people who lived long lives, and without physical or mental anomalies. On my father's side, too, I don't remember any cases of mental or physical degeneration. (MGY 19)

The lexical choice, here—"degeneration" and "physical anomalies"—is medically influenced. The latter phrase especially echoes questions 17 and 18, which ask patients to describe abnormal appearance or deviant sexual tendencies of their close relatives. By describing what is not the case, Body therefore rejects the identity of the "degenerate."

A particularly telling instance is the concluding section of the questionnaire. Unlike the previous items, the final set of questions lists specific conditions, such as "bisexuality," "desire for minors," "sadism," "masochism," "fetishism," "erotic desire for cross-dressing," "exhibitionism," "voyeurism," "zoophilia," and others (694–95). Rather than subscribing to any of these options, Body explicitly rejects all of them. In response to sexually explicit stories told by his male colleagues at the clothing shop where he is briefly employed as an apprentice, Body remarks: "Today these stories remind me of the perverse deeds

---

50. Arnold Davidson, *The Emergence of Sexuality: Historical Epistemology and the Formation of Concepts* (Cambridge, MA: Harvard University Press, 2001), 3.

of a sadist or exhibitionist!" (MGY 95). The echoing of words taken from the questionnaire in particular, and the medical lexicon in general, emphasizes the fact that the protagonist also defines himself according to *rejected* personhoods provided by Hirschfeld's questionnaire. Here, he uses Hirschfeld's questionnaire to create a biographical prosthesis of nonpathology.

Tracing the relationship between Body's autobiography and Hirschfeld's questionnaire shows that sexual-scientific discourse provides a number of biographical prostheses for sexual-scientific life writing. These biographical prostheses include, for example, establishing a sense of heterosexual masculinity and of nonpathology. As a consequence, Body's memoir provides a coherent narrative that makes Body's own desires, identifications, and self-awareness legible to the expert reader. While Hirschfeld's questionnaire sets out the categories and therefore limits for identification, it also provides a prosthetic framework for Body's narrative to unfold. As critical disability scholar Margrit Shildrick argues about the normative and yet subversive meaning of prosthesis, "On the one hand, prosthetic devices are intended to replace or enhance normative function and appearance, figuring, in other words a Foucauldian sense of the technological disciplining and regulation of the body, but on the other, their use may be radically subverted."[51] Body's narrative exploits the normative potential of the prosthetic support of sexual-scientific discourse in order to claim subjective agency and tell a livable story where his maleness becomes legible and his ascribed female identity collapses. Livability, the balance between finding categories of recognition that hold but do not suffocate the subject, arises in the careful navigation of the sexual-scientific script. Body's engagement with Hirschfeld's questionnaire shows that agency does not require the absolute rejection of sexual-scientific knowledge, practice, and technique, but is constituted in the ability to narrate a coherent story that contributes to an active shaping of the sexual self as part of a generative process. In the following section, I explore more specifically how Body's narrative intervenes creatively and critically in sexological discourse in order to shape a livable life.

3. Narrative Prosthesis

Agency in sexual-scientific life writing can be determined by tracing efforts to make prosthetic use of sexual-scientific discourse. The latter is used as pros-

---

51. Margrit Shildrick, *Dangerous Discourses of Disability, Subjectivity and Sexuality* (Basingstoke: Palgrave Macmillan, 2009), 133.

thetic support for telling a coherent narrative that achieves a sense of livability, a narrative that, as explored in the previous chapter, can be confessed to, and understood by, a community and readership. Nonetheless, there are instances in Body's memoirs in which the narrative complicates the clearly categorized schema of the questionnaire and refuses to simply rely on its prosthetic support.[52] Despite Body's seemingly clear-cut male identity, a sense of uncertainty and incoherence arises at times. "The old doubts appeared anew. What was I? Boy or girl? If I was a girl, then why . . . didn't I suffer this 'disease,' which I found disgusting, yet desired nonetheless as a clear sign to define my sex? If I was a boy, why the girl's name?" (MGY 79). The definition of what it means to be a girl or boy in Body's situation is particularly interesting. As a girl, he lacks the perceived physical signifiers of womanhood: breasts and menstruation here referred to as a disease. Yet he is prohibited from being a boy by one word: his name. This word is given immense power; although his physicality suggests otherwise, Body is regarded as a woman because of his female name, which interpellates him into an identity as seen by others. Because words position an individual in a way that can be painful, a single word—"Norbert"—can cause Body immense happiness, while another—"Nora"—causes intense pain. A male identity is impossible to narrate adequately, because every attempt to attribute masculine terms to himself signifies a certain gap between the way in which he sees himself and the way in which the world sees and genders him.

When his female colleagues at the clothing shop where Body works begin to date men and talk about their experiences, Body comments: "Secretly, I wished for such an adventure, too; of course, just so I would have something to contribute to their conversation" (MGY 73). Body here momentarily desires to pass as a woman, just like his colleagues, by wishing for a heterosexual encounter *as* woman. Yet this statement is immediately followed by a qualifying statement, which nullifies any claim of female identification, and gives a reason that is more coherent with his male desire to spend time among his female col-

---

52. Not only Body, but other patients of Hirschfeld, too, critically engage with the latter's sexological theories. Looking at Hirschfeld's *Die Transvestiten*, Darryl B. Hill notes that Hirschfeld may have wanted to present his understanding of transvestitism as separate from homosexuality, but that the first-person cases he presented often contradicted this categorization. Mr. I, for example, claims that he does not have homosexual tendencies, but then goes on to say that he feels differently when dressed as a woman: "I deeply despise Urnings and effeminate men. The idea of penetration without being in costume seems to me abominable." Magnus Hirschfeld, *Die Transvestiten: Eine Untersuchung über den erotischen Verkleidungsstrieb* (Berlin: Alfred Pulvermacher und Co., 1910); Darryl B. Hill, "Sexuality and Gender in Hirschfeld's *Die Transvestiten*: A Case of the 'Elusive Evidence of the Ordinary,'" *Journal of the History of Sexuality* 14, no. 3 (July 2005): 326.

leagues. The same argumentative structure is repeated several times. Body, for example, asserts: "Our interest in these strange creatures with short hair increased. I say 'our,' although I was only interested in their outward appearance" (MGY 73). As much as masculine attributes seemed fraudulent before, the "I," introducing a female identity, is certainly a sham.

Nonetheless, there are instances in which Body fully embraces a female identity. When his girlfriends at school called him a "foul boy," Body "raged and screamed and tried to convince the girls that [he] really was a girl" (MGY 42). This is a kind of calling into existence, what Denise Riley calls an "aggressive interpellation, which simultaneously demands consent and incites refusal."[53] Another instance reiterates this: when his male playmates ask him whether he "would . . . like to be a real boy," Body "beg[ins] to brag that girls are much better off and how happy [he] was to be a girl" (MGY 63). At the moment when Body is called a boy, he violently refuses this identity. Yet Body's male identity never ceases to exist. Judith Butler writes: "Called by an injurious name, I come into social being, and because I have a certain inevitable attachment to my existence . . . I am led to embrace the terms that injure me because they constitute me socially."[54] At the moment of aggressive interpellation, where Body refuses to be a boy and insists on his female identity, he has also been called a boy and cannot forget his boyishness. Although he apparently rejects any association with a potential male self and never sees his male friends again after this incident, the desire to be a "real boy" remains throughout the narrative.

At the same time, moments of female identification remain and emerge again when Body begins to socialize with his classmates at school. He says: "At the ice rink we met our protectors, who carried out all sorts of chivalrous deeds. For us, they were the representatives of a strange world, which we loved and admired, and we were happy to be allowed to fulfill their wishes" (MGY 73–74). No qualifying statement follows this description; Body appears to thoroughly identify with these views. Consider also another passage later on: "We were certainly scared of men, because they appeared barbaric to us, every one an unfaithful brute, even the husband, who surely raped his wife anew every day—every woman a saint, who had to sacrifice herself to such a monster" (MGY 93). Body perceives these stereotypes as a woman, but what also

---

53. Denise Riley, *The Words of Selves: Identification Solidarity Irony* (Stanford: Stanford University Press, 2000), 85.

54. Judith Butler, *Excitable Speech: A Politics of the Performative* (London: Routledge, 1997), 104, cited in Riley, *Words of Selves*, 126.

becomes evident is that he speaks of his female identity only in the plural, suggesting that, in the singular, the "I" cannot, without committing fraud, express an identity as woman. Body claims both a male and a female identity at times, yet cannot maintain either one without qualifying, denying, or emphasizing it. To be, in the words of Butler, "that for which there is no place within the given regime of truth" leaves his identity noncoherent and fluid, never truly male and never unconditionally female.[55] Within the logic of Hirschfeld's questionnaire, this does not appear a viable option.

There is another reason why Body's attempts to appear as unquestioningly male might have been particularly urgent, and his nonetheless ambiguous positioning might have been particularly problematic for him. Sander Gilman reads in Body's descriptions of his gender identity a fear of being read as a feminized man. When Body presents his changing voice during adolescence as a sign of tuberculosis, he refers to the fears, common at the time, that tuberculosis feminizes men. As a consequence, however, he introduces the hope that such somatic feminization might be cured. Gilman sees a parallel between such a fear of the feminized male body and the attention drawn to Body's French Catholic appearance, which Body argues can be guessed from his outward appearance. Karl Baer was Jewish, rather than French Catholic, a substitution, Gilman argues, that sought to divert attention from the existing sexual stereotype of the feminized Jew: "For Baer, and for the world in which he loved, the 'damaged' genitalia of the male Jew, damaged through circumcision . . . meant that the male Jew is already neither truly male nor actually female."[56] As a consequence, Body had to defend his male identity against a twofold challenge: his female naming at birth and antisemitic stereotypes of Jewish men as both feminized and prone to illness.[57]

Oskar Panizza's grotesque novella *Der operirte Jud'* (*The Operated Jew*)

---

55. Butler, *Undoing Gender*, 58.

56. Sander Gilman, "Whose Body Is It, Anyway? Hermaphrodites, Gays, and Jews in N. O. Body's Germany," in N. O. Body, *A Man's Maiden Years*, trans. Deborah Simon (Philadelphia: University of Pennsylvania Press, 2006), xxi.

57. Sander Gilman, "Jews and Mental Illness: Medical Metaphors, Anti-Semitism, and the Jewish Response," *Journal of the History of the Behavioral Sciences* 20, no. 2 (April 1984): 150–59. The International Holocaust Remembrance Alliance recommends the spelling of "antisemitism" over "anti-Semitism" "in order to dispel the idea that there is an entity 'Semitism' which 'anti-Semitism' opposes. Antisemitism should be read as a unified term so that the meaning of the generic term for modern Jew-hatred is clear." I follow their recommendation. See "Memo on Spelling Antisemitism," International Holocaust Remembrance Alliance, accessed March 24, 2021, https://www.holocaustremembrance.com/sites/default/files/memo-on-spelling-of-antisemitism_final-1.pdf

vividly satirizes this antisemitic stereotype of the damaged physiognomy of the Jew.[58] The novella depicts the typecast Jewish character Faitel, who undergoes invasive surgery that includes the breaking and setting of bones in order to enable what Joela Jacobs calls "physiognomic passing."[59] Ultimately, Faitel's transformation fails and he is described as reverting back into his "monstrous" former self. While some critics understand Panizza's novella as an antisemitic text, Jacobs argues that it satirizes both stereotypes of Jewishness as well as the constructed nature of German national identity.[60] It certainly draws a vivid image of antisemitic stereotyping of Jewish physiognomy as evident and unalterable, which subsequently makes passing as well as assimilation impossible. Such antisemitism permeated German culture broadly and medical sciences and medico-scientific professions in particular.[61] Making Body—and his body—French Catholic, rather than Jewish, is a direct response to such antisemitism typecasting. This is despite the fact that his Jewish identity played an important role in his professional as well as private life, as I will explore further in Chapter 3.

If the presentation of Body's life as perfectly in line with Hirschfeld's questionnaire shows, on the one hand, an eagerness to conform, do divergences from the questionnaire, such as the threat of feminization, on the other hand, mean that the narrative breaks down by failing to tell a coherent story? Applying the metaphor of prosthesis, I want to argue that Body's narrative shows an engagement with the normative potential of Hirschfeld's prosthetic questionnaire, which offers Body the chance to reject feminine traits and narrate a coherent story of normative masculinity, while at the same time it resists the uncomfortable fit of Hirschfeld's questionnaire, which asks for definitive answers about sexual and gender characteristics. Applying the prosthetic metaphor in this way again complicates the structure-agency binary.

For Butler, a situation in which the "I" is forced to appear coherent causes "a certain ethical violence, which demands that we manifest and maintain self-

---

58. Oskar Panizza, *Der operirte Jud'*, in *Der Korsettenfritz: Gesammelte Erzählungen*, ed. Bernd Mattheus (Munich: Matthes & Seitz, 1981).

59. Joela Jacobs, "Speaking the Non-human: Plants, Animals, and Marginalized Humans in Literary Grotesques from Oskar Panizza to Franz Kafka" (PhD diss., University of Chicago, 2014), 169.

60. Jacobs, "Speaking the Non-human," 170.

61. Gilman, "Jews and Mental Illness"; Christina von Braun, "'Der Jude' und 'das Weib': Zwei Stereotypen des 'Anderen' in der Moderne," in *Deutsch-jüdische Geschichte im 19. und 20. Jahrhundert*, ed. Ludger Heid and Joachim Knoll (Stuttgart: Burg, 1992).

identity at all times and require that others do the same."[62] This can only be countered by "suspending the demand for self-identity or, more particularly, for complete coherence."[63] If violence is done to those who narrate a coherent story of themselves, then Body is certainly a victim of such violence: his urgent desire to tell a consistent story precipitates an overemphasized description of maleness, while also prompting awkwardness about womanly behavior. Without directly responding to individual questions of the psychobiological questionnaire and yet nonetheless in response to the questionnaire's call for a clearly defined, quantifiable gender identity, Body's narrative succeeds in resolving this conflict. He states: "The fabric of my life was made from tangled threads until suddenly and with great force the inner nature of my masculinity tore through the veils and half-truths that my education, habits, and the desperate circumstances of my life had spun tightly around me." (MGY 8). This veil is a comprehensive symbol—and one appropriate to the masquerade of gender—that includes all the noncoherent statements, the lack of knowledge as to his own identity, the nonexistence of the self. Thus, Body's attempt to give an account of himself as coherent with the gendered expectations of the questionnaire still allows for the presence of experiences and emotions that exceed the questionnaire. The image of the fabric or veil symbolizes all signs of noncoherence and externalizes them as something done to the "I," which had been subjected to the veil's opacity. To narrate himself in such a way causes violence to some extent, because any noncoherent experience must be externalized and rejected in this account. Nonetheless, these noncoherent components do remain part of the text in the form of the symbolic veil, which can eventually be removed.

The veil appears again shortly after the doctor (who likely represents Hirschfeld) informs Body: "'You are as much a man as I am!' Only a bit of minor surgery was necessary, which he explained to me" (MGY 146). Although the surgery itself is never explained or further narrated—Marion Hulverscheidt suggests that the "minor surgery" mentioned in Body's narrative could indeed refer to circumcision—within the logic of the text it does take place: immediately after the doctor's announcement, the veil is removed from Body's eyes— "It was as if dark veils fell from my eyes" (MGY 146)—and Body succumbs to a fever that lasts for several days.[64] When he recovers, he is determined to

---

62. Judith Butler, *Giving an Account of Oneself* (New York: Fordham University Press, 2005), 42.

63. Butler, *Giving an Account*, 42.

64. Marion Hulverscheidt, "Zu den medizinhistorischen Aspekten der Lebensgeschichte von Karl Martha Baer oder What a doctor could tell about Nobody," in N. O. Body, *Aus eines Mannes Mädchenjahren*, ed. Hermann Simon (Berlin: Hentrich & Hentrich, 2022).

pursue life as a man. The narrative fabric or tissue is here fashioned into a kind of genital prosthesis grafted onto the body, thereby performing the surgery Hirschfeld promised. Again, the narrative plays with the double meaning of prosthesis as both normatively restoring the body (offering a surgery that makes Body as much of a man as the doctor) *and* subversively refashioning it (enacting the creative potential of narrative prosthesis).

While medical discourse is thus presented as responsible for revealing what lies beyond the confusions of a wrongly assigned gender identity, the autobiography nonetheless succeeds in incorporating all noncoherent desires, identifications, and insecurities in the form of the symbolic veil, which is swept aside but does not disappear from the body of the text. How appropriate, then, that Haraway calls such prosthetic devices "visualization technologies."[65] The prosthetic veil is described as clouding Body's vision, but its presence as catch-all for incoherent aspects of Body's narrative is vital, and, as the narrative here shows, if it is to succeed, the prosthetic veil must remain part of the body of the text. Those aspects represented by the prosthetic veil—aspects of Body's life and experience that contradict the normative expectations of masculinity—also remain a part of the life of the author after completing the narrative. Telling of his acquaintance with the author of *A Man's Girlhood Years* as a child, Hermann Simon reports that he was always referred to as Karl *M.* Baer. This abbreviated middle name intrigued Simon, who found out that M. stood for Martha, the name given to him at birth.[66] It is impossible to speak for Karl M. Baer and say what his "girlhood years" meant to him. The narrative makes clear that his childhood experience of misrecognized gender caused pain and suffering. But just as the narrative obscures but does not exclude those aspects of Body's life and experience that contradict the normative expectations of masculinity in the form of the veil, Baer keeps his former name, obscured in its abbreviated form but nonetheless a part of him that remained significant even after he had been legally recognized as a man.[67]

---

65. Haraway, "Situated Knowledges," 594.

66. Hermann Simon, "Wer war N. O. Body?," in N. O. Body, *Aus eines Mannes Mädchenjahren* (Berlin: Edition Hentrich, 1993), 170.

67. In spring 2019 I participated in a series of workshops for the Transformations project, which engaged young trans and nonbinary people in conversations about visual and textual material relating to the history of sexual sciences. In one of our workshops, we discussed Body's autobiography and the fact that Karl M. Baer kept his dead name as middle name. The comments and discussion that took place during the workshop helped me understand the complexity of Body's gendered life, which cannot be reduced to normative expectations of masculinity. I want to thank the participants for their contributions.

Another instance in which the narrative draws attention to its literariness is the moment in which Body must inform his mother of his metamorphosis. At that moment of disclosure, Body recounts: "My mother began to tell me of my birth" (MGY 151). The mother, never entirely convinced of her child's *Geschlecht*, reconsiders Body's life and begins to tell the story of her child—now a male—anew, a *mise en abyme* that reflects what the larger story has been about all along: Norbert, not Nora. The story of Body's mother exemplifies what Body has conducted on a larger scale: at the moment of narration, in which the consistency of a male gender identity is vital, both tell a coherent story. In *The Words of Selves*, Denise Riley notes this moment in which the "I" regards itself in retrospect with a particular conviction in mind: "I hovered on the brink of an admission, of a decisive act of signing myself up; but only now that I've arrived securely on its far shores do I realise how committed in advance I'd been to my plunge. . . . Perhaps I always was what, gladly, I now realise I am."[68] When asked to give an account of itself, the twenty-two-year-old self—immersed in the idea of always-already maleness and determined to achieve the best possible outcome for the current self—received the retrospective narrative in such a way that the moment of birth presents a gender identity that is consistent with the narrator's present.

Jana Funke has noted that throughout the memoirs and in this instance, Body makes use of a mixture of "straight" and "queer" time. "Baer uses the queer temporal mechanism of anachronism to straight ends—straight in the double sense of affirming a heteronormative masculinity and producing a coherent narrative of emergence despite anachronistic leaps."[69] That this retrospective revision of Body's birth is not a rebirth but a retrospective fabrication, a manipulation and machination, does not diminish Body's narrative achievement. Funke confirms this by arguing that Body's complex and strategic use of queer and straight time supports the construction of a stable heterosexual masculine self, without simplifying the complicated story of Body's life.[70]

Such an organization of life as internally coherent and externally noncoherent allows for a narrative that presents a consistent identity that can be utilized to achieve a desired outcome—legal change, the support of medical authority—while retaining another truth, an unwanted, yet existent reality somewhere outside the self. Body's autobiography allows for the telling of a

---

68. Riley, *Words of Selves*, 32.

69. Jana Funke, "The Case of Karl M.[artha] Baer: Narrating 'Uncertain' Sex," in *Sex, Gender and Time in Fiction and Culture*, ed. Ben Davies and Jana Funke (London: Palgrave Macmillan, 2011), 149.

70. Funke, "Case of Karl M.[artha] Baer," 133–34.

story that is true in relation to existing norms and expressions, while also permitting noncoherent, inexplicable expressions of the self. What makes this narrative cohere in this way is not simply the scientific framework represented in narrative form but an artistic and literary engagement with the story of a life.

The employment of formal techniques is evidence of a literary crafting that highlights a calculated and reflective engagement with the process of telling a life and presenting oneself as a certain kind of person. Yet this level of literary agency might not only endanger the status of the narrative as autobiography, but also conflict with Hirschfeld's expectations of those filling in his questionnaire. In a chapter introducing his questionnaire, Hirschfeld explains his methodology further, and reasons: "The interviewee must trust the interrogator completely, must know that the whole truth is indispensable for the correct evaluation of, and counseling for, his or her condition" (683). As Ivan Crozier argues, this trust of the patient in the doctor—and the subsequent trust of the doctor in the patient's testimony—is foundational to the practice of sexology.[71] It seems that the correct way to respond to the questionnaire is to put trust, not in oneself, but in the practitioner by giving the whole, uncontaminated truth over to that authority, who turns experience into condition and, in this sense, is the true agent of gender.

Although such a filling in of the questionnaire may be cumbersome, Hirschfeld adds that "many notable and educated persons feel an interior satisfaction, a kind of relief, to be able to give an account of themselves in such a way" (696). Hirschfeld sees the case as an opportunity for the patient to engage in a cathartic act of self-representation. To do so, however, he argues that patients must be given every opportunity to speak the truth about their feelings without being influenced by the methodological format in any way. Therefore, the interviewer must conceal the conclusions that might be drawn from the questionnaire (683). Yet Hirschfeld himself often fails to adhere to this. His questions are leading to the point of appearing farcical, when he asks, for example: "Do you take small, slow, bouncing steps, or big, firm, dignified steps?" (688). But this relation between practitioner and patient also illuminates an unresolved tension: on the one hand, the practitioner must set the rules of the patient's cathartic experience and attempt to hide the scientific agenda, so as to avoid self-diagnosis by the patient, which might distort the truth of their condition. Yet on the other hand, as already mentioned, Hirschfeld emphasizes that the patient must have great trust in this practitioner, akin to a religious confession.

---

71. Crozier, "Pillow Talk," 387–90.

Hirschfeld's support of cathartic confession implies that he does indeed believe that sexual desires must surface so that patients may know the full truth about themselves and thereby "shatter the silence and the veils of propriety in which human sexual desire was enshrouded."[72] Yet, as argued before, Hirschfeld understands the voicing of desires—the unveiling of homosexuals, hermaphrodites, cross-dressers, and so on as people in their own right—as a crucial step that allows him to argue for the innateness of sexual conditions, to compose statistical data and to establish a social agenda that accepts all sexual orientations. For Hirschfeld, confessional discourse supports his liberation movement: in return for his confession, the patients receive the right, the sexual-scientific proof, that their condition is not pathological but an innate part of their bodies and souls. Any response to the questionnaire, as Hirschfeld understands it, offers catharsis through confessional anamnesis. By putting sex into discourse, Hirschfeld not only regulates his patients' sexual and gender expression in the quasi-emancipatory moment of therapy, but also establishes power relations between doctor and patient, normal and deviant sexualities and gender identities that remain functional throughout N. O. Body's autobiography.

What is notable is that it might be in its very literariness—which at first seems to compromise the status of Body's text as truthful autobiography—that the narrative most centrally incorporates Hirschfeld's sexological approach. The shrouding of sexuality through common propriety is reflected in Body's narrative as the main factor of Body's experience of incoherence and doubt, all removed in the final moment of *aletheia* when a veil is pulled from his eyes. The scene of confession itself also appears in the narrative: despairing about his inability to marry Hanna, Body considers attending confession. "The day before I had, hesitantly, gone to a Catholic church to confess—to pour out my heart to one of the priests who didn't know me and whom I would never have to see again. . . . I was reflecting on this as I lay in bed, waiting for the doctor to arrive" (MGY 144–45). The previous attempt at religious confession is on Body's mind as he waits for the doctor to arrive, and is indeed finally realized in a medical setup, as the doctor (an anonymized version of Hirschfeld himself) prompts Body to unburden himself through medical confession (MGY 145). This medical confession offers the relief promised by Hirschfeld's essay, and although patient and doctor do not know each other personally, Body reminds himself of his professional vow of discretion—and trusts the doctor: "His calm, fine face turned toward me with an expression of friendly compassion, and his manner in general encouraged my trust. I remembered my desire

---

72. Mancini, *Magnus Hirschfeld*, 10.

to confess" (MGY 145). By including this scene of medical confession in its narrative, Body's text makes space for the representation and support of Hirschfeld's methodological beliefs, while allowing for a literary and creative engagement with the life described.

Investigating the relationship between life, autobiography, and scientific discourse through the metaphor of prosthesis, it becomes evident that Body actively and creatively engages with Hirschfeld's biographical prosthetics by accepting but also critiquing and creatively altering normative expectations of heterosexual manhood and masculinity. But the narrative, too, can be considered a prosthetic device. When the veil is pulled from Body's eyes and his mother tells the story of his birth anew, the narrative functions as prosthetic device that creatively engages with and enhances the lived life and experience of the life writer. In doing so it creates the possibilities for a livable life.

4. Prosthetic Afterlife

In this final section, I want to investigate one further prosthetic relationship, which I call the prosthetic afterlife of Body's narrative. By prosthetic afterlife I mean the reappropriation of Body's narrative as a prosthetic support for medico-scientific thought. Body's narrative becomes a reference point for future sexual-scientific discussions and, in its creative use of narrative, pushes the boundaries of precisely the sexual-scientific discourse that had functioned as prosthetic support in the first instance. In this way, Body's narrative constitutes a hinge text in what Gayle Rubin calls the "sedimentary layers of queer knowledge."[73] Body's memoirs show that queer knowledge is accumulated through sexological encounters that form the sedimentary building block for following strata of queer knowledge production.

Inasmuch as sexological discourse forms prosthetic support for sexual-scientific life writing, case studies of patients form part of sexological knowledge production as part of the feedback loop described earlier in this chapter. Ivan Crozier argues that "case histories are not neutral reports, but are the basis for sexological thought: selected, manipulated, and framed in order to establish sexological facts which will be taken up by other members of the field."[74] Here case histories become prosthetic devices that support sexological theories.

---

73. Gayle Rubin, "Geologies of Queer Studies: It's Déjà Vu All over Again," in *Deviations: A Gayle Rubin Reader* (Durham, NC: Duke University Press, 2011), 351.

74. Crozier, "Pillow Talk," 396.

Rainer Herrn has shown that Hirschfeld strategically selected cases that most clearly supported his theories, while excluding others. Herrn shows that in his writing on "transvestitism," Hirschfeld failed to mention individuals whom he had previously mentioned in other publications because they did not fit his categories. Katharina T., for example, who dressed as a man and was sexually attracted to women, was not mentioned in his study of transvestitism because T. did not fit with the understanding of transvestitism as a heterosexual phenomenon not linked with homosexuality.[75] N. O. Body's autobiography formed a suitable contribution to Hirschfeld's work: giving a detailed description of an educated and successful young person with a strong sense of justice and compassion, Body's narrative also reflected well upon Hirschfeld's practice and the acceptance of those who were perceived to deviate from sexual or gender norms. Indeed, Body became a case study in several sexological publications. However, as in my preceding analysis, I want to argue that the case study as prosthesis, despite being carefully selected to fulfill a certain purpose, as argued by Crozier, nonetheless alters sexological theories in small but significant ways. In tracing this influence of autobiographical case study over sexological theories, I show that Body's narrative is not a simple prop that passively supports sexual-scientific theories, but in fact actively provides prosthetic support that enhances but also critically intervenes in sexual-scientific discourse.

Body's autobiography does not simply replicate a preexisting discourse without affecting, disrupting, and so in some way acting upon the medico-scientific representation of himself. The impact of Body's narrative goes beyond the mere perpetuation of previously established medico-scientific categories. Hirschfeld supplied a medical report in support of Baer's application to have his birth certificate amended. This report was published in slightly amended form in 1906.[76] A decade after the publication of Body's autobiography, Hirschfeld published his *Sexualpathologie* series, a trilogy that dedicates each chapter to a different sexual type, and once again includes his report on Baer. In the chapter on "hermaphroditism" in the second volume, Hirschfeld presents the scientific progress of recent years and revises earlier views: "Not only the categorization of hermaphroditism in male and female, but also the widely accepted distinction between *verus*- and *falsus*-, *true* and *pseudo*-hermaphroditism, cannot be maintained in the light of advanced scientific

---

75. Rainer Herrn, *Schnittmuster des Geschlechts: Transvestitismus und Transsexualität in der frühen Sexualwissenschaft* (Gießen: Psychosozial-Verlag, 2005), 63.

76. Hulverscheidt, "Zu den medizinhistorischen Aspekten der Lebensgeschichte von Karl Martha Baer," 174–77.

findings."[77] Very simply put, Hirschfeld here argues that the variety of conditions related to "hermaphroditism" are more diverse than the simple distinction he seeks to refute. "*True* hermaphroditism" refers to the theory that a person may have both testicles and ovaries; "*pseudo*-hermaphroditism" distinguishes between "masculine hermaphroditism" and "feminine hermaphroditism," where a person has either testicles or ovaries, but where other characteristic do not coincide with male or female sex glands.[78] Hirschfeld argues that these distinctions do not suffice to describe the variety of "hermaphroditic" conditions. Although hesitant to suggest a new series of categories to distinguish the variety of conditions, Hirschfeld settles on four subtypes of "genital hermaphroditism" that are surprisingly similar to the categories he seeks to refute: "masculine hermaphroditism" (gonads and female external genitalia); "feminine hermaphroditism" (ovaries and male external genitalia); "neutral hermaphroditism" (rudimentary sex glands that are neither male nor female with either male, female, or ambiguous external genitalia); and "dual hermaphroditism" (sex glands that are partially male, partially female [ovotestes] with either male, female, or ambiguous external genitalia).[79] In addition to this, he tentatively suggests three further groups: *hermaphroditismus genitalis glandularis* (sex glands are a mixtures of male and female); *hermaphroditismus genitalis tubularis* (the excretory ducts are a mixture of male and female); and *hermaphroditismus genitalis conjugalis* (the tissue connecting the genital apparatus is a mixture between male and female).[80] I do not intend to explain Hirschfeld's categorization of "hermaphroditism" in detail here, but this outline seeks to show that Hirschfeld understood "genital hermaphroditism" as a variety of intermediate stages between the perceived categories of "man" and "woman."

In order to refute the distinction of "hermaphroditism" into true and pseudo, as well as male and female "hermaphroditism," Hirschfeld lists a series of case studies. The case of Friederike S. outlines a case that is extremely similar to Body's: Friederike prefers to play games typically associated with boys; her breasts do not develop but instead she grows a beard; she is exclusively attracted to women; she wishes she was "born a man'; her ambiguous genitalia indicate internal testes and she ejaculates. However, one of the few details of this case that distinguish her from Body's is that Friederike ultimately decides

77. Magnus Hirschfeld, *Sexualpathologie: Ein Lehrbuch für Ärzte und Studierende*, vol. 2, *Sexuelle Zwischenstufen: Das männliche Weib und der weibliche Mann* (Bonn: A. Marcus und E. Webers, 1918), 25.

78. Hirschfeld, *Sexuelle Zwischenstufen*, 78.

79. Hirschfeld, *Sexuelle Zwischenstufen*, 79.

80. Hirschfeld, *Sexuelle Zwischenstufen*, 79–80.

against the legal change from woman to man.[81] Hirschfeld diagnoses Friederike with "erreur de sexe," erroneous determination of sex, based on "masculine pseudo-hermaphroditism."

A few pages later, Hirschfeld lists the case of Anna Laabs, which he reveals to be another pseudonym for the author of *A Man's Girlhood Years* and notes as an instructive addition to this collection of cases. Although Friederike S. and Anna Laabs share many similarities, Hirschfeld's diagnosis of Laabs is communicated rather differently:

> This study has shown that Anna Laabs's sex was, without a doubt, erroneously determined as female at birth. The patient's genitals, secondary sexual characteristics, and sexual desire confirm that Laabs is, in truth, a man. These findings demand that the patient's official records should be rectified immediately and his gender registered as male.[82]

Whereas Hirschfeld uses medical terms such as "erreur de sexe" and "male pseudo-hermaphroditism" to describe Friederike S., he does not use these terms to describe Body but simply states that Body has always been a man and was simply misrecognized at birth. But here, Body's case simply does not seem to fit: virtually all other cases in this chapter describe a case of misrecognized sex at birth due to "pseudo-hermaphroditism" (the subchapter in which these cases of hermaphroditism are described is called "irrtümliche Geschlechtsbestimmung," "mistaken determination of sex/gender"). In contrast, the final diagnosis of Body's/Laabs's case seems to indicate that this misrecognition is simply a mistake unrelated to genital ambiguity *even though* Hirschfeld's description of Laabs's case includes descriptions of hypospadias, a common birth defect where the urinary opening is not at the head of the penis, but within or near the scrotum.[83] Marion Hulverscheidt suggests that Hirschfeld purposefully diagnoses an erroneous determination of sex, because he knew that this would support Baer's application to have his birth certificate amended, whereas a diagnosis of (pseudo)hermaphroditism would have complicated Baer's case.[84]

Hirschfeld's evaluation of Laabs's case echoes precisely the narrative description of this instance in Body's autobiography. As Body narrates, at his birth the midwife is inexperienced and cannot decide the child's sex (MGY

---

81. Hirschfeld, *Sexuelle Zwischenstufen*, 25–30.

82. Hirschfeld, *Sexuelle Zwischenstufen*, 47.

83. Hirschfeld, *Sexuelle Zwischenstufen*, 46.

84. Hulverscheidt, "Zu den medizinhistorischen Aspekten der Lebensgeschichte von Karl Martha Baer."

10–11). A subsequent examination by a local doctor remains superficial. This determination of the child's sex is presented as unreliable and Body's father pays the midwife and doctor to ensure their confidentiality. The "erreur de sexe" is here shown to be human error. The "unhappy child" (MGY 11) is thus forced to live life as a girl. Hirschfeld, in his discussion of Laabs in *Sexualpathologie*, repeats the narrative presented in *A Man's Girlhood Years* above and beyond his own sexological theories: Laabs is not described as "hermaphroditic" and her misrecognition at birth is a human error. Unlike Friederike S., Body seeks legal recognition and furthermore writes openly about his strong identification as man. There are many reasons why Friederike S. may have chosen not to seek legal recognition, for example because it could have threatened access to secure employment or threaten to unsettle kinship ties. Body's more "straight" narrative, as Funke described it, provided a better fit with Hirschfeld's theoretical work. Nonetheless, the dynamic interrelation between autobiography and sexological publication shows that the narrative did, in turn, have a profound influence on Hirschfeld's theories and functioned as prosthesis that supported, but also complicated and contradicted, Hirschfeld's sexological theory.

In another example of prosthetic afterlife, Body's case is referenced in the first volume of Helene Deutsch's *The Psychology of Women: A Psychoanalytic Interpretation*.[85] Helene Deutsch was a psychoanalyst, colleague of Sigmund Freud's, and founder of the Vienna Training Institute before fleeing to the United States, where she continued to work as a psychoanalyst.[86] In *The Psychology of Women*, Deutsch refers to the case of a supposedly homosexual woman whom she reveals as the author of a book that she calls *The Girlhood Years of a Man*, clearly a reference to N. O. Body's *A Man's Girlhood Years*.

Deutsch's two-volume work discusses female sexuality in its developmental stages and possibilities, including a large section on female homosexuality. Both volumes are themselves cyborg-like creatures with case studies pieced together from various source materials. "The material used in this book is not restricted to my personal observations in the course of psychoanalytic therapy," Deutsch explains. "It is taken from case and life histories recorded by other observers—physicians and social workers—not prejudiced in favour of

---

85. As Hulverscheidt notes, Body/Baer's case is also taken up by several other medical professionals, including Friedrich Gottfried Mannel, Iwan Bloch, Georg Merzbach, and Franz Ludwig von Neugebauer. Hulverscheidt, "Zu den medizinhistorischen Aspekten der Lebensgeschichte von Karl Martha Baer."

86. For more information about Helene Deutsch's life, see her autobiography: Helene Deutsch, *Confrontations with Myself: An Epilogue* (New York: Norton, 1973); Paul Roazen, *Helene Deutsch: A Psychoanalyst's Life* (London: Routledge, 2019 [1985]); Brenda S. Webster, "Helene Deutsch: A New Look," *Signs* 10, no. 3 (Spring 1985): 553–71.

any psychologic theory."[87] In this way, her methodological approach aligns itself with that of previous sexual-scientific publications that rely on a heterogeneous archive of case studies.

In the chapter discussing types of female homosexuality, Deutsch presents what she describes as two distinct types of homosexuality among women. The first kind, she argues, comprises

> those individuals who display pronounced masculine traits in the choice of objects as well as in all other manifestations of life. The physical structure of women belonging to this group may also be more or less masculine. In some, the structure of the sexual organs has a hermaphroditic character, in others we are confronted with more or less prominent aberrations of the secondary sex characteristics ... such as the vocal cords, the hair growth, etc. Many cases are characterized only by the absence of certain feminine sex characteristics, such as breasts.[88]

The second type of female homosexuality described by Deutsch refers to those who "show no physical signs of abnormity and whose bodily constitution is completely feminine. The causes of their inversion are obviously psychogenic."[89] Both types of homosexuality here strikingly combine sexological and psychoanalytic thinking, as she combines both physical and psychogenic origins of female homosexuality. The first type of homosexual portrays a conflation of gender and sexuality that is symptomatic of both contemporaneous sexological and psychoanalytic thinking and one that is firmly rooted in a binary system of gender. This first type is reminiscent of theories of gender inversion known from German sexology, where homosexuality is one form of (psychological and physical) sexual intermediacy.

It is this first type that Deutsch assigns to the case of the author of *The Girlhood Years of a Man*, a story that she retells—and rewrites—at length:

> Others, on the contrary, negate their masculinity, even if they are urged in that direction by their biological structure. As regards this point, the following personal observation of an androgynous woman whose homosexual tendencies had an unambiguously somatic basis, may be instructive.
>
> She was a girl of about 25, delicately built, with very feminine features

---

87. Helene Deutsch, *The Psychology of Women: A Psychoanalytic Interpretation*, vol. 1 (New York: Grune & Stratton, 1944), xii.

88. Deutsch, *Psychology of Women*, 325.

89. Deutsch, *Psychology of Women*, 325.

and fair complexion, but with a deep voice and hair on her face. Among her women friends, her conduct was irreproachably feminine; she dressed coquettishly, tried in every way to remove the hair on her face, and often complained bitterly about her organic constitution. She was very success-ful as an executive in an international organization, showed great energy in her chosen field, and all her professional behaviour, despite her pro-tests, revealed an absolutely masculine-active character.

. . . The epilogue was unexpected: the case aroused the interest of a well known sexologist, who discovered that the girl in question was a real her-maphrodite; he succeeded in transforming her into a man by an operation. The success of the operation was confirmed when the woman whom the "girl" had courted divorced her husband and was married and impreg-nated by the newly created man. The latter had had—he declared—no idea of his peculiar structure, and had considered himself a homosexual woman. He later wrote and published a book called *The Girlhood Years of a Man*.[90]

Deutsch presents Body's case as an exemplary representation of the first type of masculine homosexual woman, which covers a variety of subcategories of the masculine female homosexual: those whose sexual organs are hermaph-roditic, those whose secondary sex characteristics are aberrant and tend toward the masculine, and those who lack feminine characteristics. Body, who is implied to have hermaphroditic sexual organs, a hoarse voice and beard, and a flat chest, confirms every single one of these subcategories, presenting an over-determination of the type. In fact, Body's case shows that such overdetermina-tion of the masculine female homosexual eventually leads to Body simply being a man. If this is really an exemplary case of masculine female homosexu-ality in Deutsch's regard, then masculine female homosexuality dissolves; he is, finally, a man misrecognized as girl.

But Deutsch's description, especially nearing her concluding paragraph, reveals her own categories to be slippery: continually referring to the writer of the book as a "girl" and "androgynous woman" with "homosexual tendencies," the description of the case ends with Body, postsurgery, who is now recognized as a man and requires male pronouns. This gender confirmation is made pos-sible by an operation, conducted by a "well-known sexologist," who discov-ered the girl to be a hermaphrodite. How might we understand Body, then, in this account of the case? Homosexual girl, hermaphrodite, and finally also

90. Deutsch, *Psychology of Women*, 328–29.

such an authentic man that, in this exaggerated version of Body's case, he is able to prove his heterosexual masculinity by impregnating his wife? To only complicate things further, Deutsch emphasizes Body's futile attempts to resist his clearly masculine nature when spending time with his female friends. But precisely this resistance to his inherent masculinity—in this instance emphasized to prove that his masculinity bursts through even his most desperate attempts to satisfy the demands made of him by friends, family, and society to be a "real" woman—is then later ascribed to underlying feminine characterization, when Deutsch notes that "the person in question, although organically a fully-fledged male, displayed many feminine characteristics in his behaviour."[91] In this reference to his behavior Body becomes the fully-fledged male, with female characteristics in this instance, reminiscent of preconceptions of the effeminate man, the male homosexual.

Responses to Body's narrative ascribe a variety of conditions and identities or sexual categories to Body. Hirschfeld's *Sexualpathologie* suggests that Body's/Laabs's case could describe a case of "erreur de sexe" due to "masculine pseudo-hermaphroditism," but shies away from making this argument explicit, instead arguing that Body's case was one of human error. Deutsch describes him as androgynous woman, overdetermined female homosexual, hermaphrodite, and finally seemingly a misrecognized man. None of these medically specific identities are ever mentioned in the narrative itself, but all could, in some way, be concluded from the narrative. Body's narrative finally allows itself to function as prosthetic support for various sexual-scientific theories—it contains all the right building blocks—but its narrative flexibility ultimately undermines whatever theory it is made to fit.

Even in Deutsch's jumbled version of the narrative, Body's body retains its shape. It forms a foreign object in the body of Deutsch's text that has its own will and that cannot be made to fit entirely. Deutsch finally summarizes the story by referring to it as "the case of our sensational lover" and shows that Body's affliction had taken on the nature of a sensational story, a medico-scientific melodrama, the status of a myth.[92] And here again, Body's prosthetic narrative recalls the cyborg as aspirational myth, which does not strive for a sense of wholeness but survives by "seizing the tools to mark the world that marked them as other."[93] Abandoning the idea of wholeness and seizing upon such prosthetic support from other sources, such intertextual connections can-

91. Deutsch, *Psychology of Women*, 330.

92. Deutsch, *Psychology of Women*, 330.

93. Haraway, "A Cyborg Manifesto," 141.

not be removed and instead remain a deeply lodged part within the narrative self: "The machine is us, our processes, an aspect of our embodiment."[94]

Conclusion

Body's narrative quite clearly engages with sexual-scientific discourses in more ways than simple reproduction of preexisting categories. The question remains as to why he puts so much effort into subordinating himself to a discourse that clearly cannot summarize him in an entirely satisfactory way. In finding his place within Hirschfeld's sexological theorization, to what extent does Body's narrative confirm a discourse bestowed with incredible power, as prevalent scientific discourses always are, and inadvertently reinforce the strict gender binary, portraying categories stereotypically? As Helga Thorson points out in her essay on Body's autobiography, Body's heterosexual male identity is reinforced by a repeated characterization of misogynist feelings, such as exasperation over a friend's "girlish foolishness" (MGY 28) and sadistic dreams about killing his lover, Harriet. Both the autobiography and Hirschfeld's case study of Anna Laabs, Thorson argues, "tend to situate the human body within a binary system of sex."[95] Kirsten Leng's reading of Anna Rüling's speech, mentioned in section 1, argues that Rüling supported stereotypical views of the lesbian woman as more masculine and therefore superior to the heterosexual woman. This might have somehow improved the image of the lesbian, Leng comments, but only by reinforcing a stereotypical binary of the sexes.[96]

Yet the specific circumstances of Body's text shed light on this surprising aspect of the narrative. Body, who sees the impossibility of marrying his girlfriend Hanna as a reason for suicide, wants nothing more than to gain the right to act upon his sexual desires and form a relationship with the woman he loves without fear of persecution. In order to achieve this, Body must secure the necessary official support to execute his change if he wants both his and Hanna's life and their relationship to be recognized. Not surprisingly, to change one's gender at the age of twenty-two under Wilhelmine law was not without complications: following the consultation of a doctor, Body reports that he has to turn to a lawyer, who urges him to request medical certificates issued by

94. Haraway, "A Cyborg Manifesto," 146.
95. Helga Thorson, "Masking/Unmasking Identity in Early Twentieth-Century Germany: The Importance of N. O. Body," *Women in German Yearbook: Feminist Studies in German Literature and Culture* 25, no. 1 (2009): 151.
96. Leng, "Anna Rüling."

well-established authorities. A first application to the minister of the interior is unsuccessful, and only upon renewed pressure from the lawyer do the authorities agree to change Body's gender in the town register.[97] There is evidence that he was successful: Hermann Simon discovered Karl Baer's birth certificate, which includes an amendment to Baer's *Geschlecht* and first name.[98]

That the narrative has an ultimate aim that transcends Hirschfeld's activism and his theory of sexual intermediate stages is evident. What Body needs, in short, is the support of the law that can sanction his gender change and thereby normalize him and bestow him with rights and protections against violence and exclusion. Only once Body is medically proven to have been a man all along can he gain the right to live and be recognized legally and legitimately as a male. To speak from a position not recognized by powerful legal discourse—from the position of abnormal woman or lacking man—brings no adequate recognition of his life. Inconsistent or malleable identifications, particularly when they concern gender identity, contradict a deeply rooted sense of intrinsic, binary identification manifested within the law. As Joanne Meyerowitz succinctly notes about another case of gender deviance, that of Earl Lind, "The hierarchy here is not male over female but one in which gender-normative people (feminine women and masculine men) are accorded privileges denied to gender transgressors."[99] Body, faced with two options—to remain a powerless and unrecognized transgressor, or to subordinate himself to a legal and scientific system that at least allows for some formal recognition—chooses the latter as the more livable option.

By understanding the relationship between life, narrative, and sexual-scientific discourse as a prosthetic assemblage, I have shown the various possibilities for agency presented in *A Man's Girlhood Years*. Body's autobiography makes productive use of Hirschfeld's questionnaire, which functions as prosthetic support for the creation of a normative, legible gender identity as heterosexual man. Beyond this straightforward compliance with Hirschfeld's questionnaire, Body's autobiography engages various narrative strategies to creatively alter normative expectations of sexual-scientific discourse. In doing so, these narrative strategies—the veil that is pulled from Body's eyes, his mother telling the story of *his* birth anew—can be considered prosthetic

---

97. For a thorough overview of the legal situation that Baer had to navigate to achieve the amendment of his birth certificate, see Konstanze Plett, "N. O. Body im Recht," in N. O. Body, *Aus eines Mannes Mädchenjahren*, ed. Hermann Simon (Berlin: Hentrich & Hentrich, 2022).

98. Body, *Aus eines Mannes Mädchenjahren* (2022), p. 137.

99. Joanne Meyerowitz, "Thinking Sex with an Androgyne," *GLQ* 17, no. 1 (2010): 101.

devices that engage with and enhance the lived life and experience of the life writer. Finally, Body's narrative account becomes a prosthetic device that is used to support but that also disrupts the sexual-scientific theories of Hirschfeld and Deutsch.

Body's prosthetic afterlife shows the importance of paying close attention to the sedimentary layers of queer knowledges. Body's narrative forms a dense layer and a shaky foundation for Hirschfeld's writing on hermaphroditism and Deutsch's writing on sexuality. It disrupts any straightforward incorporation into sexual knowledge production. By "mining" (as Rubin suggests we might) this stratum of queer knowledge production, I have drawn attention to the importance of life writing and subtle agency in sexual knowledge production after 1900. My analysis of *A Man's Girlhood Years* shows that the negotiation of lived experience and sexual-scientific discourses in the form of autobiographical narrative presents various opportunities for agency, where narrative writing and sexual-scientific theories are utilized by the life writer to create the possibilities for a livable life. My hospitable reading has shown that Body is no less an agent of his gender for making use of prosthetic support in the form of sexual-scientific discourse. Body shows his agency, perhaps most strongly and rather surprisingly, through an act of conformity that indicates that he knows exactly how to subordinate himself firmly to a system whose dichotomies may be of as little interest to him as the validity of Hirschfeld's claims. Body's narrative amounts to a literary, strategic positioning that takes those systems that imposed themselves on the individual—social structures, scientific discourse, and legal power—as a prosthetic support that an embodied subject may rely on but can nonetheless engage with critically, creatively and actively. In the next chapter, I investigate further frameworks of recognition that sexual-scientific narratives seize on in pursuit of creating the conditions for a livable life. Specifically, I examine how sexual-scientific life writing uses visual and haptic descriptions of masking, veiling, and clothing to inhabit an embodied, livable sense of queer subjectivity.

CHAPTER 3

Frames of Livability

Sexual-Scientific Encounter, Photography,
and the Department Store

In *A Man's Girlhood Years* (*Aus eines Mannes Mädchenjahren*, 1907), the author relates one of his earliest childhood memories: "I looked up and noticed that the two girls stared at me, whispered, and laughed. They pointed at my dress, which had ridden up during the game. I stood up, feeling frightened and ashamed" (MGY 40). Dori, the protagonist of *Diary of a Male Bride* (*Tagebuch einer männlichen Braut*, 1907), is employed as a shop clerk when they are asked to perform a peculiar task by their employer: "He had begun to frequently use me as a model. If a customer wants to buy a cloak or a coat, it will be placed around my shoulders. . . . Then I have to walk up and down in front of the mirror with dainty steps. This often causes the customers to laugh" (DMB 48–49). In both scenes, the protagonists' growing awareness as queer subjects is recognized by others via a supposed mismatch between body and clothes. In both cases, bodies are framed as ill-fitting, at odds with normative expectations. Themes of looking and *Schaulust* or scopophilia are reinforced as Body's friends and Dori's customers look at their bodies inquisitively and with desire.

This relationship between displayed bodies and an inquisitive audience is a recurrent theme that appears in two contexts that I will explore further in this chapter: the sexual-scientific encounter and the department store. These seemingly different spaces, I will show, share a number of similarities. As medico-scientific patients, Body's and Dori's bodies are examined in a clinical space. This scene of clinical display is captured in medical photographs that accompany sexological publications, and both the clinical encounter and its photographic documentation present the deviant body—by which I mean a body that is considered to deviate from a perceived norm—to an audience or readership. Similar themes of looking and exhibition arise in the context of the department store, in which both protagonists find themselves as shop assistants. Here, the line between consumerism and scopophilia blurs and the deviant body becomes an object to be looked at and to be desired. Framed in these two different settings—as a patient in a medico-scientific context and as a shop assistant in the department store—Body's and Dori's bodies are assigned meaning (as object of desire, as ridiculous outsider). At the same time, both narratives also claim these frames through the medium of life writing, which presents bodies, experiences, and desires in autobiographical form and functions as its own framing device that negotiates a sense of queer livability.

In this chapter, I will analyze how sexual-scientific life writing presents these and other frames in order to establish a sense of queer livability under often impossible and unlivable conditions. I will investigate how visual, haptic, and contextual concealment and masquerade can be considered through the concept of the frame, with reference to Judith Butler's work. I will ask: how does the frame's focus on and exclusion of certain aspects of queer life contribute to but also complicate how we might understand queer livability in the early twentieth century? In the first section of this chapter, I will analyze how the queer body is framed in the encounter between sexual-scientific practitioner and patient by drawing on research on early twentieth-century medico-scientific photography, which literally as well as epistemologically frames the body. In the second section, I will investigate how contextual framing functions in the specific realm of commerce and commodification in the fashion and department store after 1900. Here, I will also consider the conflicting and dangerous results of further framing devices. Antisemitic stereotyping as violent framing connects both texts as well as the medico-scientific frame and the frame of the department store. Body conceals his Jewish identity in order to deflect stereotypes that associated Jewishness with effeminacy (see also Chapter 2). In *Diary of a Male Bride*, antisemitic tropes, based on the coding of the early twentieth-century department store as Jewish, serve to frame experiences of harassment and abuse. These examples of antisemitic stereotyping show that the frame can be a dangerous and potentially violent tool to be used in the pursuit of queer livability.

1. Framing the Queer Body in Life Writing and Photography

In film, photography, and literature, the frame is a powerful tool that draws attention to the central aspects of an event, scene, or person. At the same time, the frame always excludes what lies outside this center. The frame always makes a cut. In *Frames of War*, Judith Butler considers epistemological frames that make certain lives appear livable and grievable. Butler argues that these "frames through which we apprehend or, indeed, fail to apprehend the lives of others as lost or injured (lose-able or injurable) are politically saturated. They are themselves operations of power."[1] Butler here makes the distinction between recognition and apprehension. Whereas the former implies full cognition, apprehension senses and perceives, without fully knowing. Apprehension is therefore more suitable to sensing the limits of norms and frames and the possibility of a remainder of life beyond the scope of norms.

Such an apprehension of the frame also poses the ontological question of what makes a life, thus framed, a life at all. As Butler argues, a life cannot be considered outside of "the operations of power" or the social significations of the body, so outside of the frame.[2] Accordingly, framing is intimately tied to livability, as Butler argues: "The epistemological capacity to apprehend a life is partially dependent on that life being produced according to norms that qualify it as a life or, indeed, as part of life."[3] Here, the framing of a life according to certain norms creates a sense of livability, whereby norms are not deterministic but remain flexible and dynamic. Recognition of subjects depends on this framing, but subjects can exceed or cut across various frames. In the case of turn-of-the-century sexual-scientific life writing, frames of gender, biological, and medical research and consumerism all offer competing framings of livable bodies. In addition to this, the subject can exceed the norms that structure such frames and so whatever lies outside the frame can still be immensely meaningful.

When we think about images, the frame guides our interpretation, but we can also call into question what is left out.[4] As Butler points out, images and texts leave their frame or context all the time and, in doing so, elicit a different response. The context in which I read sexual-scientific life writing today is very different from the one it was originally received in (see my discussion in Chapter 1 for a discussion of reception over time). Furthermore, photographs produced in the context of sexual sciences were circulated widely among professionals but also a much wider nonprofessional readership. Breaking out of the frame of medico-scientific observation by being regarded by nonprofessional audiences as well as scholars today does not release the subject from

---

1. Judith Butler, *Frames of War: When Is Life Grievable* (London: Verso, 2009), 1.
2. Butler, *Frames of War*, 1.
3. Butler, *Frames of War*, 3.
4. Butler, *Frames of War*, 8–9.

constraints—reading sexual-scientific life writing now does not lessen the pain of discrimination, marginalization, and exclusion—but it might make such exclusion less acceptable.[5]

While remaining attentive to the negative, restrictive, and normative ways in which the frame can effect power over the subjects thus framed, in this chapter I want to explore how frames are used in sexual-scientific life writing to make sense of the queer body and subject. This forms part of a hospitable reading that seeks to understand the agency of the writing self, not only as resistance to dominant discursive frames, but also through more complex, creative, and productive uses of framing devices. Butler's discussion of the frame is important here because it reminds us that livability is not an unproblematic achievement. If frames rely on power to construct their content by making use of norms and thus produce certain forms of life that are livable and grievable, such livability necessarily excludes other forms of life not yet recognized as livable and grievable. Something or someone is always left out.

One definitive frame of sexual-scientific life writing is that of sexual-scientific discourse itself. Such discourse forms an epistemological frame that has the power to determine how bodies can be recognized. In *Diary of a Male Bride*, the following scene takes place:

> I was at the doctor's. I wanted to be absolutely sure. Herr Wehldorf had been right. The doctor confirmed it. It seems I am a particularly interesting phenomenon (*Erscheinung*) in this area. I had to undress completely and the learned man examined my body in the most meticulous manner and made a whole set of notes. I found this examination extremely embarrassing. It was the first time in my life that I had had to undress in front of a stranger in that way. The doctor asked me if, in the interest of science, I was willing to be presented by him to a group of medical doctors and students. (DMB 67)

It is at this moment that the deviant body is undressed for the first time in a medical context. Dori is presented to a medical audience and closely examined. Yet this moment of bodily encounter is marked by a peculiar absence of

---

5. Butler uses the example of images of and poetry by Abu Ghraib prisoners that circulate outside the prison. "Even though neither the image nor the poetry can free anyone from prison, or stop a bomb or, indeed, reverse the course of the war, they nevertheless do provide the conditions for breaking out of the quotidian acceptance of war and for a more generalized horror and outrage that will support and impel calls for justice and an end to violence." Butler, *Frames of War*, 11.

the naked body that is here discussed. Instead of a description of bodies or body parts, the narrative pays particular attention to the reactions to this body: Dori's friend, Herr Wehldorf, had first spoken to Dori about their "condition," which, on the previous page, is summarized as follows: "So this is the kind of creature (*Geschöpf*) I am: not man, not woman. And there is no cure for this, no help, no surgery" (DMB 66). Dori here becomes a *Geschöpf*, a creature neither male nor female.

Yet while the body escapes physical alterations—surgery, the text states, is impossible—it is also so obviously different that its presentation will contribute to scientific knowledge. Dori becomes part of the doctor's collection of cases, collected under a category that Dori does not seem to know, a diagnosis that—from Dori's point of view—misplaces rather than places the body, which is not described at this point in the narrative. From the perspective of life writing, Dori's body becomes the remainder that lies outside of the frame. The narrative refuses recognition to the reader, allowing only a form of apprehension—sensing and acknowledging its presence. Although the deviant body is the central object of the epistemological frame of sexual-scientific discourse, the narrative presents the body as lying outside of the frame. In that way, life writing itself becomes a way to frame bodily experience and the harmful and unsettling effects of the medical encounter.

A very similar scene of undressing under the medico-sexological gaze takes place in *A Man's Girlhood Years*:

> Then he [the doctor] asked me some more questions. I told him the story of my childhood, the secret of my body, spoke about the endless suffering and humiliation of the past. . . . The doctor listened silently, then he said that I would have to let him examine me closely. When he was finished, he spoke to me with kind words. . . . "You are as much a man as I am!" Only a bit of minor surgery was necessary, which he explained to me. (MGY 145–46)

The reader is confronted with the story of childhood and a secret of the body, but the exposed body itself is lacking; we read about the prompt and the verdict, but no body. In a way similar to *Diary of a Male Bride*, Body's doctor places him in a system that categorizes him, but here, too, noncoherence arises: If Body is a perfect man—which, in this instance, is evidently a judgment based on physical examination—then why does he require surgery? And what kind of *minor* surgery could it be that could initiate the confirmation of Body's gender? If the patient is a man just like the doctor, but nonetheless needs surgery, does the doctor also require surgery? As already discussed in the previous chapter, Body's narrative invents a family of French Catholics in order to conceal the author's Jewishness, because the Jewish body was inscribed with antisemitic stereotypes of effeminacy and damaged masculinity.[6] As such, the concealment of the body at the moment of surgery is a double concealment that seeks to hide the sexually ambiguous body as well as a body that is coded as effeminate because it is read as Jewish. Like Dori's body exposed in front of the medical gaze, Body's body is both the central object to be framed and yet is represented as unrecognizable, as lying outside the frame. Here the deviant body is obscene "in the literal sense of being off (*ob*) the public scene," as described by film scholar Linda Williams.[7] If the reader is meant to look for the body here, then contradictory demands on the queer body overlap and leave the body only as narrative gap.

Such an absence of bodily description is peculiar when considering the sexual-scientific discourse within which these narratives are firmly rooted and the medical encounter that is described, which frames the body as the focus of its inquiry. As discussed in detail in the previous chapter, *A Man's Girlhood Years* is entwined with Magnus Hirschfeld's sexological methodology. An afterword by Hirschfeld is published alongside Body's narrative, which furthermore responds to Hirschfeld psychobiological questionnaire, and Body reappears as case study in Hirschfeld's as well as others' sexual-scientific work. *Diary of a Male Bride*, too, stands in relation to sexual-scientific discourses more broadly, as Dori shows familiarity with sexual-scientific terminology when they refer to themselves as a "homosexual" or, more specifically, "Uranian" (*Urning*) (DMB 68). As Jens Dobler points out in his afterword to the 2010 republication of *Diary of a Male Bride*, Hirschfeld was also personally acquainted with Dina Alma de Paradeda, the historical figure who influenced the writing of the *Diary* and whom Hirschfeld met at one of the *Urningsbälle*, the dance events for self-described transvestites and homosexuals in

---

6. Sander Gilman has worked extensively on the relationship between Jewishness, sexuality, and gender. See Sander L. Gilman, *The Jew's Body* (London: Routledge, 1991); Sander L. Gilman, *Freud, Race, and Gender* (Princeton, NJ: Princeton University Press, 1993).

7. Linda Williams, "Porn Studies: Proliferating Pornographies On/Scene: An Introduction," in *Porn Studies*, ed. Linda Williams (Durham, NC: Duke University Press, 2004), 3. See also Linda Williams, *Hard Core: Power, Pleasure, and the "Frenzy of the Visible"* (Berkeley: University of California Press, 1999), 281; Linda Williams, *Screening Sex* (Durham, NC: Duke University Press, 2008), 7.

Berlin (see also my discussion in Chapter One).[8] In his 1910 publication, *Die Transvestiten: Eine Untersuchung über den erotischen Verkleidungstrieb* (*Transvestites: The Erotic Drive to Cross-Dress*), Hirschfeld refers to Paradeda at length as one of his case studies.[9]

Recent scholarship on the interdisciplinary history of sexual sciences has shown that sexual sciences not only relied on medico-scientific training and methods, but also drew significantly on anthropological data and literary sources.[10] Nonetheless, sexual scientists most often trained in areas of medical specialism that grew out of established nineteenth-century disciplines, including physiology, dermatology, psychiatry, and neurology. They also continued to draw on emerging medico-scientific disciplines, including genetics, endocrinology, and psychology. Biology and medicine remained influential disciplinary frames for sexual-scientific thinking. In Hirschfeld's sexological work, questions relating to sex, sexuality, and gender are discussed with relation to the physicality of the body. Deviation from the sexual and gender norm was summarized under the term *drittes Geschlecht* (third sex), showing that *Geschlecht* incorporated both sexual and gender diversity and variation. Hirschfeld's theories of the third sex build on the works of German writer Karl Heinrich Ulrichs (1825–1895), who uses the term "Uranian" to describe a person who encompasses a female soul in a male body. Yet Hirschfeld's *Zwischenstufentheorie* (theory of sexual intermediacy), which he developed and publicized in his *Sexualpathologie* (*Sexual Pathology*) series and throughout the twenty-year publication of his *Yearbook of Sexual Intermediacy* (*Jahrbuch für sexuelle Zwischenstufen*), goes beyond Ulrichs's theories by arguing that all people are located on a scale somewhere between the opposing poles of man and woman—neither of which is reached completely in any one person—and that all people, to varying degrees, contain both female and male characteristics.[11] This connection between sex and desire again suggests a link between

---

8. Jens Dobler, afterword to Walter Homann, *Tagebuch einer männlichen Braut* (Hamburg: Männerschwarm Verlag, 2010), 154.

9. See Magnus Hirschfeld, *Die Transvestiten: Eine Untersuchung über den erotischen Verkleidungstrieb* (Berlin: Alfred Pulvermacher, 1910), 189–92.

10. See, for example, Kate Fisher and Jana Funke, "British Sexual Science beyond the Medical: Cross-Disciplinary, Cross-Historical, and Cross-Cultural Translations," in *Sexology and Translation: Cultural and Scientific Encounters across the Modern World*, ed. Heike Bauer (Philadelphia: Temple University Press, 2015).

11. Magnus Hirschfeld, *Jahrbuch für sexuelle Zwischenstufen*, 1899–1923; Magnus Hirschfeld, *Sexualpathologie: Ein Lehrbuch für Ärzte und Studierende*, 3 vols. (Bonn: A. Marcus & E. Webers, 1917–20).

physical morphology and sexuality. Indeed, Hirschfeld coins the term *Seelen-zwittertum* (hermaphroditism of the soul)[12] and confirms that he perceives homosexuality to be parallel to the physical condition of hermaphroditism. Sexual intermediate types are located somewhere between these poles in both mind *and* body. When talking about what will later be called sexuality, the body is always already implicated and framed as the central focus of sexual-scientific inquiry.

For Hirschfeld, all categories of sexual deviance were fundamentally related to the physicality of the body, although, as the following discussion will show, this body often eludes comprehension. Yet despite Hirschfeld's self-positioning of sexology as a biological science, German sexology after 1900 was still an emerging field without institutional affiliation. Biology and medicine act as disciplinary frames that support the recognition of sexology as a serious, professional, scientific discipline. Dealing with a subject matter that was often considered indecent and veering into the pornographic, the framing of sexual sciences as biological science supported sexual scientists' claims of authority and professionalism.[13] In order to make his particular approach to sex research scientific, Hirschfeld and others like him felt the necessity to convince the skeptical research community of the validity of their claims. Hirschfeld not only was reliant on the physical examination of his patients, but, believing that a physical diagnosis was able to yield scientifically valid data about human sexuality, also had to find a way to present his findings in a credible way to the scientific community. As a sexologist he was therefore not only concerned with the body, but also with the *representation* of this body so that it might function as evidence, based on which theories of sexuality and its deviations could be developed and proven to be legitimate.

For these reasons, Hirschfeld in particular became interested in the new, indexical medium of photography, which promised to show things as they really were and offer proof beyond doubt, and so support the scientific presentation of sexual research that might otherwise be questioned. Recent scholarship in the history of sexual sciences has begun to examine the "visual archive of sexology" and the ways in which photography was used as evidence by

---

12. See Klaus Müller, *Aber in meinem Herzen sprach eine Stimme so laut: Homosexuelle Autobiographien und medizinische Pathographien im neunzehnten Jahrhundert* (Berlin: Verlag rosa Winkel, 1991), 301.

13. On the close relationship between sexology and erotic print culture and how this relationship is policed by sexual scientists in order to present sexology as a respectable scientific field, see Sarah Bull, "More Than a Case of Mistaken Identity: Adult Entertainment and the Making of Early Sexology," *History of Human Sciences* 34, no. 1 (February 2020): 10–39.

sexual scientists.[14] As Katie Sutton summarizes, sexology's "almost exclusive reliance on subjective textual evidence began to change when technological developments in photography and its mass reproduction combined with an expanding patient base in ways that enabled sexologists to embrace this seemingly more empirical form of evidence."[15] Such photography was not only a central part of Hirschfeld's publications, especially *Geschlechtsübergänge* (*Sexual Transitions*, 1905), *Die Transvestiten* (1910), and his *Sexualpathologie* series (1916–20), but would go on to become the centerpiece of his Institute of Sexology in the 1920s. The *Zwischenstufenwand* (wall of sexual intermediates), a collage of photographs divided into sexual groups and kinds, formed its central focus.[16] With this orientation, medico-scientific photography aligned the epistemological framing of the body with a visual framing of bodies that relate and differ from one another.

Despite this effort to use photography as an indexical and empirical tool, however, these images are self-consciously aestheticized and draw on specific stylistic convention that run counter to the expectation of unbiased scientific representation. Here the parallels between sexual-scientific life writing and medical photography become clear. Both frame queer and trans lives and bodies within the framework of medico-scientific discourse, but both use literary and visual tools to counteract these frameworks. Specific moments in sexual-scientific life writing point toward the scenography of medical photography. Dori recounts the doctor's request to exhibit them in front of a medical audience. Such an exhibition for the purpose of medical education and comparison of deviant bodies is precisely the intended purpose of sexual-scientific photography, too. Although photographs of queer and trans individuals were certainly not restricted to the medical realm, in this chapter I consider photographs that appear in a medical context in particular because they represent the same scene of medical encounter as presented by Body and Dori in their respective narratives.[17] Such an analysis

---

14. "The Visual Archive of Sexology" was the title of a symposium at Birkbeck in 2017, organized by Heike Bauer and Katie Sutton, which brought together scholars in the history of sexology to examine the use of images and visual evidence in historical sexology. See also Heike Bauer, Melina Pappademos, Katie Sutton, and Jennifer Tucker, eds., "The Visual Archive of Sex," special issue, *Radical History Review* 142, no. 1 (January 2022).

15. Katie Sutton, "Sexology's Photographic Turn: Visualizing Trans Identity in Interwar Germany," *Journal of the History of Sexuality* 27, no. 3 (September 2018): 442.

16. On Hirschfeld's *Zwischenstufenwand*, see Rainer Herrn, "Ge- und erlebte Vielfalt— Sexuelle Zwischenstufen im Institut für Sexualwissenschaft," *Sexuologie* 20, nos. 1–2 (2013): 6–14.

17. For scholarship that highlights how photographs of sexually and gender-diverse indi-

follows Butler's argument that we must pay attention to the ways in which existing frameworks of recognition—in this case sexual-scientific methodology and its use of visual aids—operate and fail if we want to understand the conditions of livability.

In sexual-scientific photographs, the body is framed epistemologically as a type of body with a unique diagnosis. Kathrin Peters describes how in *Geschlechtsübergänge* and elsewhere, Hirschfeld does not just rely on photographs of his own patients, but relies on existing photographs that he recirculates.[18] Peters discusses how one such image, taken by photographer Wilhelm von Gloeden, reappears in Hirschfeld's work. Whereas von Gloeden's photograph shows a naked male-presenting person in front of an artistic floral background, in Hirschfeld's publication the image has been retouched by stripping out the background and placing the person at the center of the photograph against a white, clinical background. The demand of sexual sciences to be neutral, clinical, and scientific is here communicated by literally reframing the body at the center of the photograph.

In her essay on the sexological utilization of photography, Katharina Sykora argues that Hirschfeld's photographs show a modern scientific commitment to the discovery of nature by enacting the lifting of veils and unfolding of layers (of clothes and skin) in his photographs. In doing so, Hirschfeld develops his own metaphorics of discovery.[19] The photographs of medical examination that Hirschfeld includes in his publications are meant to be viewed with a coolly medical gaze that enables one to access the truth of nature, which can be found behind the veil of clothes, or even layers of skin revealed in each image. Yet this medical gaze is highly aestheticized. As Sykora argues, the mode of revelatory viewing presented in photographs used by Hirschfeld adds up to a set of metaphoric discoveries built into the experience of viewing such photographs.

---

viduals stand in relation to science, art, and (sub)culture, see David James Prickett, "Magnus Hirschfeld and the Photographic (Re)invention of the 'Third Sex,'" in *Visual Culture in Twentieth-Century Germany: Text as Spectacle,* ed. Gail Finney (Bloomington: Indiana University Press, 2006); Sutton, "Sexology's Photographic Turn"; Kathrin Peters, *Rätselbilder des Geschlechts: Körperwissen und Medialität um 1900* (Kempten: Diaphanes, 2010); Kathrin Peters, "Anatomy Is Sublime: The Photographic Activity of Wilhelm von Gloeden and Magnus Hirschfeld," in *Not Straight from Germany: Sexual Publics and Sexual Citizenship since Magnus Hirschfeld,* ed. Michael Thomas Taylor, Annette F. Timm, and Rainer Herrn (Ann Arbor: University of Michigan Press, 2017).

18. Peters, "Anatomy Is Sublime," 171.

19. Katharina Sykora, "Umkleidekabinen des Geschlechts: Sexualmedizinische Fotografie im frühen 20. Jahrhundert," *Fotogeschichte: Beiträge zur Geschichte und Ästhetik der Fotografie* 24, no. 92 (March 2004): 15–30.

Such an act of discovery is visualized by presenting several photographs alongside one another in a narrative series that frames the body as a certain type of body. Medical photographs are frequently presented in the form of a triptych, which shows a naked individual in the middle, with two further photographs of the individual dressed in typically male and female attire respectively on either side.[20] Sutton notes how "such 'compare and contrast' images mark the beginnings of a distinct and at times distinctly problematic trend in Hirschfeld's representation of gender-atypical subjects that becomes particularly evident in his later series on *Sexualpathologie*."[21] Hirschfeld's methodology changes to accommodate his desire for a clearer visualization of sexual intermediacy. These triptychs may well make nakedness the center of attention, framed between two images of the subject dressed in traditionally female (left) and male (right) attire, an arrangement that also mimics Hirschfeld's theory of sexual intermediacy.

The choice of a triptych in the presentation of intermediate stages of human development is telling in itself. Not only does the medical triptych have a dissonant association with the religious triptych, but it also recalls the mirrors of a dressing table, offering intense yet fragmented multiplanar reflections and confirmations of the self that are framed in multiple reflexive ways. Such dressing table mirrors give the illusion of a total view of self when someone is seated in front of them and provide a narcissistic confirmation of this self. Yet the triptych also gives a sense of a false method: a flat mirror would never be sufficient in the creation of the made-up self, which requires a triple view. This confirms the meticulous labor that goes into performing gender. The triple mirror also splits the self into multiple fragments or frames, reflecting back a composite image of selfhood that relies on multiple forms of framing of a subject not otherwise "fully formed."[22]

At first glance, such a set of photographs seems to reveal the secret of the subject's body through this method of discovery. What is obscene, or off-

---

20. I have chosen not to reprint these images here, as it is unclear whether the subjects consented to having their photographs printed in this form. This is an ethically ambiguous choice. On the one hand, choosing not to reprint the photograph here might avoid the further display of queer individuals as bodies to be diagnosed. On the other hand, Amanda B. might have chosen to be represented in this way and my refusal to honor this self-portrayal presents a paternalistic interference in trans people's right to self-definition.

21. Sutton, "Sexology's Photographic Turn," 465.

22. Benjamin Kahan, *The Book of Minor Perverts: Sexology, Etiology, and the Emergences of Sexuality* (Chicago: University of Chicago Press, 2019), 7ff. See also my discussion of subjects that are not yet fully formed in the introduction to this book.

scene, here appears "on/scene," a term coined by Linda Williams "to describe the way in which discussions and representations once deemed obscene—as an excludable hard core easily excised from supposedly decent public space—have insistently cropped up, and not only in the realm of pornography."[23] Such photographs move that which is usually concealed into the center. However, the image of the naked person in the center only gains significance when put in the context of both photographs in which the same person is clothed. If viewed by themselves, neither image shows any sign of morphological difference. The act of revelation is enacted purely by the constellation of photographs next to each other. Even though the naked body is on/scene (rather than ob/scene or off/scene), it nonetheless exceeds its epistemological framing. Simply showing the naked body in photography, then, cannot reveal the truth about this body, which is always mediated by photographic framing. In this way, sexual and gender ambiguities can only be achieved by means of staged or photographic construction.[24] For *Geschlecht* (sex/gender) to be recognizable, it requires the framing of the body and its arrangement in a certain visual narrative space.

This does not mean that the individual thus portrayed escapes its sexual-scientific framing. Such a frame always makes a cut. Here, for example, the sexual-scientific frame does not allow an understanding of gender and sexuality that does not require a diagnosis. However, this failure to make individuals fully recognizable opens up the way for further and multiple readings of gender. The individuals portrayed can be read as outside the gender binary, or indeed as transitional and thus at least to some extent able to live in their chosen gender. The sexual-scientific frame opens up the possibility of livability at the same time as it frames and thereby restricts the ways in which livable queer lives can be apprehended. These ambiguities are important because they reveal the ways in which depicted subjects might have used their photographic framing to express themselves. Examining depictions of cross-dressing and male intimacy in Third Reich photography, Jennifer Evans and Elissa Mailänder argue that the expectation of photographs to reveal fixed and firm identities obscures important ambiguities of identity. In the case of police photographs, for example, they see not only violence and trauma but also the possibility for resistance on the part of the depicted subject.[25] Such a hospitable reading

23. Williams, *Screening Sex*, 7.

24. Sykora, "Umkleidekabinen des Geschlechts," 18.

25. Jennifer Evans and Elissa Mailänder, "Cross-Dressing, Male Intimacy and the Violence of Transgression in Third Reich Photography," *German History* 38, no. 2 (June 2020): 25–43.

acknowledges the agency of the photographic subject to attempt a livable life, even under unlivable conditions.

Photographic subjects can work with and against the visual method of sexology. Using Butler's distinction between recognition and apprehension, and apprehending these bodies as lying outside of the binary and yet refusing recognition as a certain kind of body (despite the caption assigning a diagnosis), we can understand such photographic subjects as exceeding the frame of sexual-scientific photography without fully escaping from its confines. For the viewer, the erotic potential of these photographs, showing naked bodies in a boudoir-like scene, overlaps with the clinical frame of these photographs. Erotic desire and desire for knowledge merge in the act of looking. In this way, the metaphorics of discovery cultivated in these images effect both the functioning of the sexual-scientific frame as well as its fragmentation.

This excursion into the use of photographic evidence in sexual-scientific publications shows that the use of photography as evidence always requires a kind of framing, literally in the way that images are cropped and retouched, in their composition as part of a triptych, or as epistemologically framed by sexual-scientific theories and methods. Yet as Butler argues and my analysis has shown, such frames "can and do break with themselves":[26] In the remainder of this section, I return to Dori's and Body's narratives in order to analyze how sexual-scientific life writing work with but also break the frame of sexual-scientific discourse.

When Dori is first called a "homosexual," they respond: "das klingt mir so *unfaßbar*"—"that sounds so unfathomable" (DMB 66). *Unfaßbar* means the inability to understand or represent in words a certain matter, but it also refers to an inability to be grasped or held, and so it can also mean to have no *Fassung*, no hold or frame. Dori cannot grasp the meaning and implications of this interpellation, because, as is repeated on the next page, it makes them *fassungslos*, without hold or frame (DMB 67). In the moment that their body has been designated as a kind of body, a homosexual body, it can no longer be grasped—understood *or* touched—which is made clear when, at the moment of medical examination, the body escapes all representation. This loss of framing is a loss of context as well as narrative and sociability, because Dori is not only removed from a normative framing that would make sense to them, but is also left there in solitude as they lose first their family and closest friend and later their partner because of a perceived anomaly.

Throughout the narrative, there are instances where Dori is framed as different, but this difference fails to take on livable forms of personhood for Dori.

---

26. Butler, *Frames of War*, 12.

During adolescence, Dori is called names such as dolly (*Puppe*), eunuch (*Eunuch*), and whore (*Hure*) (DMB 15, 25, 42). These are hurtful interpellations that refer to Dori's body as deficient and different: as *Puppe*, Dori's friends call them fragile, as *Eunuch*, Dori's brother accuses them of a lack of virility, and as a *Hure*, the stranger who names Dori such not only mistakes them for a woman, but a sex-working woman with a profession that situates her on the social margins. It also shows Dori's body to be desirable and, accordingly, not only marks the relationship between Dori and their friend Kurt, who accompanies Dori in this instance, as homosexual, but also calls into question the interpellator's sexual orientation. Such interpellations function as powerful frames that enact violence and harm on the subject thus framed.

In the final scene of Dori's narrative, their body is positioned in a peculiar way as they face themselves in a mirror—a scene akin to that of a photographic self-portrait—only moments before their suicide. In order to see themselves, Dori looks at the reflection of their body in the mirror, like another person, through the eyes of another and sees an impossibility: "But I am a liar, have been a liar since birth. I lied when I tried to convince people that I was a man, and I lied when I put on women's clothes. My whole life is a lie, and I will die from it" (DMB 9). Dori cannot be the man that they were expected to be, cannot be the woman they attempted to be, because Dori is always seen as different and deviant. In this moment of reflection Dori cannot see their own body, because something is missing. They see their body through the eyes of another as a body that must always stand outside the norm while performing the normal, an act that Dori perceives as an unlivable lie. The parallel between mirror image and medical photography here emphasizes the harm done by visual scrutiny and the violence enacted by the diagnostic frame.

Dori's struggle for livable circumstances, then, can be understood as an attempt to reframe their body, to reestablish a relation to a body that combines visibility and recognition with internal desires. A sense of community with others of their "kind"—what is referred to in the text as *gemeinsames Unglück* (shared unhappiness) (DMB 71)—thus offers livable moments by reframing Dori in the context of those who are similarly rejected. Yet this also highlights the reasons for Dori's tragic end: living as a woman engaged to a man, Dori had to fabricate a heritage and identity that is under threat of being revealed by their partner's jealous family. The threatened removal of this "framing" promised by their most precious relationship seems unbearable to Dori as they commit suicide.

When Body, on the other hand, is teased and made fun of because of his supposedly abnormal looks, the situation becomes *unerträglich* (unbearable)

(MGY 90), and Body feels *niedergedrückt*, sad or literally pushed down by the weight of the matter (MGY 89). To be confronted with an understanding of one's body as abnormal is here not expressed as a lack of framing, as it was in Dori's narrative, but as excess, an unbearable burden or weight that bears heavily on Body. After Body's transformation into Norbert, the reader is finally presented with one direct bodily description: "My body, no longer held back by constricting items of clothing, flourishes more freely and more powerfully. . . . [P]hysically, nothing should remain from my girlhood years but a faint mark from my corset" (MGY 154) The unlivable conditions of life as a woman have left marks on his body.

In another instance, Body's friends comment on his body and exclaim, "Look, Nora is so very different (*anders*) from us" (MGY 24). The word *anders* not only refers to a simple morphological difference but also carries connotations of homosexuality. Richard Oswald's film *Different from the Others* (*Anders als die Andern*, 1919), for example, uses the term *anders* to describe the abuse and maltreatment of homosexuals, precisely because they are perceived to be different.[27] Yet it would go too far to suggest that Body is here accused of homosexuality. Rather, the term *anders* shows an interesting modality. It can be used as a variable code for a variety of kinds of sexual or gender otherness. Body is not interpellated as homosexual here, but his *Anderssein* is clearly marked as belonging to the sexual realm. In this scene, Body's *Anderssein* is symbolized by the metonymic object of the dress. The dress is associated with the body, but it is not the body itself that is described here. And neither does the body need to be revealed to show what is really at stake: that Body's body is simply *anders* and therefore outside the norm. In the narratives discussed here, a photographic way of looking at the undressed body can be detected that echoes the simultaneous revealing and blurring of bodily particulars.

The unbearable burden of gender assignment also becomes visible in some of Hirschfeld's photographs, in particular a triptych depicting Amanda B.[28] In the center, the triptych shows an image of B. naked, of medium height and with hands placed on hips. To the right, B. is significantly taller, dressed in male attire and stands with upright posture, with a cane in one hand and a hat in the other. The image and the subject's posture communicate comfort in male

---

27. On Hirschfeld's involvement in *Anders als die Andern* see Ina Linge, "Sexology, Popular Science and Queer History in *Anders als die Andern* (Different from the Others)," *Gender and History* 30, no. 3 (2018): 595–610.

28. Magnus Hirschfeld, *Sexualpathologie: Ein Lehrbuch für Ärzte und Studierende*, vol. 2, *Sexuelle Zwischenstufen: Das männliche Weib und der weibliche Mann* (Bonn: A. Marcus & E. Webers, 1918), Plate 1.

clothes. The image on the left shows B. in a cowered pose, figuratively and literally weighed down by the burden of femininity. The original cover image to Body's memoirs shows an image that is similar to Amanda B.'s cowered pose. The image by Lucian Bernhard shows an example of his famous *Plakatstil* (poster style), an early version of poster art that developed in Germany around 1900.[29] The image shows two girls in the background looking at a larger person (presumably Body) in the foreground. Body's eyes appear nervous as they look back toward the girls. His body, dressed in a blouse with a gigantic bow tight around the neck, is cowered and gives off the appearance of a person who is very uncomfortable in these clothes. The clothes frame Body's body as being at odds with the gendered norm they express.

When Body accepts the doctor's help and legally becomes Norbert, he deals differently with his now incoherent past. He visits his mother and, at that moment of disclosure, says that his mother retells the story of his birth. This story is vital, part of the life and body implicated in it, and must be retold. Norbert Body emphasizes this when, a few pages later, he says: "I would have been spared so much suffering and so many battles if just one person, at home or at school, had spoken with me about my gender honestly and sincerely!" (MGY 158). Talking about the body, giving language to the body so that this body can be situated in the family, before the law, before others, is here revealed to be a vital contributor to Body's sense of livability. In his mother's narrative, Body's life is reframed in a more livable way.

As the excess of the unbearable burden of womanhood is removed to restore a sense of livable and bodily framing, another kind of framing also occurs: "Around this time I had my photograph taken for the first time and sent it to Hanna" (MGY 153). Body's transformation, framed as such by the photographic medium, is met with approval. "On the whole, people thought that I had changed to my advantage" (MGY 153). Livability is bestowed on Body as the burden of femininity is lifted. Notably, the final scene in which Body's masculinity is ultimately secured, he, as Norbert, pulls off the veil of femininity, discarding Nora. Yet as with Dori, Body experiences a sentiment of bodily loss that is clearly expressed when the narrative is published under the pseudonym N. O. Body, *no body*.

In this scene, the photograph, taken in a private rather than medico-scientific context, parallels the possibilities for agency offered by the medium of life writing. Katie Sutton traces the similarities and differences between

---

29. On Lucian Bernhard, see Ruth E. Iskin, *The Poster: Art, Advertising, Design, and Collecting, 1860–1900s* (Hanover, NH: Dartmouth College Press, 2014), 239–42.

medico-scientific photography of trans subjects and self-representation of trans subjects as it emerged in subcultural contexts in Germany, arguing that "subcultural actors appropriated, adapted, and rejected sexology's solidifying visual conventions to suit an emerging minority politics focused less on medical explanation and more on public recognition and respect."[30] Body's photograph shows him in his legally transitioned state as a heterosexual man engaged to Hanna. The response he receives is positive and confirms the overall approval of his transition, and the photograph gives Body the agency to present himself in the way that he wants to be seen and to ask for recognition as such. Such calls for recognition, as I have argued in Chapter 1, form part of a call for hospitable reading. In recording Body's intentions, the ekphratic photograph stands in for the narrative as a whole, which uses the first-person narrative to frame Body's life in livable ways.

This livable framing of Body's body through private photography and narrative framing, as well as the two differing understandings of unlivable condition as lack or excess of framing, express the conditions of livability. Dori's emphasis on lack expresses the withdrawal of a functioning relation with bodily norms and with others around them and shows the violence of the frame, which offers no possibilities for a livable life. Body cannot bear the excess of assigned categories that frame his body and therefore foreclose and contradict more suitable identifications. Medical categories, relations to others, and norms hold us, but unlivable conditions arise when they frame the subject too loosely or too tightly, when they do not fit the subject that is set in its frame. The prospect of livability is never foreclosed by the existence of categories or ensured by the absence of the same, but depends on the particular way in which a subject relates to categories of recognition, and this relation is, in the case of Dori and Body, facilitated by medical practitioners who employ such categories. Whereas in the scene of disrobement, Body reports how the doctor "spoke to me with kind words" (MGY 146), Dori's doctor hardly speaks to them and only asks Dori to become an object of scientific display.

My analysis of medico-scientific photography as well as sexual-scientific life writing reveals that the body put on display gains meaning only through framing, veiling, and staging. Such framing can threaten to expose the subject to unlivable forms of power, for example when Body feels devastated by being framed as abnormal by friends and family or when Dori is framed violently through hurtful interpellations. At the same time, the framing of Body's life as a boy in the narrative of his mother and as a man in the photograph sent to

---

30. Sutton, "Sexology's Photographic Turn," 478.

Hanna provides a livable narrative frame. These examples show that frames are ambivalent and that they can be used to create both livable and unlivable conditions. Reading these texts in a hospitable way acknowledges the agency and active participation of life writers in navigating such frames to create livable lives and the call for recognition that this framing demands.

2. Sex Sells: (Re)framing Queer Livability at the Fashion and Department Store

The epistemological, visual, and sartorial framing I have discussed, which strongly influences the meaning of medico-scientific photography and patients' understanding of their own bodies and desires, is strikingly repeated within the space of the department store. Just as gendered clothing functions as an important frame for the individuals depicted in medical photography, Dori and Body report how gendered clothing (and other accoutrements of gender) in the space of the department store functions as a variously (un)livable frame for diverse gendered identities. The sexual and gendered difference that makes Dori and Body the central focus of sexual-scientific knowledge production also makes them of central interest to the world of commerce, commodification, and desire. For both Dori and Body, consumerism and desire in the department store offer another central frame through which sexual subjectivity can be understood. Just as discussed previously, such frames exert power over the individual thus framed and can cause harmful as well as livable moments. In this section, I follow both Dori's and Body's experiences as queer objects on display in order to deepen the understanding of the frame as ambivalent tool to achieve livability.

The entanglement of consumer culture and sexual-scientific discourses and methods is strikingly portrayed in Til Brugman's "Warenhaus der Liebe" ("Department Store of Love"). In this satirical piece, the Dutch author describes a thinly veiled version of Hirschfeld's Institute of Sexology as a department store that caters to its customers' extraordinary sexual desires.[31] In the piece, written around 1931, one customer asks for a chamber pot and finds the desired item among a large collection of pots. Another customer, a kleptomaniac, visits the Department Store of Love to steal items for a small fee. Others come to buy bottles of urine or feces made of sugar. Brugman, at the time of writing in a

---

31. Til Brugman, "Warenhaus der Liebe," in *Das vertippte Zebra: Lyrik und Prosa*, ed. Marion Brandt (Berlin: Hoho, 1995).

relationship with Dadaist artist Hannah Höch, might have sympathized with Hirschfeld's activism in support of sexual intermediate types, but her satirical take on the Institute of Sexology also lends a critical lens to the perceived commercialization of sexuality. Brugman's piece was written the same year that Hirschfeld published a pamphlet advertising the benefits of *Titus-Perlen*, a potency pill that contained hormone supplements.[32] Brugman's piece alludes to this commercialization of sexual desire and potency as she describes the various objects and experiences for sale at her Department Store of Love.

Brugman's piece makes a connection between Hirschfeld's institute and department stores as two quintessentially modernist German institutions that are both ambivalently placed. Opinions about the department store were split between those who were enthusiastic about the new possibilities and freedoms it offered and antimodernist reactions against consumerism and commerce. Opinions were similarly split about Hirschfeld's institute. While many appreciated that the institute supported new possibilities and freedoms for sexual/gender identification, some who held conservative views about sexuality understood it as a refuge for perverts and degenerates, with Hirschfeld and his colleagues as agitators for illicit sex under the guise of sexual education.[33] In comparing the department store, a place coded as Jewish, with the Institute of Sexology run by Hirschfeld, a Jewish practitioner, Brugman also points out the growing antisemitism that permeates responses to both Hirschfeld's institute and the department store.

As I will show in this section, *Diary of a Male Bride* and *A Man's Girlhood Years* anticipate these themes of commercialized sexuality, ambiguity toward the department store, and antisemitism. Both Dori and Body start their work as shop clerks when their families can no longer cover the costs of further education. Both receive low wages, and both fear that they cannot meet the demands of their new job and employer. They are members of a new generation of working-class girls starting out on their lifelong career as shopgirls—except that, in the eyes of their peers, family, and the majority of their contemporaries, they are not ordinary, because they are not considered—nor do they consider

---

32. Magnus Hirschfeld, *Titus-Perlen: Wissenschaftliches Sexual-Hormon-Präparat nach Vorschrift von Sanitätsrat Dr. Magnus Hirschfeld unter ständiger klinischer Kontrolle des Instituts für Sexualwissenschaft* (Berlin: Berlin-Pankow Titus Chemisch-pharm. Fabrik, 1931[?]). In Promonta (no. 21), Sammlung zum Institut für Sexualwissenschaft und Magnus Hirschfeld, Schwules Museum Archive and Library.

33. Rainer Herrn, "Outside in—inside Out: Topografie, Architektur und Funktionen des Instituts für Sexualwissenschaft zwischen Wahrnehmungen und Imaginationen," in *Metropolenzauber: Sexuelle Moderne und urbaner Wahn*, ed. Gabriele Dietze and Dorothea Dornhof (Vienna: Böhlau, 2014), 26.

themselves—to be girls. Consequently, their work for a large retailer exposes them as oddities and opens the way for gossip, harassment, and abuse. But the specific conventions and provisions of the department store also influence the very identity of those who enter into its space: the large business that aims at dominating the market through ever greater advertising efforts and extravagance also determines that, much like the commodity goods displayed, the bodies of those who work on the shop floor are implicated in this entanglement of customers' desire and retailers' competition and become commodified as marketing tools to incite the desire of potential customers. However, it is not my aim here to equate commodification with a lack of agency. Instead, I propose a more hospitable reading. Just as the framing of medical photography can be understood to violently expose and displace the subject, as well as offer opportunities for the subject to appear in more livable ways—by avoiding a clear subjugation to the gender binary—the commodification of bodies in the space of the department store offers a kind of framing that, although ambivalent and potentially harmful, offers meaningful ways for self-presentation and thus for livability.

As consumer paradise and entertainer of masses, early twentieth-century fashion and department stores are places imbued with commerce, entered for the purpose of consumption—or to dream of consuming; they are places that have their own peculiar rules and functions that make everything appear possible and purchasable. Yet, as Raymond Williams notes, such commercial activity requires more than the simple display of goods. Elaborate product advertisement reveals that "we have a cultural pattern in which the objects are not enough but must be validated, if only in fantasy, by association with social and personal meanings."[34] With increased competition among department stores and large retailers comes the need to make product and shop appear ever more exciting, to develop marketing tricks and consider everything as a selling point that might attract consumers in greater numbers, appealing not just to their identities as buyers, but also to their social and personal aspirations.

The department store was also a space of sexualized desire that was particularly feminized. As Rita Felski argues, "Whereas female sexuality remained a problematic notion throughout the century, its existence either denied or projected onto the deviant figure of the femme fatale, women's desire for commodities could be publicly acknowledged as a legitimate, if

---

34. Raymond Williams, "The Magic System," *New Left Review* 1, no. 4 (July–August 1960): 23.

often trivialized, form of wanting."[35] At the same time, sexualized consumption was projected onto female shop clerks. Discussing one of the most well-known representations of the department store in literature, Émile Zola's *Au Bonheur des Dames* (*The Ladies' Paradise*, 1883), Paul Lerner describes how "the image of decapitated mannequins with price tags above their necks acutely symbolizes the ways in which the department store commodified women and female beauty and indeed did violence to women. Zola describes the dummies as 'women for sale,' suggesting a slippage between inanimate mannequins and actual women."[36] As such a commodifier, the department store offered both new possibilities for female desire and agency and new forms of objectification.

It is such a feminized space of sexualized desire for consumer goods that Dori and Body both enter as shop clerks. When his father dies and leaves his family without money, Body becomes a *Lehrmädchen*, literally a girl apprentice, although here we might conceivably understand it as apprenticing as a girl. Body's apprenticeship takes place at a big-city department store – Hermann Simon's research into Body/Baer's biography suggests that this might be the Warenhaus Gottschalk in Bielefeld[37]— a place that he simultaneously fears and has hopes for: "The farewell to my home was made easier by the fact that I would now come to a strange city where no one knew about my secret" (MGY 84). Thus, Body enters the shop floor at a time of both financial insecurity and uncertainty about the recognition of his gender identity. In *Diary of a Male Bride*, too, the retail space arises as a setting for important events in the protagonist's life. Raised as a boy, Dori is continually interpellated as effeminate. Dori becomes enamored with a male musician, claiming to not quite know what the social connotations of such a love might be. Their work at a women's fashion boutique introduces them to a life in which the performance of femininity becomes possible, expressed and legitimized in their subsequent work as shopgirl responsible for trying on outfits in front of female clients. Both Dori and Body work in a space dedicated to commerce, an emporium that is highly specialized and departmentalized, and both work in a section of the business that focuses on female attire. In both texts, the time spent in the retail space coincides with the turning point from adolescence to adulthood through the

35. Rita Felski, *The Gender of Modernity* (Cambridge, MA: Harvard University Press, 1995), 65.

36. Paul Lerner, *The Consuming Temple: Jews, Department Stores, and the Consumer Revolution in Germany, 1880—1940* (Ithaca, NY: Cornell University Press, 2015), 125.

37. Hermann Simon, "N. O. Body – Karl M. Baer", in N. O. Body, *Aus eines Mannes Mädchenjahren*, ed. Hermann Simon (Berlin: Hentrich & Hentrich, 2022), 140.

crucial time of puberty during which, Body reports, physical changes exacerbate his marginalization and his understanding of difference.

Both Dori and Body learn very quickly that life on the shop floor functions according to its own rules. When Herr Markus, the owner of the Damenkonfektionsgeschäft der Firma Markus & Bernstein, a fashion boutique, hires Dori as his new shop assistant, Dori's difference—long blond hair and feminine gait—which elsewhere triggers questioning looks and misunderstandings, seems to have business value when placed on the shop floor: "My mother said I would have to have my hair cut, but Herr Markus disagreed. He wanted me just so, just the way I am. That would be something different; it would please his female customers" (DMB 38). Herr Markus wants Dori just the way they are: different. The modality of the word "different" becomes clear here, a difference that is nonetheless clearly found in relation to Dori's sexual or gender identity. Considering that Dori had previously experienced the transgression of sexual and gender norms as highly problematic and that, as the owner of a large high-street business, Herr Markus would certainly have been able to find another employable woman for his shop, it is quite extraordinary that the lure of Dori's otherness seems to outweigh any doubts Herr Markus might have had about hiring them. Yet Herr Markus orders Dori to stay the way they are, not in order to allow for Dori to be an autonomous agent in the presentation of their body, but because this body, the way it is, signifies something different and other, a feature to impress and entertain the customers. This difference, which elsewhere untethers Dori as they are teased by their peers, leads in this instance to a particular kind of recognition of otherness as interesting and alluring. This framing of the queer body as desirable, a framing that is supported by the commodification of Dori's bodily difference, gives Dori a space to exist "on/scene," and without hiding, albeit under problematic conditions.

Similarly, when Body presents himself at the *großstädtischer Geschäftspalast*, the big-city business palace in which Herr Werner's boutique is situated, his difference is noted. His new employer comments, "Ho! You have the voice of a man," but immediately qualifies this statement, describing Body's difference as a potential asset for his business: "Well, it won't hurt, I should hope it will impress the customers" (MGY 85). Asserting that there is no harm to his business involved in hiring Body appears to show an understanding of the common apprehension of deviance as disadvantage, but he concludes that he can renegotiate this difference once it enters the space of his department store, where it can be presented in such a way as to make a lasting impression on the customer. However, unlike Dori's case, where the attention drawn to their physical appearance offers opportunities for livable gender performance, in Body's case the public performance as shopgirl causes apprehension and anxiety and does not, in this instance, provide a livable framing.

Inside the shop, items are arranged in order to frame the customer's relation to products through a desire to own and consume them. To catch the customer's gaze is therefore one of the most important tasks of the shop. That this is the case is shown by the exceptional position of the *Schaufensterdekorateur*, the window dresser responsible for framing the shop's goods in the shop window: "Today, it is no longer enough to pile up different goods in the shop window, but the eyes of the big-city dwellers must be drawn to modern color compositions and fairy-tale-like clouds of silk" (MGY 87). The window dresser of Dori's shop "has the task of tastefully arranging the splendors of the company in eight large shop windows" (DMB 65). Notably, the window dresser, Herr Wehldorf, is also a queer figure who reveals to Dori that, like himself, Dori is a "homosexual" (DMB 65), a word that Dori had not previously been aware of and that gives a language to his difference. In Body's narrative, the window dresser, with "long curly hair and a velvet jacket" (MGY 87), functions as a paradigmatic exponent of queer (window) dressing that both Dori and Body will experience. The appearance of the window dresser in both narratives as a visibly queer figure who is quite literally responsible for the frame of the shop window and also has agency over it anticipates that the frame of the department store offers a livable space for those who visibly deviate from the norm and facilitates an exchange of knowledge between them.

Indeed the department store features as a setting for homosexual encounters in various other texts from the same period. Hans Ostwald's short text from 1904, entitled "In der Passage" ("In the Arcades"), tells of an encounter between two men in the arcades of the Friedrichstraße in Berlin:

> A big man with a gray beard approaches from the other end of the arcades. He has shadows under his gray eyes, which were searching, searching just like the eyes of the younger man. But the older man's gaze moves blankly over the dressed-up ladies and the many nicely dressed, young girls. . . . Then the gentleman's eyes fall on the young man, his shabby gentility, and his pale-pink tie. And a languishing, enticing smile surrounds the soft mouth of the young man. The gentleman winks and soon enough they stand next to each other in front of the jeweler's shop and whisper to one another like bride and groom.[38]

---

38. Hans Ostwald, "In der Passage," *Das neue Magazin* (1904): 438–42. My own translation.

The department store functions as a make-believe space that enables the queer figure to play out their fantasies. Again, the shop window frames an opportunity for queer encounter that merges the lover reflected in its surface with the expensive jewels displayed behind and turns him into a precious (and, it is suggested, consumable) object of desire. Attraction and consumerism merge in this moment of framing. The older of the two men searches the other out like one of the objects displayed, and the department store becomes a queer matchmaking service, similar to Brugman's Department Store of Love, which unites visitors with their objects of desire.

In the shop window, beautiful products offer themselves to the customers, encouraging passersby to window-shop—*schaufensterbummeln*—and thereby cultivate a desire to look, a *Schaulust*, so to speak. It is in this space—one in which everything seems to offer itself to the customer, where everything can be touched, tried, desired, a space where displays must keep the customer captivated—that the queer body is prompted to work its magic. Dori's and Body's bodies are thus exhibited and put on display (*zur Schau gestellt*) as goods, commodified to work as just another selling point that complements the commercial flair of the shop and to lure in *schaulustige* customers who, entering a space so saturated in commerce, intuitively know just how to react.

In *Diary of a Male Bride*, this scene of display takes place as follows:

> Since I am fulfilling my function at the company . . . to the satisfaction of Herr Markus, he has been much friendlier to me. He now frequently uses me as a model (*Probier-Mamsell*). If a customer wants to buy a cloak or a coat, it will be placed around my shoulders. . . . Then I have to walk up and down in front of the mirror with dainty steps. This often causes laughter, which encourages the lady customers' *Kauflust*, their desire to buy. This idea isn't entirely unprofitable for me. It is pleasant for me insofar as I no longer have to deliver so many parcels, because I have become indispensable in the shop. (DMB 48–49)

This reference to *Probier-Mamsell* (literally a young woman, a mademoiselle, trying something on or trying something out) possibly refers to the function of the mannequin, inanimate dummies displayed in shop windows and elsewhere in the shop, as well as the use of living models who tried on dresses for interested customers before the introduction of changing rooms.[39] Dori's performance is reminiscent of a later occurrence, already cited, where Dori—"in the

---

39. Lerner, *The Consuming Temple*, 125.

interest of science"—is asked "to be presented . . . to a group of medical doctors and students" (DMB 67). Whereas I argued that this scene in front of the medical practitioner is perceived as unlivable by Dori, their role as model is perceived quite differently. Dori acknowledges that their role as mannequin benefits them because they no longer have to perform other physically demanding jobs.

Dori's performance as *Probier-Mamsell* becomes a sort of trademark for Herr Markus's shop that leads Dori to perceive themselves as a business asset with indispensable value as it inspires the customers' *Kauflust*, their desire to buy. This *Kauflust*—which Body also mentions in the context of the *Rücksichts-losigkeit kauflustiger Frauen* (the inconsiderateness of women who are driven by their desire to buy) (MGY 96)—expresses an amalgamation of desire and consumption. *Kauflust*, as Paul Lerner explains, "became a leitmotif in department store representations of all kinds, an explanation for the stores' ability to enthrall customers and entice passersby."[40] This leitmotif, Lerner argues, expresses contemporary anxieties about women's insatiable desire to consume.[41] Indeed, when the coat is placed around Dori's shoulders and frames their physique, it becomes unclear whether customers desire Dori or the coat that surrounds them. Here, the customers' desire is queered as the object of desire fluctuates between body and fetishistic object and the female customers' desire is at least partially drawn to the female-presenting Dori. As the customers look on, it is thus unclear whether they are primarily guided by *Schaulust* or *Kauflust*. This amalgamation of desire is reminiscent of medical photography, which merges erotic desire and desire for knowledge. Dori's awareness of the erotic potential of their performance also indicates agency in navigating the frame of the department store by seizing on opportunities to create livable moments for themselves.

If the body is thus implicated in the *Kauflust* of customers, the desire to consume takes on more overtly sexual tones, an aspect that is foreshadowed by the psychoanalytic connotations of *Schaulust*. In his *Drei Abhandlungen zur Sexualtheorie* (*Three Essays on the Theory of Sexuality*), Sigmund Freud introduces *Schaulust*—here "scopophilia"—as an aspect of sexual behavior: "Visual impressions remain the most frequent pathway along which libidinal excitation is aroused. . . . It is usual for most normal people to linger to some extent over the intermediate sexual aim of a looking that has a sexual tinge to it."[42] To look

---

40. Lerner, *The Consuming Temple*, 5.
41. Lerner, *The Consuming Temple*, 5.
42. Sigmund Freud, *Three Essays on the Theory of Sexuality*, in *The Standard Edition of*

at the desired object is thus part of an overtly sexual act that is further stimu-
lated by the space of commerce as it emphasizes processes of looking and
displaying, two processes that are contained in what Freud points out to be
complementary "scopophilic instinct and exhibitionism."[43] The fixation on the
intermediary here also substituted the desired object with a simulacrum of the
real thing and reinforces the link of *Schaulust* to commodity fetishism.

In a short satirical piece in the lesbian magazine *Die Freundin* (*The Girlfriend*) from 1930 entitled "'Er' und 'sie' kaufen ein" ("'He' and 'She' Go Shopping"), Elsbeth Killmer describes a lesbian couple—referred to as "he" and
"she" to emphasize their respective butch and femme characteristics—on their
shopping spree to the Tauentzienstraße, a major shopping street in Berlin.[44] In all
likelihood this is the Kaufhaus des Westens (KaDeWe), a department store
founded in 1907 by Abraham Adolf Jandorf. In the story, the space of the department store is used to enable the playing out of the couple's stereotypically gendered relationship. "She" wants to go shopping, "he" would rather fix the car.
While "she" wanders around the various departments of the KaDeWe, trying to
tick items off her shopping list but getting hopelessly lost among the items displayed, "he" is more interested in the shopgirls: "In his thoughts he was preoccupied with the little saleswoman and had to insist that this cute little person
really did have a heavenly patience and a beautiful, angelic face."[45] Yet "she" is
also distracted: "She had suddenly noticed that the saleswoman in front of her
had fabulous eyes, a fabulous boyish figure, and threw her fabulous glances. That
was why she was certainly intending to buy some of the plaid woolen fabric,
which the saleswoman had so 'fabulously' praised."[46] Here the department store
is a space that enables queer desire by allowing the fluid performance of gendered behavior and notably a desire that mixes *Schaulust* with *Kauflust*: "she"
wants to buy the item displayed because she desires the shopgirl.[47]

---

the *Complete Psychological Works of Sigmund Freud*, trans. James Strachey, vol. 7, *1901–
1905: A Case of Hysteria, Three Essays on Sexuality and Other Works* (London: Hogarth,
1953), 123–246, 156–57.

43. Freud, *Three Essays*, 166.

44. On Elsbeth Killmer, see Heike Schader, *Virile, Vamps und wilde Veilchen: Sexualität,
Begehren und Erotik in den Zeitschriften homosexueller Frauen im Berlin der 1920er Jahre*
(Sulzbach/Taunus: Helmer, 2004).

45. E. Killmer, "'Er' und 'sie' kaufen ein," *Die Freundin* 6, no. 16 (1930): no pagination.
Spinnboden Lesbenarchiv.

46. Killmer, "'Er' und 'sie' kaufen ein."

47. In Patricia Highsmith's *The Price of Salt*, the department store similarly functions as
a space for the queer encounter between protagonist Therese Belivet, who works in the toy

Kauflust, too, offers a continuation of the sexual theme. Turn-of-the-century discussions of female shoplifters, for example, note what they perceive to be connections between shopping and sexual desire. In her discussion of kleptomania, Karen Nolte shows that the desire to steal was understood as closely linked to female desire, a desire that only increased with the arrival of the department store. The Berlin neurologist Siegfried Placzek hypothesized that kleptomania was an expression of the drives and an anomaly of the sexual life, which involved the arousal of sexual desire and satisfaction.[48] The reason for this is, by now, a familiar one: the open presentation of goods was meant to awaken a feeling of desire.[49]

In Joe May's 1929 film *Asphalt* the reasons for protagonist Else's shoplifting are not explained by necessity, but by a compulsion that is ultimately linked to her desire for sexual attention and romantic fulfillment.[50] Fittingly, the opening scene of May's film shows a scarcely clad woman displayed in a high-street shopping window trying on and taking off stockings, while consumers, with a mix of *Kauf-* and *Schaulust*, look on. If shopping and the interactions with displayed goods are sexually arousing, then the combination of real-life model or mannequin with tantalizing sexual ambiguity and desirable clothing is a recipe for unprecedented arousal. The simultaneous *Kauflust* of customers, flitting between desire for body and goods displayed, does not even need to differentiate between object and subject, because the space of the shop implicates Dori's body in its exhibition of commodities.

Commodified as display dummy, placed on the shop floor by their employer, and asked to walk up and down in front of aroused customers, Dori's situation seems an unlikely condition for a livable life. The performance as model or mannequin provokes laughter, suggesting that it is enjoyable precisely because it is not normal but extraordinary and incongruous. The shop floor does not offer to normalize queer performance; Dori remains *anders*. Yet it is here that Dori's *Anderssein*, this difference, is given a platform to perform otherwise deviant behavior as an act with a purpose and justification. Dori's performance on the shop floor enables them to leave the shop and continue being different but valued:

---

department, and her future lover, Carol Aird. Patricia Highsmith, *The Price of Salt* (New York: Coward-McCann, 1952).

48. Karen Nolte, *Gelebte Hysterie: Erfahrung, Eigensinn und psychiatrische Diskurse im Anstaltsalltag um 1900* (Frankfurt am Main: Campus, 2003), 255.

49. Nolte, *Gelebte Hysterie*, 257.

50. Joe May, dir., *Asphalt* (1929; London: Eureka, 2005), DVD.

Certainly, I know that people will stop in the street to look at me. I know
that I am a living advertisement for Herr Markus, but I don't care. Let
them all know that I am not one to follow the crowds (*kein Herdentier*). I
have my oddities (*Absonderlichkeiten*). And why shouldn't I? (DMB
54–55)

Note that Dori does not leave the shop dressed in women's clothing. Such an
act is still impossible and can take place on the shop floor only. Yet something
has changed: Dori's passing through the shop as place of consumerism has
endowed their difference with value, a value that may be monetary in character
for Herr Markus, but certainly goes beyond that for Dori. Within the frame of
department store commodification, Dori's body and gender performance is
framed as being in the right place, albeit highly commodified.

Outside of the department store, Dori's difference is continually
pointed out during their school years, but hardly ever in positive terms. Yet
when Dori becomes aware of their difference by noticing the customers'
reaction to their bodily and gendered performance, Dori starts engaging
with it differently and to great effect. Thus, when Dori walks back and forth
"with dainty steps" and a woman's coat draped around their shoulders, they
put on a performance of otherness by purposefully citing female behavior.
To argue that the department store offers livable moments in which Dori's
gendered performance can be recognized and appreciated within the frame
of commerce is not to say that Dori always identified as a woman. Although
their later life as *Damen-Imitator* (female impersonator) suggests that Dori
desires to take on a certain feminine role, their situation is too complex to
be described as *weibisch* (womanish), an interpellation by their friend Kurt
that Dori rejects (DMB 54). The term *Probier-Mamsell* aptly expresses this
by drawing attention to the fact that Dori tries on female behavior for size,
thereby merging the lexica of commerce and gender. The female attire
serves as a facilitation of cross-dressing, allowing Dori to try on a female
role, a performance that is enhanced by the ready-to-wear items in stan-
dardized sizes offered by the turn-of-the-century department store.
Repeated patterns and shapes and multiple copies of the same dress in
themselves form a means of citation in the Derridean sense that Dori taps
into when they put on a women's coat, thereby performing an already
established and already cited form of femininity.

This inability of the customers to separate Dori's body from the dress that
surrounds it points once more to the fact that the bodily intelligibility—the
livability—of the deviant self is intricately linked to the robes and veils that

frame or dress it. This is once more reminiscent of medical photographs, where the dress frames the viewer's understanding of the person depicted in each photograph and gives meaning to the bodies displayed. For Dori, the queer performance of modeling that draws the attention and delight of customers provides a framing for the queer body that is not without complications but that, in this instance, offers a livable frame in which the queer body appears as desirable. As will be shown, this act of livability will come with detrimental side effects, but it is the beginning of an attempt that will lay the foundation for major events in Dori's life. Just as the subjects of medical photography are framed in sometimes unlivable terms, they can and do use this framing to create opportunities for livability. In a similar way, within the constraints of the frame Dori is able to achieve livable moments. Dori's time at the store is a crucial moment for the formation of Dori's own gender and sexual identity and their attempts to make life livable.

Body understands the commodification of his body on the shop floor very differently. When he is not happy to make use of his special "skill"—his voice—the shop owner Herr Werner is not pleased: "I trembled when I had to offer my help to such a customer. People stared at me, whispered, and laughed loudly. My boss interpreted this fear of customers as laziness and was therefore not particularly impressed by his new shopgirl apprentice" (MGY 89–90). The stares and laughter at Body as *Lehrmädchen* (literally "apprentice girl," or apprenticing as a girl) here recall Dori's experience as model, yet for Body this does not seem to be a livable circumstance. This is partially due to his very different identification during childhood and adolescence: although Body was raised as a girl, he describes how his body and interests are unfeminine and more those of a boy. Certainly, Body's experiences could be described as very similar to those of Dori; yet unlike the latter, Body's name and legal sex are changed at the end of the narrative and he is thus able to live life as a man without fear of discovery as the veil of femininity is pulled away, not from Nora, but from Norbert: "It seemed as if dark veils had been torn from my eyes. The doctor was right. Physically I was a man. And I had been told many times that I was male in mind and spirit" (MGY 146). Body understands himself as always already male, an identity that is disregarded on the shop floor, where he is expected to be and act as a woman.[51] Whereas the department store frames

---

51. This final moment of disrobing, however, also allows a different reading: the suggestion that the dark veil of femininity obscured his body and the world around him until it fell away poses the question whether Body might have manipulated this veil in the past as feminine masquerade.

Dori as the rightful center of attention and desire, Body is framed as at odds with his surroundings.

Part of Body's refusal to act out the queer performance asked for by Herr Werner is that the shop floor is a space that carries female connotations, as it offers women a certain freedom to spend time in public by themselves and to socialize with others.[52] In her discussion of the pathologization of female shop-lifters as an expression of modernist fears brought on by female emancipation, Rachel MagShamhráin even characterizes the department store as an "Amazon city," a space in which it is primarily women who work, shop, and socialize.[53] Although some critics understand women's intimate relationship with consumer culture and fashion as an outcome of women's manipulation by patriarchal institutions, Felski highlights how "more recent arguments within feminism and cultural studies have rejected this manipulation thesis, insisting that greater weight be given to the potential for active negotiation and recontextualization of meaning in the process of consumption."[54] We can see that this is certainly the case with Dori, whose feminine performance opens up opportunities to matter in the space of the department store.

When Body, however, is placed in the department store as masculine girl, his masculinity cannot be acted out in the same way as Dori's femininity. Whereas Dori's difference cites the norm of the shop floor, Body's difference distances him even further from that norm. There are two contradictory demands made of Body: unlike Dori, he cannot be the queer mascot, because the performance of femininity is precisely the one he wants to escape, but he also cannot be a normal shop "girl." Thus, for Body, the space of the department store is one that cannot create livable conditions because it frames him as different from the other girls.

In this unlivable condition, Body suffers under the mask he has to put on as shop-girl, an outer layer he has to add onto his self, which encourages him to put on a performance of compliant, normal shop-girl when he feels entirely unable to live up to this role. He writes:

> So much has been said about the actor who has to laugh on stage even if his heart is full of sadness; so many touching stories have been written

---

52. Nolte, *Gelebte Hysterie*, 257.

53. Rachel MagShamhráin, "The Ambivalence of the Department Store Kleptomaniac: On the Juridico-Medical Treatment of Cases of Middle-Class Female Theft around 1900," in *The Berlin Department Store: History and Discourse*, ed. Godela Weiss-Sussex and Ulrike Zitzlsperger (Frankfurt am Main: Peter Lang, 2013), 75.

54. Felski, *The Gender of Modernity*, 63.

and read about the poor theater extra and the dancing girls who have to smile even if one of their loved ones lies ill at home. And yet no one ever recognizes that the faces of shopgirls are often just a mask that covers up pain and suffering. While the actress is only forced to feign a strange smile for a few hours on stage, these poor creatures are never allowed to discard their masks. (MGY 95)

For Body, the shop floor is a stage that demands an impossible performance. Framed as a girl, he is forced to play this role relentlessly. He draws parallels between this unlivable gender performance and the unlivable performance of all shopgirls, as they are forced to hide their emotions and personal difficulties in the interest of customer service. What Body describes here is the "emotional labor" of shop work. Arlie Hochschild coined this seminal term to describe scenarios such as these where the worker has to create and sustain feelings such as sympathy, goodwill, and command in order to deliver a corporate service.[55] Hochschild also argues that emotional labor responds to specific economic and class markers: "In each job the worker must be attuned to the economic status of the customer."[56] This attunement to the customers' wealth or lack thereof further emphasizes the economic situation of the shopgirl.

Although this commodification of the body in ways that do not represent his own desires seems unlivable to him, passing through the department store does allow Body to live out certain desires by opening up another space to him: the female staff dormitory. Here, as Nora he lives as one of the girls, but he can also fulfill the tentative sexual relations he desires. Living in this space of semi-suspended reality in which only females exist, he becomes the replacement male, fully female and yet object of desire for many girls there. Once his flat chest is mistaken as a sign of malnutrition by the unknowing girls, Body is excluded from the girls' playful comparison of bust sizes so as not to make him feel upset about his own morphology. Body is thus left to watch and enjoy. When a female colleague is prescribed massages for a lump in her breast, Body administers these. Behind the scenes of the customer-clerk relationship that outs him as different, his life among female staff allows him to live out his sexual desires. What makes life livable for Body during his time at the dormitory is not a provision of a space in which he can act and be perceived as male—a gender identification that, at this point in the text, does not entirely

---

55. Arlie Russell Hochschild, *The Managed Heart: Commercialization of Human Feeling* (Berkeley: University of California Press, 2012 [1983]), 137–38.

56. Hochschild, *The Managed Heart*, 138.

represent Body's desires. Interestingly, it is acting like a full, though malnourished, "normal" girl that represents Body's transitional gender identity better than the queer performance on the shop floor. Thus, for Body, life on the shop floor is unlivable, whereas life in the girls' dormitory offers friendship, desire, and sexual arousal, while letting Body's self remain intact. The shop floor is not a space in which norms are suspended, but in which the tactical playing with the norm through compliant performance is utilized as a marketing tool. Cheerful and playful deviance is tolerated, but signs of trouble are not.

The frame of commerce and commercialization, which implicates sexual desire and gender performance, is ambivalent. Dori thrives on being given a platform that puts their gender performance center stage and recognizes this performance as meaningful within the space of the department store. For Body, the framing as shopgirl draws attention to his *Anderssein* and enacts a painful and unlivable exposure. Yet life behind the scenes in the women's dormitory allows his sexual desire and attraction to women to unfold. Sexual desire permeates both the department store and life at the staff dormitory. Not just sexual desire, but the close relationship between desire and consumption, *Kauf-* and *Schaulust*, which develops on the shop floor, begins to permeate the professional and private lives of Dori and Body in other ways. Both become aware of the close relationship between work as a shopgirl and sexual aggression and harassment, sex work and social inequality. As I will show later, both Dori and Body actively reframe their experiences at the department store in order to understand these various intersections of sex, work, and inequality, but they do so in very different ways.

Hearing a story told by his colleagues, Body realizes that some shopgirls have to supplement their income with sex work:

> Social misery is particularly prevalent among the salespeople in the big city. We were told the following true story: a gentleman in Cologne on the Rhine hired a saleswoman. "I'll pay you twenty-five marks a month." "But I cannot live on that," the girl said. "That is your problem, dear child, and by the way, you are busy here only during the day (!!)." (MGY 96)

Body dramatically punctuates his indignation at this suggestion, but his outrage is somewhat ambiguous: he is upset that the "gentleman" suggested that a shopgirl should engage in illicit sex work, yet his statement also suggests outrage at the thought that an already overworked shopgirl should complement her day job with yet another occupation. At the same time, the gentleman's comments show his understanding of salespeople's bodies as commodities, where the shop owner decides that shop work can easily be replaced with sex work without regarding the salesperson's preferences. This plays into a critique of the department store as a place that has lost all connection with morality and workers' rights. As one critic of the department store, Johannes Steindamm, wrote in 1904, "Here a human being is nothing but a workhorse (*Arbeitstier*)— once exhausted (*verbraucht*), they are simply gotten rid of."[57] This *Arbeitstier* resonates with the earlier *Herdentier* mentioned by Dori, an indication that the employee's life is threatened with being reduced to unlivable, inhuman conditions (a condition that Dori refuses by claiming not to be a *Herdentier*). For Body, this unlivability is expressed in the social misery of the salesperson forced to supplement a meager income with sex work.[58]

This story told to Body, which reveals the close relationship between shop work and sex work, also offers a comment on the already low social status of the shopgirl. As Dorothy Rowe argues in her monograph on sexuality and early twentieth-century Berlin, it was not unheard of that some salespeople supplemented their income with sex work:

> Procuring, like prostitution, was not an exclusive activity for many of its practitioners; it was most often a phase that many working-class men and women went through on their way to setting up other businesses such as street and market trading, finding alternative employment, supplementing their existing incomes.[59]

Evidently some working-class men and women understood sex work as an entrepreneurial opportunity to enter more respected and established trades related to work in business and sales. Body understands this close connection between shop work and sex work, although he focuses on the social inequality that leaves sex work as the only option for some women and men. He tells the story of a sex worker who visits the department store. As some of his colleagues express their disgust at their customer's profession, Body and others "pitied this person, who was so poor that she had to endure the torments of

---

57. Johannes Steindamm, *Beiträge zur Warenhausfrage* (Berlin: E. Ebering, 1904), 25, cited in Detlef Briesen, *Warenhaus, Massenkonsum und Sozialmoral* (Frankfurt am Main: Campus Verlag, 2001), 16. Translation my own.

58. For a cultural history of sex work in Berlin during the late Wilhelmine and Weimar periods, see Jill Suzanne Smith, *Berlin Coquette: Prostitution and the New German Woman, 1890–1933* (Ithaca, NY: Cornell University Press, 2013).

59. Dorothy Rowe, *Representing Berlin: Sexuality and the City in Imperial and Weimar Germany* (Aldershot: Ashgate, 2003), 100.

debauchery every day" (MGY 93–94).[60] Body's pity and empathy shows that he sees in the situation of the sex worker part of his own commodification as shopgirl from which he cannot escape. The *soziale Elend*, the social misery of the shopgirl, is linked to that of the sex worker, who is here presented as a tormented victim of sexual violence and social exclusion. In Body's narrative, the *Kauflust/Schaulust* that takes place on the shop floor is clearly linked to the sex work that takes place outside of, but related to, work on the shop floor.

For Body, the time at the department store provides an insight into the social injustice and economic difficulties faced by working-class girls and women, in particular, and he embarks on a short-lived but nonetheless significant career as political activist and feminist speaker. Still employed as a shop assistant, Body seeks out education as a distraction from his menial tasks. At the library, he comes across books on feminism and women's rights and begins to volunteer for charitable causes. This soon draws the attention of Stadtrat O., a city councillor, who supports Body's education. For two years, Body studies political economy in Berlin and publishes articles on social issues related to sex work and immigration, focusing in particular on the plight of girls and women. His articles draw the attention of a German-American newspaper, which hires him to travel to Poland, Siebenbürgen (today in Romania), Hungary, the Ukraine, and Turkey. Here Body researches women's social issues, including lack of education, bad working conditions, and class difference roughly during the years 1903–4.

In his memoirs, Body's later political interests come as a direct result of the work and hardship encountered during his time as a shop assistant, although for reasons of anonymity he does not expand on this. Researching the biography of the person behind the pseudonym N. O. Body, Karl Baer, Hermann Simon shows that in 1903 Baer, then still legally recognized as female, moved to Hamburg in order to train as a social worker.[61] In Hamburg, Baer also joined the Zionistische Ortsgruppe Altona, a Jewish charitable organization. As one of three ambassadors representing the group, Baer is sent to Galicia, a region in modern Poland and Ukraine. In Lviv (today in Ukraine) Baer is tasked with

---

60. In Christopher Isherwood's novel *Mr Norris Changes Trains*, the department store is explicitly described as the site of queer sex work, as the characters are well aware that "the speciality of the Kaufhaus des Westens" is "the whores on the corner . . . who dress up to excite the boot-fetishists." Christopher Isherwood, *Mr Norris Changes Trains* (London: Hogarth Press, 1952), 54–55.

61. The following biographical sketch is taken from Hermann Simon, "Wer war N. O. Body?," in N. O. Body, *Aus eines Mannes Mädchenjahren* (Berlin: Edition Hentrich, 1993).

tackling the issue of the *internationaler Mädchenhandel*, the so-called white slave trade, or sex trafficking. Social reformers since the late nineteenth century were concerned with this supposed criminal trading of Central European girls and women that forced them into prostitution. As Dietmar Jazbinsek has argued, the prevalence of sex trafficking has been largely disproven, but claiming its existence was used to engender xenophobic hostility as well as to deny sex work as a recognized profession.[62]

Baer himself was tasked with educating local women in Lviv with the aim of improving their economic and moral constitution. He published a report on his research on the topic as *Der internationale Mädchenhandel* (*The International White Slave Trade*).[63] Baer's report was published in Hans Ostwald's popular series Großstadt-Dokumente (Metropolis Documents), where Magnus Hirschfeld had published his influential ethnography of homosexuals in Berlin, *Berlins drittes Geschlecht* (*Berlin's Third Sex*).[64] The series published a number of sociological studies of groups on the margins of society, including sex workers, homosexuals, and anarchists, and covered a wide range of social issues, for example, gambling, people smuggling, and religious sects.[65] In his memoirs, Body mentions his studies and the subsequent travel and speaker tour through Eastern Europe, but he does not mention that his travels were related to the fight against "white slavery." Similarly, in his report Baer does not mention his own time spent in Galicia. It is likely that the reason for both cases was that he wanted to remain anonymous.

For Body, the frame of the department store, which frames him as oddity, creates few opportunities for a livable life. Instead, Body introduces social injustice as a framework for thinking about his experiences in the department store. By drawing on this framework of social justice, Body is able to frame his experiences at the department store as an insightful learning

---

62. Dietmar Jazbinsek, "Der internationale Mädchenhandel: Biographie eines sozialen Problems," WZB Discussion Paper, No. FS II 02–501, Wissenschaftszentrum Berlin für Sozialforschung (2002).

63. M. Baer, *Der Internationale Mädchenhandel*, in *Großstadt-Dokumente* 37 (Berlin: Hermann Seemann Nachfolger, 1908). Baer published further articles on the topic. See K. M. Baer, "Über den Mädchenhandel," *Zeitschrift für Sexualwissenschaft* 1, no. 9 (1908): 513–28; M. Baer, "Mädchenhandel," *Arena* 3, no. 5 (August 1908): 549–55.

64. Magnus Hirschfeld, *Berlins drittes Geschlecht*, in *Großstadt-Dokumente* 3 (Berlin: Hermann Seemann Nachfolger, 1904).

65. Dietmar Jazbinsek and Ralf Thies, "Großstadt-Dokumente: Metropolenforschung im Berlin der Jahrhundertwende," *Schriftenreihe der Forschungsgruppe Metropolenforschung des Forschungsschwerpunkts Technik-Arbeit-Umwelt am Wissenschaftszentrum für Sozialforschung* 98 (1997): 45.

experience that sets up his future career as speaker and social rights campaigner. That which remains off/scene and ob/scene on the shop floor—the social inequality experienced by working-class women—is reframed as Body's central object of inquiry, one that shapes Body's politics and eventually leads to his legal transition as he meets his future wife, Hanna, on one of his travels through Eastern Europe. Ultimately, the pursuit of social justice provides a frame for Body's experiences that presents them in a useful way for his development. Whereas Dori uses the existing frame of the department store and manipulates it in such a way that it provides livable moments, Body transitions to another frame that offers him a way out from the unlivable conditions of life at the department store.

Like Body, Dori, too, comments on the close relationship between shop work and sex work. Commenting on a letter from their friend, Kurt, Dori says: "He writes that in the company Markus & Bernstein only the street girls make their purchases. . . . But he's right. I now know the kind of well-dressed women who shop here" (DMB 49). Dori, although they do not seem to be pleased about their customers' profession, certainly does not seem very surprised. Notably, it seems that Kurt mentions that sex workers shop there in order to highlight the bad reputation that the shop has for its lack of moral integrity and urges Dori to find employment elsewhere.

I read Dori's lack of outrage as an indication that Dori relates to them: if sex workers masquerade as well-dressed women of a higher social status, Dori is then not the only one who engages in a kind of cross-dressing in the department store. This parallel also suggests that the trying on of clothes under the guise of Dori's role as *Probier-Mamsell* is not only a kind of cross-dressing in gender terms, but also in terms of class: Dori tries on clothes that they would never be able to afford but their work in the shop enables Dori to temporarily imagine stepping out of the role of working-class shop assistant and into that of wealthy middle-class consumer. This class-transgression is aspirational. After leaving the department store Dori becomes a *Damen-Imitator* (female impersonator). Upon wearing one of their ball gowns to the opera, Dori is propositioned by a variety of men and becomes a quasi-escort in exchange for expensive gifts (DMB 90–95).

Although Body and Dori do not further engage in sex work, they are not protected from unwanted approaches. Body reports how he befriends a fellow apprentice, but how this friendship does not last long "because the lad, misled by my comradely trust, became impertinent as we were working together in the basement one day. I gave him a good slap in the face" (MGY 96). Having worked at the shop only briefly, Dori experiences an event that makes them determined to leave both home and workplace. Dori does not explicitly describe the details of the event, but it is suggested that the shop owner, Herr Markus, sexually harassed Dori. When Dori reports the *widerliche Szene* (disgusting scene) (DMB 60) to their mother, she does not, as Dori had hoped, terminate their contract with Herr Markus but blackmails him into paying a large sum of money so that she can open a shop in the family house—commerce, it seems, is parasitic.

In the days that follow, Herr Markus retreats to his office, but Dori's colleagues begin to laugh and point, and one male colleague even approaches Dori and asks "whether we want to go for a stroll this evening. We could celebrate the good deal from the day before with a bottle of wine" (DMB 61). That Dori was previously mistaken for and painfully interpellated as "whore" thus turns out to be a sinister premonition of things to come. The harassment of Dori over access to their body represents, to their family, only a business opportunity. The *Kauf-* and *Schaulust* fostered on the shop floor is here represented as permeating Dori's private relationships. Although the commodification of their difference on the shop floor initially enables Dori to arrange for a life more livable, the intense form of commodification required to maintain such a presentation leads to abuse and assault. The *Schmutz* of their workplace that sticks to the "dirty fingers of Herr Markus" (DMB 60) becomes unbearable.

Here, Dori's initial enthusiasm for consumer culture and performance as commodity is exchanged for antimodernist tropes that understand the department store as moral danger. Detlef Briesen argues that the perception of the department store as a place of moral danger is based on assumptions of the department store as detrimental to economic behavior, cityscape, culture, and more.[66] One particular reason for the fear that department stores might endanger good economic practice emerges: it is assumed that, with their dubious practices, they destroy the order, decency, and morality of business life. It is not a big step from there to assume that the department store might then also destroy the morality of the consumer and salesperson.[67] Thus, Briesen notes that the economic immorality of the business also spills over into the personal lives of customers and employees. Besides sex work and sexual harassment, Briesen points out that opponents of the department store also criticize another aspect that supposedly challenges the moral integrity of the population, namely that the department store functioned as a space where people could meet and

---

66. Briesen, *Warenhaus, Massenkonsum und Sozialmoral*, 15.
67. Briesen, *Warenhaus, Massenkonsum und Sozialmoral*, 15.

initiate intimate encounters.[68] Dori confirms this: "Many salespeople also have lovers among our female customers. Oh, what filth" (DMB 49). Viewed through the lens of moral danger, the commodification of bodily potential, neatly paraded and presented on the shop floor, provokes a ravenous desire for ever more bodies and ever more satisfaction. The *Schmutz* as by-product of glamorous goods and exotic bodies is cleared from the shop floor, but finds its release in the secret interactions between customers and staff, or among the staff themselves: the "shop boys . . . told the filthiest stories, boasted about their sexual adventures, and loved to tell their unambiguous stories in the presence of the girls" (MGY 95). Like an infectious disease, the illicit "filth" of sex work, sexual harassment, and verbal abuse exceeds the department store and spreads behind the facade of the elaborately decorated shop windows.

This framework of moral danger is borrowed from antimodernist critiques of the department store and consumer culture more broadly, both of which were closely tied to antisemitic tropes.[69] As Paul Lerner summarizes, "Jews held, or at least started, the overwhelming majority of department stores and clothing and fashion houses throughout the country. Yet, beyond these empirical realities, writers, cultural critics, political agitators, and shoppers associated department stores with Jews in a variety of ways."[70] Department stores and fashion houses were often Jewish-owned, but more importantly the association between Jews and the department store was firmly assumed, even where this was not the case. Antimodernist critiques of department stores often seized on the association between the department store and Jewish ownership and imbued their critique with antisemitic stereotypes that depicted the department store as a place for intense capitalism, profit-making, and commodification.[71] Commodity capitalism was linked to sex work and human trafficking, again engendering antisemitic stereotypes.[72] Jewish business owners were depicted as sexual predators.[73]

With this in mind, the turn of Dori's narrative toward an evidently anti-

---

68. Briesen, *Warenhaus, Massenkonsum und Sozialmoral*, 16.

69. For an important reading of how German-Jewish authors offered counternarratives to an antimodernist rhetoric of the department store that was closely tied to antisemitic tendencies, see Godela Weiss-Sussex, "Confronting Stereotypes: Department Store Novels by German-Jewish Authors, 1916–1925," in *Tales of Commerce and Imagination: Department Stores and Modernity in Film and Literature*, ed. Godela Weiss-Sussex and Ulrike Zitzlsperger (Oxford: Peter Lang, 2015).

70. Lerner, *The Consuming Temple*, 5.

71. Lerner, *The Consuming Temple*, 10.

72. Lerner, *The Consuming Temple*, 135.

73. Lerner, *The Consuming Temple*, 19.

modernist critique that presents sex work, sexual assault, and overall filth as a result of the department store culture makes visible the antisemitic stereotypes engendered in the narrative. The name "Markus & Bernstein" suggests that Dori's workplace is a Jewish-owned business. As already discussed in Chapter 2, antisemitic stereotyping ascribed both effeminacy as well as hypersexuality to Jewish men. Such effeminacy expresses itself in variously lacking forms of masculinity, from myths of the menstruating Jew to accusations of homosexuality.[74] At the same time, Jewish men were stereotyped as having an insatiable sexuality. In addition to this, Lerner's monograph shows how, in its specific relation to the department store, Jewishness has been stereotypically and pervasively linked to greed and consumerism. The Jewish store owner was often represented as power-hungry and as a "demonic seeker of domination."[75] Dori's description of Herr Markus subtly engenders all three stereotypes: Dori explains Herr Markus's decision to hire them as driven by his desire to make money, a desire that initially supports Dori's need for self-representation but is then revealed to show a complete disregard for Dori's well-being or safety. If Dori describes Herr Markus's initial desire to hire them—"He wanted me this way, exactly the way that I am"—as a desire to commercialize Dori's queerness, the sexual assault signifies Herr Markus's sexual desire for Dori and insinuates antisemitic stereotypes of Herr Markus as simultaneously effeminate third sex and hypersexualized assailant. Finally, this amassing of antisemitic stereotyping culminates in the description of Herr Markus's "dirty fingers," symbolizing both sexual degradation and his greed for money.

Herr Markus's potential Jewishness is never explicitly mentioned, but the recognizable use of antisemitic stereotypes complicates Dori's narrative. Here, antisemitic tropes provide another narrative frame that Dori seizes on to explain their own failure of livability in the commercialized space of the department store. This shows the pervasive spread of antisemitism in prewar Germany. It also makes for an uncomfortable reading of Dori's account of sexual assault. This is not to say that Dori's accusation of sexual assault against Herr Markus is grounded in false accusations, but that the reason for the assault is explained with veiled reference to antisemitic stereotypes of insatiable queer sexuality.

---

74. On the historical association between Jewishness and homosexuality, see Jay Geller, "Freud, Blüher, and the *Secessio Inversa*: *Männerbünde*, Homosexuality, and Freud's Theory of Cultural Formation," in *Queer Theory and the Jewish Question*, ed. Daniel Boyarin, Daniel Itzkovitz, and Ann Pellegrini (New York: Columbia University Press, 2003); George L. Mosse, *Nationalism and Sexuality: Middle-Class Morality and Sexual Norms in Modern Europe* (Madison: University of Wisconsin Press, 1988); Gilman, *Freud, Race, and Gender*.

75. Weiss-Sussex, "Confronting Stereotypes," 95.

Dori seizes on pervasive antisemitic stereotypes as a framework for thinking through hardship, victimization, and assault experienced as a salesperson.

Conclusion

Neither Dori nor Body works as a shopgirl for very long. Nonetheless, life after the department store remains intricately linked to the experiences on the shop floor. For Body, the time at the department store provides an insight into the social injustice and economic difficulties faced by working-class girls and women and allows him to transition to a different career and, ultimately, a different gender. Dori's life, too, remains influenced by their experiences as shop assistant—although with a different outcome: Dori's life continues to center on the commodification of their body as they take on work as a medical manne-quin, exhibiting their body to a group of eager students, and later as a *Damen-Imitator*, where Dori's movement up and down the stage is strongly reminis-cent of their shop floor routine. Dori not only continues to cross-dress, but also continues to transgress the boundaries of class. Long after leaving Herr Markus's business, Dori remains caught up in the commerce and imagination promised by the shop, and—enticed by consumerism—spends first hundreds, then thousands of marks on extravagant costumes.

The hospitable reading that I have pursued in this chapter is attentive to the (im)possibilities of achieving a livable life in sexual-scientific life writing. Talking about the questions that must be asked with regard to livability, Butler suggests that "we must ask . . . what humans require in order to maintain and reproduce the conditions of their own livability. And what are our politics such that we are, in whatever way is possible, both conceptualizing the possibility of the livable life, and arranging for its institutional support?"[76] With regard to the first of Butler's questions, Body's and Dori's narratives show that livability relies on the livable framing and staging of the body in relation to its social and normative surroundings. A livable life, in these narratives, is one that matters, both in the sense of having received recognition from others around it and in the sense that it has a bodily weight and bodily contours. Both too much and too little *Fassung*, or framing, is problematic, just as livability is endangered by categories that hold too tightly or offer no hold at all. As the photographs that appear in Hirschfeld's publications show, the framing of the queer body—both visually and textually—through a focus on and exclusion of certain bodily

---

76. Judith Butler, *Undoing Gender* (London: Routledge, 2004), 39.

aspects, through composition, and through epistemological framing can create both possibilities and impossibilities for livable queer lives.

By using the meta-frame of self-authored narrative, both texts give a powerful account of the various ways in which dominant frames can and do break. Giving an account of how the dominant frames of sexual sciences and consumer capitalism work, Dori's and Body's narratives break out of these frames by presenting their narratives to a wider readership. This does not lessen the pain of their experiences—Dori's suicide is a stark reminder of the ultimate unlivability of their circumstances. However, it does offer an important insight into the ways in which dominant frames can affect the livability of queer lives. It also reveals possibilities for agency, where queer subjects use, manipulate, and break the frames that define them in order to achieve livability.

The frame has the power both to make queer life possible and to relegate it to the realm of the off/scene or obscene, that which is excluded from the intelligibility of the frame. At the same time, the frame can be redrawn to make otherwise obscured aspects of queer life become intelligible, for example, when Body's narrative focuses on the invisible lives of working-class girls and women in order to establish a career that takes him out of the unlivable life of the department store and makes a different, more livable life possible. Some frames help to situate the individual thus reframed, but at extreme costs to the livability of others. This is strikingly evident when Dori draws on antisemitic stereotypes in order to make sense of their experiences of harassment. The frame operates within systems of power that always threaten to make a cut, distinguishing between those who are recognizable and therefore livable and grievable, and those that are not. Dori's use of antisemitic tropes shows that they have internalized this function of the frame. This example of Dori's utilization of antisemitic stereotypes reveals the importance of the political and institutional support, as outlined by Butler, which is in place to support the conditions for a livable life and how they function or fail. The absolute pervasiveness of antisemitism in Germany in the early twentieth century, expressed in Dori's casual mobilization of antisemitic stereotypes, anticipates how state politics will go on to frame some lives as unlivable (Jewish lives and queer and trans lives, as well as multiple others). This example shows the powerful potential of politics and institutions to support and police the livability of queer lives. These political and institutional frames (and the lack thereof) will be discussed in the following chapter.

CHAPTER 4

Trans-investiture

Writing Gender Transition in the 1890s and 1920s

In *Christopher and His Kind*, Christopher Isherwood's autobiographical text about his years in Berlin, the protagonist describes the Institute of Sexology in the following way: "Sex, in this sanctuary, was being treated with seriousness. How could it not be? Over the entrance to the Institute was an inscription in Latin which meant: Sacred to Love and to Sorrow."[1] The Institute of Sexology bore the Latin inscription *Amori et Dolori Sacrum*, dedicated to pain and to love.[2] In Isherwood's words, the institute is described as a safe space, both a place of refuge and safety, but also like a temple or holy place. A sanctuary commonly offers refuge or safety and so is a place that protects life, or ensures that life remains livable. This particular emphasis on protection suggests that not all institutions offer such refuge to queer lives. Institutional framing, like the frames discussed in the previous chapter, can provide both livable and unlivable conditions for queer lives.

In this chapter I investigate the institutional framing of queer and trans lives and institutional procedures whereby such refuge and sanctity might be ensured but also endangered and the ways in which sexual-scientific life writing navigates this framing in order to achieve a sense of queer livability. In particular, this chapter is concerned with trans life writings that narrate their experience of gender identity as a process of transition and examines the ways in which this experience is institutionally framed. The key theoretical impulse for this chapter builds on Eric Santner's study of "investiture," the performative

---

1. Christopher Isherwood, *Christopher and His Kind* (London: Eyre Methuen, 1977), 19.

2. Volkmar Sigusch, *Geschichte der Sexualwissenschaft* (Frankfurt am Main: Campus-Verlag, 2008), 346; Florence Tamagne, *A History of Homosexuality in Europe*, vol. 1 (New York: Algora, 2004), 83. The institute's inscription is likely inspired by the same inscription on a villa on Capri, a favorite visiting spot of self-identifying Uranians. See Magnus Hirschfeld, *Die Homosexualität des Mannes und des Weibes* (Berlin: L. Marcus, 1914), 571.

awarding of social status via social and legal rites. When this investiture fails, a crisis of investiture can be triggered, leading to serious mental distress. I argue that sexual-scientific life writing recognizes this crisis, but that it also appropriates rites of investiture in order to establish new social realities and, in doing so, create the possibilities for a livable life. In this investigation, I reconsider this concept of investiture to illuminate the investiture of gender transformation, which I call *trans-investiture*. I argue that the act of writing, in particular the process of *Umschreibung* (roughly: transcription) critically enhances and corrects such trans-investiture. In doing so, I show how specifically trans forms of self-expression and identification can be negotiated via life writing. To be clear, my argument here is not that sexual-scientific life writing describes queer or trans identity (or becoming) as inevitably about transformation or transgression of gender boundaries. Instead, I argue that in order to navigate rigid and normative expectations of gender as binary, some life writers appropriate and repurpose externally imposed narratives of transgression in order to establish a livable life.

I will analyze the relationship between medico-scientific institutions, writing, and trans-investiture with reference to two texts from two different historical contexts. The first text I will discuss is Daniel Paul Schreber's *Denkwürdigkeiten eines Nervenkranken* (*Memoirs of My Nervous Illness*, 1903), in which we learn about Schreber's experiences in the 1890s as a patient in the University Clinic of Leipzig and later the Sonnenstein Asylum in Pirna near Dresden. During this time, Schreber experiences a periodic transformation into a woman and tries to make sense of this experience. Schreber's memoirs became famous when Sigmund Freud made Schreber's account the basis of one of his detailed case studies. *Und dennoch Ja zum Leben* (*Life Nonetheless*, 1981) was published pseudonymously under the name Erich Amborn.[3] Although it was not published until the early 1980s, it tells the story of Martin, a young person in the 1920s and 1930s who is assigned female at birth but later transitions to live as a man while working with Magnus Hirschfeld at the Institute of Sexology in Berlin.

The two narratives discussed in this chapter are very different from one another in terms of genre, age of protagonist, and experience with gender transition. Schreber's *Memoirs* was written at the turn of the twentieth century by a person who enjoyed the respect and privilege of a middle-class, middle-aged

---

3. *Und dennoch Ja zum Leben* bears no relation to Victor E. Frankl's . . . *trotzdem Ja zum Leben sagen: Ein Psychologe erlebt das Konzentrationslager* (*Yes to Life, in Spite of Everything*). To avoid confusion, I translate *Und dennoch Ja zum Leben* as *Life Nonetheless*.

bourgeois man with a respected career as a judge. Schreber's experiences of becoming a woman feature heavily in the narrative, but do not culminate in externally recognized transition. Martin's narrative is a piece of life writing not easily categorized as novel or autobiography, which tells the story of an adolescent and young adult during World War I and the interwar years who succeeds in having his gender confirmed both medically and legally.[4]

However, as I want to argue in this chapter, both narratives give a crucial insight into the power of investiture in the realm of gender as their life writers seek to transition from one gender to another. The outcome of this process is very different in the two cases: in one, the protagonist accepts legal and surgical changes. In the other, the life writer remains in a stage of fluctuation, or persistent change, from male to female identification. My point here is not to define a definitive end point of transition. My hospitable reading recognizes that the two protagonists transition to the extent that is possible or livable for them in their respective circumstances. In this chapter, I want to consider how these circumstances are shaped by institutional authority and care at two distinct historical moments and how each protagonist works with and against this institutional framing to achieve a sense of livability. The protagonist of *Life Nonetheless* had access to certain institutions and sexological identity categories that enabled him to explain and write about his trans-identification. Schreber, however, did not have access to the same categories for identification or community. Nonetheless, as I argue in this chapter, both individuals use the institutional framing made available through medico-scientific discourse to give an account of their trans-identifications. Accordingly, this chapter analyzes how a change of gender is performed in both texts through frameworks of institutional authority or care and how both texts appropriate this institutional investiture to create the possibilities—whether real or imagined—of a livable life.

1. Gender Transition in the 1890s: Daniel Paul Schreber's *Memoirs of My Nervous Illness* (1903)

Daniel Paul Schreber's *Memoirs of My Nervous Illness* was published in 1903 but gives a report of a period of mental ill health from 1893 to 1901. In their remarkable memoir, Schreber tells of their own experiences of gender trans-

---

4. In this chapter, I use the pronouns he/him for Martin. As the narrative is written from both the first-person and third-person singular, it is easy to determine that male pronouns are most appropriate as these are used in third-person descriptions of Martin.

gression and transformation. Schreber's periodic transformation from man into woman takes place in a carefully orchestrated network of paranoid delusions, in which Schreber becomes God's bride. Schreber's first psychotic phase, on which they briefly reflect in their memoirs, occurred in 1884, shortly after they failed to secure a parliamentary seat as a member of the National Liberal Party.[5] Schreber recovered a year later. Sometime between their first and second period of mental illness Schreber had a peculiar dream, which foreshadowed later events: in this dream, they felt that it would be pleasant to succumb to intercourse as a woman. In 1893, after an accelerated career as a judge, Schreber was appointed president of the Senate of the Superior Court of Appeals in Dresden, at which time they experienced a second psychotic phase. During this second bout of illness, which is the focus of their memoirs, Schreber found themselves assaulted by divine rays and the victim of an elaborate, paranoid system of control enacted by God. They consequently perceived themselves to be turning into a woman and, on occasion, wore female attire in private in order to inhabit this new identity.

In this chapter, I read Schreber as a trans figure and use they/them pronouns. Most psychoanalytic studies of Schreber assume that Schreber's gender transformation is part of the judge's elaborate psychosis.[6] By reading Schreber as a trans figure, my work shows the ways in which a hospitable reading that takes at face value Schreber's experiences can enrich our understanding of canonical texts that are not always thought of as trans narratives. The fact that Schreber's memoirs are rarely read as a trans narrative is also a symptom of the burden of proof imposed on historical trans people. Unless trans identity can be proven definitively, their trans status is often ignored. This is despite the fact that people may not have had access to the terminology to describe themselves in ways that would today be definitively understood as trans, nor does this burden of proof leave space for individuals like Schreber whose experience of becoming a woman was periodic. By using gender-neutral pronouns, I do not

---

5. Schreber's chances of winning a seat in this election were slim from the beginning. Schreber was standing against the incumbent and prominent Social Democratic Party candidate in Chemnitz, an industrial city with an increasing working-class population. See Zvi Lothane, *In Defense of Schreber: Soul Murder and Psychiatry* (Hillsdale, NJ: Analytic Press, 1992), 32–33.

6. Notable exceptions are Marjorie Garber's discussion of Schreber as "transsexual," a reading Garber also recognizes in Ida MacAlpine and Richard Hunter's description of Schreber in their first English translation of Schreber's memoirs. Marjorie Garber, *Vested Interests: Cross-Dressing and Cultural Anxiety* (New York: Routledge, 1992), 205–8; Daniel Paul Schreber, *Memoirs of My Nervous Illness*, trans. Ida MacAlpine and Richard Hunter (London: William Dawson, 1955).

mean to prioritize permanent transition over periodic identification, as is the case with Schreber. As I show in this chapter, the periodicity of Schreber's identification and the final return to their family as father and husband may well be due to the absolute lack of recognition of trans-identifying individuals and Schreber's fear of a loss of social status as woman. However, I also want to respect that this periodic becoming woman was simply how Schreber experienced their gender. Schreber would not have used they/them pronouns. Nonetheless, in this context at least, these pronouns are helpful in bringing out the richness of the judge's gendered life.

Although this chapter traces the ways in which Schreber's memoirs navigate their identity as a woman, it should be noted that, for Schreber, convincing their readership of the validity of their gender identity was not the main reason for publication. During Schreber's time in the asylum their wife enforced Schreber's *Entmündigung*, meaning that Schreber henceforth remained under tutelage and that their legal right to act as an autonomous subject was removed. Schreber's main goal was to convince the court to have their tutelage rescinded. Schreber's memoirs function as an appeal to a readership to be recognized as a person who can manage their own affairs. In 1900, Schreber used the memoirs, which they had likely completed that year based on previous notes, to appeal to the Superior Court of Appeals in Dresden—the same court where Schreber had previously held the highest position—and won their appeal.[7] After a brief time spent outside of psychiatric institutions, Schreber returned to an asylum in 1907 for their third and final bout of psychosis. Schreber died in 1911 in an asylum near Leipzig.

Schreber's complex memoir became well known through Sigmund Freud's essay "Psycho-analytic Notes on an Autobiographical Account of a Case of Paranoia (Dementia Paranoides)" ("Psychoanalytische Bemerkungen über einen autobiographischen Fall von Paranoia (Dementia Paranoides)," 1911).[8] Freud investigates Schreber's life in a mediated way, mediated by Schreber's memoirs. He never personally met Schreber, and his analysis of Schreber via the written account of their life therefore turns Freud into a literary or critical commentator. Freud's account of the judge's paranoia asserts that Schreber's fantasies can be understood as the result of a homosexual

7. Eric L. Santner, *My Own Private Germany: Daniel Paul Schreber's Secret History of Modernity* (Princeton, NJ: Princeton University Press, 1996), 5.

8. Sigmund Freud, "Psycho-analytic Notes on an Autobiographical Account of a Case of Paranoia (Dementia Paranoides)," in *The Standard Edition of the Complete Psychological Works of Sigmund Freud*, trans James Strachey, vol. 12, *1911–1913: The Case of Schreber, Papers on Technique and Other Works* (London: Hogarth, 1958), 1–82.

attachment to the father. This homosexual attachment is repressed and projected onto other figures, first Schreber's psychiatrist, Paul Flechsig, and then God. The Schreber case was of immense importance to Freud because the newly established discipline of psychoanalysis was still in the process of establishing itself, and Freud had to make a convincing case for psychological damage done by repressed homosexuality. Freud's authority as analyst rested on the success and believability of his analysis of Schreber.

This chapter is concerned with Schreber's memoirs rather than Freud's case. However, it is important to note that Freud's case can be considered an answer to the call for a readership that, as I have argued in Chapter 1, is a common characteristic of sexual-scientific life writing. Freud's case is a selective reading of Schreber's memoirs in which Freud presents Schreber as a respectable, bourgeois model of patriarchy.[9] Unlike most of Freud's other cases, which report the analysis and treatment of his patients, his Schreber case concerns a written account, not a personal encounter. Freud justifies this exception by arguing that Schreber's particular form of paranoia resists face-to-face therapy and that Schreber's written account is therefore an acceptable replacement that allows insight into Schreber's unconscious.[10] Indeed, Freud focuses solely on Schreber's writing at the exclusion of further biographical or psychiatric information that would have been accessible to him.[11] Despite the fact that in the case of Schreber, analyst and analysand did not meet, Santner argues that a transferential process, so typical of the psychoanalytic encounter, takes place in Schreber's writing and Freud's reading. Both experience a kind of influence anxiety, fearing that their thoughts are not original. Schreber felt the influence of God's rays over their thoughts, while Freud feared the performative power of his colleagues to change the nature of psychoanalysis.[12] This fear of influence that takes place in the textual encounter shows that text and reader are intimately and dynamically related: just as Freud's reading provides a frame that makes Schreber's life recognizable in psychoanalytic terms, Schreber's memoirs provide a case which aids the development of Freud's Oedipal model, in which the male child desires the mother but suffers under the threat of castration form the father. As critical reader rather than therapist, Freud's treatment of text suggests that he understands the mutually influential relationship that can exist between text and reader.

---

9. Freud, "Psycho-analytic Notes," 10.
10. Freud, "Psycho-analytic Notes," 9.
11. Freud, "Psycho-analytic Notes," 46. See also Santner, *My Own Private Germany*, 36.
12. Santner, *My Own Private Germany*, 19–26.

Despite the fact that Schreber never met Freud personally, Freud's psychoanalytic framing meant that Schreber's memoirs became a classic case of sexual-scientific life writing, an autobiographical text that can hardly be considered outside of the context of sexual sciences. Schreber's memoirs also became a widely read text of interest to scholars of social and cultural history and theory. Many critics have, for example, endeavored to put Schreber's illness into its cultural context. In the 1950s, William Niederland investigated Schreber's relationship with their famous father and notorious inventor of controversial child-rearing methods, Daniel Gottlob Moritz Schreber. Niederland, and later Morton Schatzmann, argue that Schreber's psychotic crisis during adulthood was triggered by their upbringing.[13] Zvi Lothane's study of Schreber explores their relationship with their psychiatrists, Guido Weber and Paul Flechsig, arguing that Schreber's relationship with these men profoundly influenced their delusions, as well as enabling their eventual release.[14] Morton Schatzmann and Elias Canetti see a parallel between Schreber's paranoia and that of National Socialism,[15] while Eric Santner understands Schreber's crisis precisely as an attempt to avert the kind of paranoid state later attained by National Socialism.[16] Jonathan Kemp casts Schreber's experience of becoming woman as a challenge to the confining and stable identity of "man," and Sander Gilman sees in it a parallel to the antisemitic figure of the castrated Jew.[17] Schreber's fame does not end here. Their memoirs and case form the basis for Jacques Lacan's development of his thoughts on psychosis and feature in Gilles Deleuze and Félix Guattari's magnum opus, *Anti-Oedipus*.[18]

Throughout these studies, we can see a sedimentation of Freud's under-

---

13. William Niederland, *The Schreber Case: Psychoanalytic Profile of a Paranoid Personality* (Hillsdale, NJ: Analytic Press, 1984); Morton Schatzman, *Soul Murder: Persecution in the Family* (New York: Random House, 1973).

14. Lothane, *In Defense of Schreber*.

15. Elias Canetti, *Crowds and Power*, trans. Carol Stewart (New York: Continuum, 1981), 434–62.

16. Santner, *My Own Private Germany*, ix–xiv.

17. Jonathan Kemp, *The Penetrated Male* (New York: punctum books, 2013); Sander L. Gilman, *Freud, Race, and Gender* (Princeton, NJ: Princeton University Press, 1993).

18. Jacques Lacan, *The Seminar of Jacques Lacan*, vol. 3, *The Psychoses*, trans. Russell Grigg, ed. Jacques-Alain Miller (New York: Norton, 1993); Gilles Deleuze and Félix Guattari, *Anti-Oedipus: Capitalism and Schizophrenia*, trans. Robert Hurley, Mark Seem, and Helen R. Lane (London: Continuum, 2004). For a detailed summary of Schreber's "readers," see Angela Woods, "Schizophrenia: The Sublime Text of Psychoanalysis," in *The Sublime Object of Psychiatry: Schizophrenia in Clinical and Cultural Theory* (Oxford: Oxford University Press, 2011), 1–59.

standing of the Schreber case through the lens of homosexuality. Although questions of gender identity gained broader interest in sexological and psychoanalytic work, most notably in the specific figure of the transvestite, the question of gender identity was not directly addressed by Freud in his analysis of Schreber's memoirs, and Freud instead read Schreber's memoirs through the lens of (homo)sexuality.[19] Translators of Schreber's memoirs, MacAlpine and Hunter, already noted in the 1950s that Schreber's case is reminiscent of "accounts for the cases of change of sex reported in the newspapers."[20] Much scholarship mentions Schreber's trans-identification in passing, but it is rarely the focus of attention. As I have mentioned, it was perhaps not the main aim of Schreber's memoirs to convince the readership of the validity of their claims regarding gender specifically, but primarily to achieve the rescission of their tutelage. Nonetheless, bracketing out gender identity from Schreber's account fails to comprehend the full range of Schreber's experience of the world. In Alex Pheby's novel *Playthings*, for example, which gives a novelized account of Schreber's inner life, no mention is made of Schreber's experiences of gender.[21] This is a remarkable exclusion that speaks to the difficulty of situating Schreber's gender within their broader experiences as suffering from ill mental health.

Whereas Freud's treatment of Schreber is tied in with the larger psychoanalytic project to assert the Oedipal model, sexological thinkers might have reacted to Schreber's plight rather differently. Hirschfeld, for example, must certainly have been aware of Schreber. He attended the Third International Psychoanalytic Congress in Weimar in 1911, where he would have heard Freud's presentation "Nachtrag zur Analyse Schrebers" (translated in the *Standard Edition* as "Postscript to the Case of Paranoia"), Freud's additional remarks on his study of Schreber's memoirs. We can only speculate what Hirschfeld might have thought of Schreber's memoirs. But in 1911, a year after the publication of his treatise on transvestitism, Hirschfeld's sexological theories certainly allowed for the recognition of the transvestite as an identity separate from and indeed unrelated to the homosexual.

Hirschfeld's influential study *Die Transvestiten* began to conceptualize the distinct phenomenon of living and dressing as a member of another sex.

---

19. For a discussion of psychoanalytic approaches to transvestitism, see Katie Sutton, *Sex between Body and Mind: Psychoanalysis and Sexology in the German-Speaking World, 1890s–1930s* (Ann Arbor: University of Michigan Press, 2019), 183–87.

20. Daniel Paul Schreber, *Memoirs of My Nervous Illness*, trans. and ed. Ida MacAlpine and Richard A. Hunter (Cambridge, MA: Harvard University Press, 1988), 404–5, cited in Garber, *Vested Interests*, 208.

21. Alex Pheby, *Playthings* (Norwich: Galley Beggar Press, 2015).

Here many of the cases described speak of someone's desire to permanently transition. Schreber's self-account is very different, because Schreber, as I will show, actively resists any volition or desire to transition, instead presenting this as something outwardly done *to* them. Schreber's trans-identification is not expressed as a fixed identity, but a periodic experience of transformation. Schreber is thus unaware of the conventions of categorization and permanent transition. Such scripts of trans-identification would crystallize much more clearly in the 1910s. By that point, Emma Heaney argues, diverse trans feminine narratives would have congealed into a diagnostic narrative that assumed a unitary experience of trans femininity.[22] Such narratives valued the concept of transness over and above the recognition of individual lives. These script, which I discuss in more detail in Chapter 2, provide structures and themes that shape behavior and identification. Even if Schreber had known others who identified like them, their middle-class identity might have kept them from expressing their gender identity in the same way, out of fear of losing their social status. Schreber's lack of such a script helps us understand why reading them as a trans-identifying individual necessarily remains ambivalent and why it does not add up to a recognizable and categorical form of identity.

This is not to say that Schreber's trans-identification is the central aspect of their memoirs. Over and above their gender transformation, Schreber tells a story of profound and painful psychological breakdown that has rightfully been examined and analyzed by scholars in a variety of fields. I also do not mean to pathologize Schreber's experience of womanhood by implying a causative relationship between Schreber's experiences of gender transformation and their psychological breakdown. Rather, I show that the difficulties and pain that Schreber experiences in the context of their trans-identification might intersect with, but are not necessarily the cause of, their psychological breakdown. Because gender transformation was couched in pathologizing discourses, the fear of punitive pathologization may well have fostered the crisis, even if there was no causal connection between psychotic delusions and gender transformation.

Here, as in all other chapters of this book, I focus on the life writer's self-perception and how the writer makes sense of themselves in order to create a livable life. By focusing on Schreber's account of trans-identification, I hope to show that their experience of transition and bodily transformation intersects

---

22. Emma Heaney, *The New Woman: Literary Modernism, Queer Theory, and the Trans Feminine Allegory* (Evanston, IL: Northwestern University Press, 2017).

with the power of institutions to invest meaning, identity, and livability. In my analysis, I understand Schreber as someone whose numerous experiences of being transformed into a woman paint a picture of transitioned sexual subjectivity, however ambivalent or temporary. Reading Schreber's experiences as an account of trans-identification, I examine how Schreber seizes on other frameworks, before the development of a psychoanalytic or sexological script. In particular, I investigate the relationship between their trans-identifications and those medico-scientific practices and institutions that ultimately make queer livability (im)possible.

1.1. Schreber's Investiture Crisis

In *My Own Private Germany*, Eric Santner discusses Schreber's memoirs and postulates that Schreber's illness came as a direct result of their experience of "investiture crisis." Investiture is the performative awarding of social status via social and legal rites, for example the process of naming or bestowing of degrees.[23] Santner argues that Schreber experiences a crisis of symbolic investiture at two points in their life: when Schreber fails to win a seat in the Reichstag in 1884, and when they are appointed as president of the Senate of the Superior Court of Appeals in Dresden in 1893. The root of this crisis lies in the fact that Schreber understood that the "performative magic"—the procedures whereby a social status is awarded—of symbolic power, what Santner calls "symbolic investiture," is faulty.[24] Santner understands this investiture crisis as paradigmatic of the broader crisis of modernity.

Santner grounds his reading of investiture in Walter Benjamin's essay "On the Critique of Violence" ("Zur Kritik der Gewalt"), in which, Santner claims, Benjamin points out the "self-referentiality of law and legal institutions."[25] This self-referentiality is exemplified by the "tautologous enunciation 'The law is the law!'" and the resulting lack of any foundations on whose grounds the law justifies its own existence.[26] The law is upheld by a

---

23. Santner, *My Own Private Germany*, xi–xii.
24. Santner, *My Own Private Germany*, xii.
25. Santner, *My Own Private Germany*, 9.
26. Santner, *My Own Private Germany*, 10. Although Santner here refers to Benjamin's work, Benjamin does not explicitly state this tautology. Instead, he points out that "in the exercise of violence over life and death, more than in any other legal act, the law reaffirms itself." Walter Benjamin, "Critique of Violence," in *Selected Writings*, vol. 1, *1913–1926*, ed. Michael W. Jennings (Cambridge, MA: Belknap Press of Harvard University Press, 1996), 242.

violence internal to it, which forcefully performs its own foundations. Schreber experiences their crises at the exact moments when they realize that such tautologies do not hold. Santner here also refers to the theoretical works of sociologist Pierre Bourdieu, whose work on symbolic power emphasizes that acts of symbolic investiture are imperative and must be repeated. Through such repetitive acts, you "become what you are" and "stay on the proper side of a socially consecrated boundary."[27]

As Santner points out, Judith Butler's theory of gender performativity is grounded in precisely this logic of symbolic investiture.[28] According to Butler, gender performativity requires a stylized repetition of acts based on social norms and taboos.[29] Transgression of such norms and taboos is sanctioned and normative gender representations are thereby reinforced, making illegible those who perform gender differently or transgress its strict boundaries. Rather than being founded in biology or any other a priori markers, the logic of gender, similar to the tautological statement "The law is the law," is self-referential and grounded in previous iterations of gendered expression. Consequently, everyone must incorporate (in body *and* soul) symbolic power, and the knowledge that such power is, in its first instance, arbitrary must be repressed.

Santner argues that Schreber's experiences of nervous illness present an attempt to reinstall meaning that was lost as a consequence of their investiture crisis. What Santner calls "Schreber's 'own private Germany' consists of his [*sic*] attempts, using the available repertoire of cultural values and valences, to interpret and to assign meaning to a maddening blockage in meaning."[30] Schreber's attempts to create meaning express themselves in a "series of aberrant identifications."[31] Santner investigates "the relation between a crisis in the domain of symbolic authority and the production of 'deviant' sexualities and gender identities."[32] Here the production of sexuality has to be understood in a Foucauldian sense, where sexuality can only be understood (and so is produced) in response to discursive and institutional practices:

---

27. Pierre Bourdieu, *Language and Symbolic Power*, trans. Gino Raymond and Matthew Adamson (Cambridge, MA: Harvard University Press, 1991), 122, cited in Santner, *My Own Private Germany*, 12.

28. Santner, *My Own Private Germany*, 94–95.

29. Judith Butler, *Gender Trouble: Feminism and the Subversion of Identity* (New York: Routledge, 1990).

30. Santner, *My Own Private Germany*, 55.

31. Santner, *My Own Private Germany*, xi.

32. Santner, *My Own Private Germany*, 17.

A crisis of symbolic function—one's inscription within a symbolic network by means of names and titles—can manifest itself in the realm of, or, to put it in more Foucauldian terms, *as sexuality*. It is almost as if Schreber himself were half-aware that his florid sexual fantasies were elaborations of the breakdown products of those symbolic resources which might have reassured him that he was legitimate in the "eyes" of the symbolic community.[33]

Santner's reference to Foucauldian discourse formation in the realm of sexuality also shows his attachment, so central also to Freud's argument, to Schreber's crisis as related to sexuality. Sexuality, here, becomes a symptom of a larger, underlying crisis.

In the section that follows, I propose an important intervention to Santner's reading of gender and sexuality as a response or symptom of underlying crisis of investiture. For Santner, Schreber's "aberrant identifications" become a method that Schreber uses to escape a crisis of investiture. Instead, in the section that follows I trace how Schreber uses the logic of investiture to create livable ways of trans-identification, however temporary. Accordingly, I argue that Schreber responds to the crisis of investiture by appropriating its very mechanism, not in the realm of sexuality but specifically in the realm of gender, in order to establish a sense of queer livability.

1.2. Schreber's Trans-investiture

Schreber's experience of gender transformation is split into two periods. During the first period, which concerns time spent at Flechsig and Pierson's asylum (roughly between 1894 and 1895), Schreber states that they were "most seriously concerned for my life, my manliness and later my reason."[34] It is during this period, which Schreber narrates at length and in detail, that they experience a process they call *Entmannung* (emasculation or unmanning):

> This process of unmanning consisted in the (external) male genitals (scrotum and penis) being retracted into the body and the internal sexual organs being at the same time transformed into the corresponding female sexual

---

33. Santner, *My Own Private Germany*, 49.

34. Daniel Paul Schreber, *Memoirs of My Nervous Illness*, trans. and ed. Ida MacAlpine and Richard A. Hunter (New York: New York Review Books, 2000), 117. All references, unless otherwise stated, are to this edition.

organs, a process which might have been completed in a sleep lasting hundreds of years, because the skeleton (pelvis, etc.) has also to be changed. (MNI 60)

For Schreber, unmanning is a bodily experience whereby their male body is physically turned into that of a woman. In some instances, this unmanning leads to the "actual retraction of the male organ" (MNI 142); in others Schreber's reproductive organs are only "poorly developed" but nonetheless lead to Schreber perceiving themselves as carrying an embryo (MNI 18 n. 1). This process is never permanently completed, but is repeated periodically.

In addition to becoming a woman, Schreber experiences, as the term *Entmannung* suggests, a profound loss of masculinity and power. They describe several attempts to resist this unmanning by exerting their "sense of manly honor" (MNI 64, 124). At this point, the process of unmanning does not propel Schreber into the realm of gender identity proper; rather, Schreber relates the change of their physical sex as part of a bodily transformation enacted on them. Although they experience their body as changing, they explicitly attempt to defend their manliness. In this effort, they demonstrably resist the performativity required of gender to function. Schreber's physical transformation into a woman goes hand in hand with the instillment of sexual desire *as* a woman, which Schreber calls voluptuousness (*Wollust*), an expression that frames active female eroticism in ambivalent terms and to which I will return. Indeed, it is this feeling of being a sexually desiring woman that Schreber understands as the foundational moment of their transformation, as they have a dream in which occurs "the idea that it really must be rather pleasant to be a woman succumbing to intercourse" (MNI 46).

Santner puts Schreber's experience of a breakdown of masculinity into the context of fin de siècle society and criticism of degeneration.[35] Max Nordau's study of *Entartung*, which describes degeneration as a general sense of decline, fatigue, and mental and physical exhaustion, is linked to existing fears around sexual disease, in particular syphilis, and the loss of virile power.[36] Responding to a long list of social ills relating to modern life, Santner proposes that "Schreber's *Memoirs* could be seen as an attempt to answer the question implicit in this list of pathologies: What remains of virility at the end of the nineteenth and beginning of the twentieth century?"[37] Here Schre-

---

35. Santner, *My Own Private Germany*, 6.
36. Max Nordau, *Entartung*, 2 vols. (Berlin: C. Duncker, 1893).
37. Santner, *My Own Private Germany*, 9.

ber's unmanning becomes a symptom of degenerate masculinity during modernity. Undoubtedly, the loss of virility, shown by Schreber's repeated reference to unmanning, played a significant role in Schreber's experience precisely because of the value of virility in a patriarchal society. Rather than understanding Schreber's loss of masculinity as a sign of crisis, however, I want to argue that Schreber, truly believing themselves to have a woman's body, understands the profound loss of masculine power and "manly honor" as they are periodically confined to life as a woman without the investiture of power, status, or suffrage. As a judge, Schreber would have felt this loss of male investiture profoundly.

One of Schreber's readers, the psychoanalyst Louis Breger, understands Schreber's transformation as a rejection of the experience of damaging masculinity from their father. The characteristics of masculinity learned in that way turned them into a man "dedicated to hard work and extremely self-denying."[38] Schreber exerted control over their sexual impulses, repressed feelings of rage and frustration, and could not follow their urge toward autonomy.[39] As a response to this inhibiting vision of manhood, Schreber's rebellion then expressed itself (although not consciously) in their transformation into a woman. However, it is unclear how a transformation into a woman—which Breger describes as a "creative struggle towards freedom"—would have solved any of Schreber's problems: certainly not more agency and autonomy, less sexual inhibition, more rebellion.[40] Breger's sole focus on masculinity obscures this fact. Becoming woman, here, is simply a turn away from masculinity. Another reader of Schreber's memoirs, Anthony Wilden, argues that Schreber understands transformation as positive, but argues that "this 'positive' aspect is simply the result of an idealization of women."[41] Considering Schreber's fear of unmanning as a loss of power, status, or suffrage, it is likely that, at this point in their transformation, Schreber's understanding of womanhood was focused on womanhood as lack, a form of stereotyping but certainly not idealization. Rather than understanding Schreber's gender transition as a sign of crisis and a loss of masculinity, their periodic womanhood becomes the plane on which fears of a loss of virility and subsequent power are projected.

Schreber's unmanning and the process of becoming woman go hand in

---

38. Louis Breger, "Daniel Paul Schreber: From Male into Female," *Journal of the American Academy of Psychoanalysis* 6, no. 2 (April 1978): 141.

39. Breger, "Daniel Paul Schreber," 142.

40. Breger, "Daniel Paul Schreber," 148.

41. Anthony Wilden, *System and Structure: Essays in Communication and Exchange* (London: Tavistock Publication, 1972), 291.

hand with an exposure to sexual violence. Schreber understands each incident of this periodic unmanning as profoundly unlivable as they describe various threats of sexual abuse:

> In this way a plot was laid against me (perhaps March or April 1894), the purpose of which was to hand me over to another human being after my nervous illness had been recognized as, or assumed to be, incurable, in such a way that my soul was handed to him, but my body—transformed into a female body and, misconstruing the above-described fundamental tendency of the Order of the World—was then left to that human being for sexual misuse and simply "forsaken," in other words left to rot. (MNI 63)

Schreber perceives this transformation into a woman as an intense form of passivity due to the loss of masculine agency. They understand this transformation into a woman as a form of abandonment: the methods enacted on their body were meant "to 'forsake' me, that is to say abandon me; at the time I am now discussing it was thought that this could be achieved by unmanning me and allowing my body to be prostituted like that of a female harlot" (MNI 96). In another example, Schreber fears that "my body, after the intended transformation into a female being, was to suffer some sexual abuse, particularly as there had even been talk for some time of my being thrown to the Asylum attendants for this purpose" (MNI 99). During this period, Schreber is mocked by repeated interpellations as "Miss Schreber" (English in original) (MNI 124) and *Luder* (wretch, but also whore) (MNI 130). Through no fault or volition of their own, Schreber is "handed over," "left . . . for sexual misuse," "prostituted," and verbally abused. Zvi Lothane argues that Schreber's unmanning is symbolic of their wife's enforcement of their tutelage. "In retrospect, Schreber had good reason to feel unmanned and raped."[42] Lothane understands Schreber's account of sexual assault as a displaced symptom of the assault on their freedom that took place when their wife enforced Schreber's tutelage. Santner understands Schreber's unmanning as a commentary on what *remains* of virility during modernity. In these readings, womanhood gains the meaning of an absence of manhood and we lose track of Schreber's complex and conflicting understanding of womanhood itself.

The repeated interpellation of Schreber expresses what Santner calls "abject femininity."[43] Schreber's fantasy of sexual pleasure as a woman and

---

42. Lothane, *In Defense of Schreber*, 57.
43. Santner, *My Own Private Germany*, 44.

their description of their female desire as *Wollust* (voluptuousness) similarly suggest an understanding of feminine erotic desire as stereotypically immoderate and excessive. Here Schreber seems to buy into a rather conventional "femme fatale" narrative that demonizes active female eroticism and expresses Schreber's own internalized misogyny. Marie Kolkenbrock argues that the position of the stereotyped "other" is often imagined as a liberating escape when the normative social destiny fails to address the subject.[44] In Schreber's case, it could be argued that, because the normative demands of masculine investiture failed, stereotypical understandings of womanhood as voluptuousness become more attractive. Ultimately, however, the position of the "other" is marginalized and only constructed to uphold the norm, and its idealization turns out to be a dead end. This is not to suggest that Schreber opts into womanhood as an escape from masculinity, but to highlight the fact that Schreber's attitude toward womanhood is ambivalent. Schreber's text contains fascination and pleasure at the thought of becoming a woman as well as resistance to it.

In November 1895, after having been exposed to painful and unlivable periods of unmanning during which Schreber resolutely tries to defend their manly honor, Schreber experiences a sudden change:

> I remember the period distinctly; it coincided with a number of beautiful autumn days when there was a heavy morning mist on the Elbe. During that time the signs of a transformation into a woman became so marked on my body, that I could no longer ignore the imminent goal at which the whole development was aiming. In the immediately preceding nights my male sexual organ might actually have been retracted had I not resolutely set my will against it, still following the stirring of my sense of manly honor; so near completion was the miracle. Soul-voluptuousness had become so strong that I myself received the impression of a female body, first on my arms and hands, later on my legs, bosom, buttocks and other parts of my body. . . . Several days' observation of these events sufficed to change the direction of my will completely. Until then I still considered it possible that, should my life not have fallen victim to one of the innumerable menacing miracles before, it would eventually be necessary for me to end it by suicide. . . . But now I could see beyond doubt that the Order of the World imperiously demanded my unmanning, whether I personally liked it or not, and that therefore it was *common sense* that nothing was

---

44. Marie Kolkenbrock, *Stereotype and Destiny in Arthur Schnitzler's Prose: Five Psycho-sociological Readings* (London: Bloomsbury, 2018), 77–117.

left to me but reconcile myself to the thought of being transformed into a woman. (MNI 163–64)

Introducing this passage with a romantic description of season and landscape, the narrative voice appears as one of calm interiority. Incidentally, several decades later Lili Elbe will contemplate the River Elbe and choose it as her namesake, as she travels to Dresden to receive gender confirmation surgery.[45]

It is in response to this final unmanning that Schreber decides to inhabit the role of woman and propels us into the realm of gender proper:

Since then I have wholeheartedly inscribed the cultivation of femininity on my banner, and I will continue to do so as far as consideration of my environment allows, whatever other people who are ignorant of the supernatural reasons may think of me. I would like to meet the man who, faced with the choice of either becoming a demented human being in male habitus or a spirited woman, would not prefer the latter. Such and *only such* is the issue for me. The pursuit of my previous profession, which I loved wholeheartedly, every other aim of manly ambition, and every other use of my intellectual powers in the service of mankind, are now all closed to me through the way circumstances have developed. . . . I must follow a healthy egoism, unperturbed by the judgment of other people, which prescribes for me the cultivation of femininity. (MNI 164–65)

Schreber's words here can be read as a commentary on the performativity of gender. It is the cultivation of womanhood that creates womanhood in the first place. Schreber's crisis, which, Santner claims, offers Schreber an understanding of the fact that processes of symbolic investiture function on the basis of Benjamin's tautological statement "The law is the law," leads them to understand precisely the foundational method of gender by realizing that gender, much like the law, is founded in a performative repetition of acts that have no foundations. Schreber's move from feeling forced into womanly embodiment to actively choosing to inhabit this role leads them to arrive at a fundamental understanding of gender as performative.

Schreber's statement that they would rather become an intelligent woman than an idiotic man also functions as a reversal of the patriarchal world order that they were raised in and continued to be exposed to. Indeed, in his Schreber

---

45. Lili Elbe, *Ein Mensch wechselt sein Geschlecht: Eine Lebensbeichte*, ed. Niels Hoyer (Dresden: Carl Reissner, 1932).

case, Freud makes a point of citing Schreber self-description as an "intellectually superior man of unusually sharp mind and sharp powers of observation," thereby confirming Schreber as a model figure of nineteenth-century patriarchy.[46] Reversing this patriarchal order, Schreber's identity as woman is made proudly visible by being transcribed onto their figurative banner, which bears witness to their identity. This figure of speech is similar to N. O. Body's veil (as discussed in Chapter 2) as carrier of a gendered identity and of the clothes that become part of Dori's performance as mannequin (as discussed in Chapter 3). But womanhood transcribed onto a banner is reminiscent also of a confident and historically feminist declaration of women's rights to public visibility and agency. By becoming an active agent of gender, Schreber also questions the determinism of biological sex in the patriarchal society in which they live. It is a revolt against the *Entmündigung*, the lack of autonomous agency that Schreber also experiences upon entering the asylum.

It is at this moment that Schreber's miraculous transformation of physical sex is invested with the performative power of gender and that Schreber claims womanhood as an active, performative identity that must be cultivated. Before this moment, the body is transformed through no will of their own, but this effects a mere change of sex only. The previous transformation of penis into vagina, effected through divine interference, does not immediately result in or cause Schreber understanding of themselves as a woman. But in the passage cited above, Schreber accepts their new womanhood by submitting to the Order of the World, which appears to be invested with the power to turn them into a woman. In a Butlerian sense of sex as that which gains meaning only as gender, when seen through the lens of gender, Schreber's changed body only gains meaning when it is imbued with the investiture of gender.

What is aimed at here is an investiture that allows Schreber to transform into another gender. This *trans*-investiture is the performative, symbolic process whereby Schreber is transformed into a woman. The prefix "trans-" is here not (only) meant to refer to Schreber's status as a transgender subject, but refers to the act of gendered transformation that occurs *in* the text. The term trans-investiture will be employed to shed light on the performative and transformative investiture bestowed by figures of authority that takes place when a subject transgresses the boundaries between one gender and another. The emphasis here is on the authoritative (legal, political, ideological) framework that facilitates such investiture. It asks: what mechanisms are perceived to be in place to legitimize or delegitimize the transformation from one gen-

---

46. Freud, "Psycho-analytic Notes," 10.

der into another? The term "trans-investiture" also emphasizes the transformative power that such an act of investiture will have to accomplish.

Despite this active cultivation of womanhood, in which Schreber's bodily transformation is invested with the performative power of gender, Schreber's transformation lacks volition. Santner rightly points out that "Schreber acknowledges that his yielding of the phallic prerogative and cultivation of femininity is really a forced choice."[47] I want to argue that this threat of violence, which compels Schreber to become a woman, also shows Schreber's insight into the policing of gender boundaries and norms. Butler notes that "gender identity is a performative accomplishment compelled by social sanction and taboo,"[48] which affirms that "there are nuanced and individual ways of *doing* one's gender, but *that* one does it, and that one does it *in accord with* certain sanctions and proscriptions, is clearly not a fully individual matter."[49] In order for gender to become a social truth, gendered acts have to be repeated, but, importantly, they are compelled by sanction and taboo, which are violently enforced. In this sense, Schreber's gender performance not only portrays a repetition of acts that are important for gender to "work," but also represents the *fear* of sanctions that is inherent in all performances of gender.

Not only does Schreber's trans-investiture mimic the outward appearance of being a woman, the repetition of gendered acts, but Schreber also perceives themselves as becoming a woman precisely by engaging in fear of punishment from God and the Order of the World, should they dare to perform differently or not at all. Gender performativity functions through sanctions of the wrong kind of performances. Schreber's reference to being forsaken and left to rot can then be understood as a punishment for refusing to inhabit their body properly, as a woman. As Santner points out: "His [*sic*] . . . most forceful argument in defense of cross-dressing is . . . that it is for him [*sic*] a religious practice, one necessitated by the special relation he [*sic*] has come to have with God."[50] God's authority over them, God's power to bestow symbolic investiture and make Schreber a woman, is therefore a direct replacement for the social, legal, and medical discourses and institutions that previously worked on Schreber in order to bestow them with an investiture as man.

Schreber's rejection of the identity of idiotic man in favor of becoming an intelligent woman is reminiscent of an earlier scene during which Schreber is

47. Santner, *My Own Private Germany*, 97.

48. Judith Butler, "Performative Acts and Gender Constitution: An Essay in Phenomenology and Feminist Theory," *Theatre Journal* 40, no. 4 (1988): 520.

49. Butler, "Performative Acts," 525.

50. Santner, *My Own Private Germany*, 82.

addressed as "Miss Schreber": "God's rays frequently mocked me about a supposedly imminent unmanning as 'Miss Schreber' [English in the original]" (MNI 124). In his analysis of the memoirs, William Niederland argues that the foreign title "Miss" has derogative connotations by designating an unmarried and disreputable young woman.[51] As a prefix, *Miss* takes on further derogative meaning: used in such words as *Missgeschick* (mishap), *Missgeburt* (miscarriage), and *Misserfolg* (failure), it implies a self-conscious awareness of deviance from a perceived norm that is brought forth by the transgression of gender. Schreber's understanding of the depreciative nature of such an interpellation might then again show that they perform their new gender authentically to the extent that they experience the threat of social retribution if they transgress gendered expectations. Yet we might also understand this interpellation as "Miss" as a reaffirmation of Schreber's visibility as a confident new woman in a double sense: both as a newly transitioned woman, but also as the feminist ideal of the New Woman who was met with suspicion and derision because she was educated, sexually autonomous, and legally and economically independent.

Importantly, Schreber recognizes that gender is invested and sanctioned not only by the Order of the World but also by medico-scientific knowledge. As Marie Kolkenbrock notes in her discussion of investiture in Arthur Schnitzler's novella *Flucht in die Finsternis* (*Flight into Darkness*), the diagnosis of the doctor, who needs to be first invested with the power to pronounce a diagnosis, is similar to a judgment spoken by a judge who is invested with the power to represent the law.[52] Judge Schreber, who was intimately acquainted with the workings of the law, would have understood the power of the doctor's diagnosis. Schreber's insight into the failure of investiture (in the realm of law) and the power of performativity (in the realm of gender) relies on the performative power of the doctor to make a diagnosis and support their trans-investiture:

> I would at all times be prepared to submit my body to medical examination for ascertaining whether my assertion is correct, that my whole body is filled with nerves of voluptuousness from the top of my head to the soles of my feet, such as is the case only in the adult female body, whereas in the case of a man, as far as I know, nerves of voluptuousness are only found in and immediately around the sex organs. (MNI 243)

---

51. Niederland, *The Schreber Case*, 44.
52. Kolkenbrock, *Stereotype and Destiny*, 88.

Schreber understands this power of medical discourse to recognize and thereby legitimize their trans-investiture. By way of a physical examination of their body, Schreber believes that they can achieve wider recognition of their gender change. This claim that their gender transformation can be observed is repeated several times, for example when Schreber writes, "My breast gives the impression of a pretty well-developed female bosom; this phenomenon can be *seen* by anybody who wants to observe me *with his own eyes*. I am therefore in a position to offer objective evidence by observation of my body" (MNI 248). Schreber here also expresses the necessity to be held (or indeed become) accountable for their gender presentation by medico-scientific figures of authority. As Schreber's diagnosis is one of mental illness, such accountability is particularly urgent. Santner here also argues that "Schreber's repeated requests that he be examined by scientists to confirm the spread of nerves of 'feminine voluptuousness' throughout his body might be understood as a distorted confirmation of Foucault's thesis that the sexual agitation he experiences is in large measure produced by such 'scientific' examinations."[53] Santner's argument here casts Schreber's sexual experience as a woman as a symptom of the overproximity between science and sexuality. Yet his argument holds that Schreber is certainly at the disposal of scientific knowledge.

Here and elsewhere, Schreber understands that medico-scientific naming has the power to invest their gender performance with meaning:

> I venture to assert flatly that anybody who sees me standing in front of a mirror with the upper part of my body naked would get the undoubted *impression of a female trunk*—especially when the illusion is strengthened by some feminine adornments. I will not hesitate to add, that once I am outside this Asylum, I would grant an opportunity for observing my body to any serious specialist whose motive is scientific interest and not mere curiosity. (MNI 248)

Their trans-invested gender performance requires this visual confirmation by a medico-scientific expert who has been invested with the power to make a diagnosis. Years of confinement at various asylums have taught Schreber the power of such a diagnosis, which Schreber here makes count in the realm of gender. As argued earlier, Schreber's writing takes place before the development of a transvestite script, which follows rules on naming and narrates transition as complete and desired. But Schreber does conform to a much older script, pres-

---

53. Santner, *My Own Private Germany*, 88.

ent, for example, in Richard von Krafft-Ebing's *Psychopathia Sexualis*, of patients writing to their doctors to describe sexual/gender symptoms and asking for diagnosis. The terminology of the transvestite did not develop until around 1910, when Hirschfeld published his work on "transvestism". Even if Schreber had had access to this text, published only a year before their death, it is unclear whether they would have identified with this terminology. Earlier descriptions of, for example, "acquired homo-sexuality" in *Psychopathia Sexualis* might have provided more suitable identifications. As one contributor, assigned male at birth, describes their condition to Krafft-Ebing, "I feel the penis as clitoris . . . the skin all over my body feels feminine . . . and I have the sensations of a woman."[54] Schreber's experiences are strongly reminiscent of these similar accounts in Krafft-Ebing's treatise.

Although I do not want to speculate whether Schreber had access to Krafft-Ebing's works, their memoirs suggest that they were keenly interested in medico-scientific developments. In several instances, Schreber cites and discusses at length the psychiatric work of Emil Kraepelin, a student of Flechsig and contemporary of Krafft-Ebing. Specifically, Schreber reviews a section of Kraepelin's *Textbook of Psychiatry* (1896) that discusses visual hallucinations. However, Kraepelin's textbook also includes a chapter on "contrary sexual instincts," in which he cites Krafft-Ebing, Albert Moll, and Albert von Schrenck-Notzing and outlines homosexuality as developing from a state of degeneracy.[55] As one of the symptoms, he mentions that "a few patients present physical characteristics indicative of the opposite sex."[56] Schreber's account thus follows the connection made between psychiatry and sexual pathology in Kraepelin's textbook. Schreber understands the power of investiture held by the medico-scientific professional to invest their gender performance with meaning. Accordingly, Schreber uses the earlier sexological/psychiatric script, writing to medico-scientific experts and asking for confirmation of a diagnosis, to construct a prototype script for trans-

---

54. Richard von Krafft-Ebing, *Psychopathia Sexualis, with Special Reference to Contrary Sexual Instinct: A Medico-Legal Study, Authorized Translation of the Seventh Enlarged and Revised German Edition*, trans. Charles Gilbert Chaddock (Philadelphia: F. A. Davis, 1894), 209.

55. Albert von Schrenck-Notzing was one of the leading figures of scientific occultism. Schreber's paranormal association with his gender transformation may indicate some connection to Schrenck-Notzing's work. However, it goes beyond the scope of this chapter to explore this connection further.

56. Emil Kraepelin, *Clinical Psychiatry: A Textbook for Students and Physicians, Abstracted and Adapted from the 6th German Edition of Kraepelin's "Lehrbuch der Psychiatrie,"* ed. Allen Ross Diefendorf (New York: Macmillan, 1904), 395.

identification, anticipating the birth of the transvestite over a decade later. Schreber at no point in the examples mentioned here recounts their experiences of actually being examined by a medical professional (although it is likely that this took place). Instead, Schreber appropriates the power of medical discourse to invest their body with meaning.

Schreber's full periodic transition to womanhood restored them to God's favors. The Order of the World demands Schreber be a woman and Schreber complies. This return to God is significant. The tautology of law ("The law is the law") is deeply linked to secularization. There is a void at the bottom of the law, as we have lost the original myth of divine investiture (the king being authorized by God). Reaching upward, Schreber uses the highest authority possible to stage their investiture by holding firm to their God, at the same time as calling on medical discourse to invest their body with meaning. Freud indicates this overlaying of medical and theistic authority when he argues that Schreber's homosexual attachment to their father (a physician) is projected onto their psychiatrist, Flechsig, who is later displaced by God.[57] Schreber's theistic theory is too complex to do justice to in this chapter, but this brief excursion shows that medical authority as well as theistic authority are invoked in order to fill the void at the bottom of the law and restore meaning to their trans-identification.

Schreber fully recognizes the power of giving an account of one's gender performance in front of an other who has the power to invest it with meaning and can thereby effect a livable life. This livability does not finally effect Schreber's permanent transition, but leads to another important result: the rescission of their tutelage. The ability to be held accountable at all, their *Mündigkeit*, is achieved by the act of writing an account of their life. Such an access to *Mündigkeit* and autonomous agency is intricately linked to one's class, status, and economic capital. In Schreber's case it also relates to their knowledge of legal proceedings. Schreber's intimate knowledge of the law as former judge at the Superior Court of Appeals in Dresden allows them to submit an application to have their *Entmündigung*, their tutelage, rescinded. Schreber provides autobiographic narrative as evidence of their ability to manage their own affairs. After reading it, the Superior Court of Appeals decides to rescind Schreber's tutelage on March 3, 1900, giving the reason that "it is not sufficient grounds for placing plaintiff under tutelage that his mental processes are mentally disturbed" (MNI 422). The reasons for this are that "the Civil Code demands . . . apart from the existence of a mental illness that the patient in

57. Freud, "Psycho-analytic Notes," 42–58.

consequence thereof is *incapable of managing his affairs*" (MNI 422–23). On July 14, 1902, the court decided that Schreber, although certainly ill, was capable of looking after their own affairs in a manner that satisfies the court's conditions. But Schreber's true trans-investiture takes place on a textual level. Here Schreber's transformation into a woman is documented, justified, and integrated into their own world order. Schreber's memoirs enable them to achieve their transformation from *entmündigt* to *mündig*. This *Mündigkeit* and its previous lack stand in direct relation to their gender transformation: during their initial physical transformation, Schreber experiences their female body only as lack (of power, authority, self-determination). Similar to their *Entmündigung*, Schreber has no agency over their own life. But as an intelligent, educated, and sexually autonomous trans-invested woman, Schreber demands *Mündigkeit*, and they finally receive it. As argued earlier, by writing the cultivation of their femininity onto their figurative banner, Schreber revolts against the *Entmündigung*, the lack of autonomous agency that they also experience upon entering the asylum.

Nonetheless, Schreber's trans-investiture is not a story marked by success. Despite their success at having their tutelage rescinded, Schreber's experience of being put under tutelage must surely have served as a warning that this action could be repeated at any time. Despite having their tutelage rescinded, Schreber would suffer from mental illness for the rest of their life and return to the asylum to die in solitude. As Santner admits at the end of his study: "Schreber's fate as a psychotic suggests that one should not, as they say, try this at home."[58] What Schreber's memoirs indicate is the importance of life writing in pointing out the requirements, but also the limits, of a livable, recognizable life. Schreber's narrative of their periodic transformation gives account of performative trans-investiture, whereby Schreber's womanhood is established but also constantly threatened by the Order of the World and medico-scientific observation and diagnosis. Schreber's memoirs give an insight into the work of livability, the effort that goes into establishing, if only momentarily, a livable queer life under extremely challenging circumstances.

As argued throughout this book, the sexual-scientific life writer's address to a readership (here the specific readership of the court) and the subsequent response are important contributors to a subject's livability, however short-lived. Schreber conducts an appeal to a readership to be recognized as a person who can manage their own affairs. In her book *Assuming a Body: Transgender and Rhetorics of Materiality*, Gayle Salamon calls this "to be asked to be seen

---

58. Santner, *My Own Private Germany*, 144.

as." This becomes a kind of radical divergence from Althusserian interpellation, where ideology interpellates or hails us as subjects (and, in Butler's reading of Althusser, gendered subjects).[59] Called into existence as (gendered) subjects, we are obliged to respond to the call. Instead, Salamon argues:

> [The] request "to be seen as" is something other than a lament about invisibility or the impossibility of ever being truly and deeply recognized beneath or beyond the categories and labels where one takes up residence in us. To ask to be seen *as* something asserts both an equivalence and an incommensurability at once, rather than asserting one at the expense of the other.[60]

Equivalence and incommensurability describe what is at stake in life writing: the narrative points out the equivalence of life and writing, but also highlights the incommensurability between both (as seen in Chapter 1).

The first half of this chapter offers a hospitable reframing and a reading of Schreber's account that takes seriously their trans-invested womanhood. If the memoirs leave doubt about whether Schreber's trans-investiture took place in the way Schreber describes it, from forced transformation to committed but temporary identity, it is important to remember that this active negotiation, this narrative agency (as discussed in Chapter 2) is a foundational part of the negotiation of narrative livability, which asks for a certain response and recognition. The fact that Schreber's manuscript effects the rescission of their tutelage and thereby a reinstallation of their autonomy as a direct effect of writing their memoirs demonstrates the power of life writing. Schreber's call for a livable life does not go unnoticed. Indeed, Freud himself comes close to expressing it in just these terms: "The paranoiac builds the world again, not more splendid, it is true, but at least so that he can once more live in it."[61] Ultimately, we might understand Freud as another ethical reader (as discussed in Chapter 1) of Schreber's memoirs who complies with Schreber's request to be examined and diagnosed. Despite the fact that Freud read Schreber's experience through the lens of sexuality, rather than gender, his Schreber case ensured that Schreber's memoirs would be read for decades and over a century to come. With his case, Freud

---

59. Louis Althusser, "Ideology and Ideological State Apparatuses," in *Lenin and Philosophy and Other Essays*, trans. Ben Brewster (New York: Monthly Review Press, 1972), 127–36.

60. Gayle Salamon, *Assuming a Body: Transgender and Rhetorics of Materiality* (New York: Columbia University Press, 2010), 124.

61. Freud, "Psycho-analytic Notes," 70–71.

authorizes Schreber's memoirs and provides a frame that makes Schreber recognizable. It is our task as reader today to recognize what Schreber "asks to be seen as" and to recognize his trans-investiture, however temporary.

2. Gender Transition in the 1920s:
Erich Amborn's *Life Nonetheless* (1981)

In the second part of this chapter I want to turn to another text that gives insight into the process of trans-investiture. *Und dennoch Ja zum Leben* (*Life Nonetheless*) was published in 1981 but narrates events that took place in the late 1910s and 1920s. *Life Nonetheless* tells the story of an individual whose gender identity is continuously questioned by himself and by others around him. Switching between first- and third-person narration, the book tells the story of Martin. At his birth at the end of the nineteenth century, he is assigned female and given the name Martina. Later in life, however, he transitions to live life as a man and first takes on the name Martin, then Toni.[62] In the 1920s he receives experimental gender confirmation surgery in Berlin.

Little was known about the author or context of publication until Rolf Thalmann and Rainer Herrn's research into the matter.[63] Thalmann and Herrn identify the author of the text, published under the pseudonym Erich Amborn, as Alex Kretzschmar (1898–1981). In 1898 Kretzschmar was assigned female at birth and only later received permission to use the first name Alex. Kretzschmar was born in Zitzschewig near Dresden, first approached Hirschfeld around 1916, and received permission to use the male first name Alex.[64] In barely anonymized form, Kretzschmar features as a case study in Hans Abraham's unpublished dissertation on transvestism from 1921.[65] He studied mechanical engineering and psychology and in the 1950s settled in Switzerland with his wife. He published books for young readers, novels, novellas, and journalistic writing. In addition to *Life Nonetheless*, the only listed publications by Kretzschmar, who also used the pseudonym Alex

---

62. I refer to Martin because it is unclear whether the name change to Toni was desired. The details of the change of name are discussed further on in this chapter.

63. Rolf Thalmann and Rainer Herrn, "Fakten und Überlegungen zur Identität des Buchautors Erich Amborn: *Und dennoch Ja zum Leben*," in *Mitteilungen der Magnus-Hirschfeld-Gesellschaft* 53 (2015): 43–49. See also Rainer Herrn, "Ge- und erlebte Vielfalt—Sexuelle Zwischenstufen im Institut für Sexualwissenschaft," *Sexuologie* 20, nos. 1–2 (2013): 6–14.

64. Thalmann and Herrn, "Fakten," 44, 47.

65. Thalmann and Herrn, "Fakten."

Alexander, are *Heini wird ein ganzer Kerl: Eine Erzählung für Zehn-bis Vier-zehnjährige und solche, die auch einmal so waren* (*Heini Grows Up: A Story for Ten- to Fourteen-Year-Olds and Those Who Were Once That Age*, 1954), republished as *Heini schafft es* (*Heini Can Do It*, 1971), and a book called *Die seltsame Frau Doritt* (*The Strange Mrs. Doritt*).[66]

Like many examples of sexual-scientific life writing discussed in this study, *Life Nonetheless* crosses boundaries not only of gender, but also of genre, positing questions about authorship, authenticity, and identity. By way of the pseudonym, the author conceals his name and identity. On the one hand, the little biographical data I have access to makes it possible to suggest (although not determine) that the text was written as an autobiography, but leaves open the possibility that the text is a historical novel, or a fictionalized account of one of Kretzschmar's psychological patients. On the other hand, the pseudonym could also be interpreted as an affirmation of authenticity: the identity of the author is concealed precisely because the text lays bare the true account of a precarious and stigmatized life. Thalmann and Herrn, for example, understand the text as an autobiography and read the name Erich as an amalgamation of the words "er" and "ich", he and I, as a veiled attempt to signal authorship.[67] In both cases the blurring of boundaries between autobiography and fiction justifies the hospitable approach to reading that was proposed in the first chapter of this study.

Additionally, unlike the texts discussed in previous chapters, it is unclear exactly under what conditions *Life Nonetheless* was written. It tells of events that took place from 1914 to 1933, was likely written in 1956, and was published in 1981.[68] This time span, beginning with the outbreak of World War I and ending with the rise of Nazism, suggests that the text was conceived, or at least published in its final version, with some historical distance that enabled the author to reflect back on these political changes. This makes it difficult to ascertain whether references to sexological concepts within the text were added retrospectively or were available to the protagonist at the time of his transition. For example, the subtitle of the text, *Die Jugend eines Intersexuellen in den Jahren 1915–1933* (*The Adolescence of an Intersex Person*) suggests that this subtitle was added with historical hindsight, as the word intersex bore

---

66. Werner Schuder, ed., *Kürschners Deutscher Literatur-Kalender* 95 (Berlin: de Gruyter, 1984), 674. I would like to thank Christa Bittermann-Wille from Ariadne/Austrian National Library for drawing my attention to this biographical information.

67. Thalmann and Herrn, "Fakten," 45–46.

68. For the year of writing, see Thalmann and Herrn, "Fakten," 44.

a different meaning in the 1910s.[69] Rather than understanding the text as recounting events that definitively happened, I instead read it as an account of what could have been possible, or was desired to be possible, under the social and legal circumstances as they are recounted retrospectively. From this viewpoint, the text offers a particularly rich archive for investigating hopes and desires for queer livability.

Since Schreber's experiences in the 1890s, sexual-scientific knowledge had evolved into a more distinct disciplinary discourse. Whereas Schreber did not have a script of trans-investiture at their disposal, the 1910s and 1920s saw a proliferation of terminology around gender and sexual diversity. Gender identity was beginning to be more firmly (although not completely) understood as a separate expression of the sex-gender phenomenon, distinct from homosexuality. *Life Nonetheless* makes explicit reference to this shift in sexual-scientific thinking by placing its protagonist at the heart of sexological activity in Berlin at the historical Institute of Sexology. When Martin moves to Berlin to seek his fortune there but is turned away by his landlady, Hirschfeld's Institute of Sexology offers the kind of refuge Christopher Isherwood's protagonist describes in the passage mentioned in the introduction to this chapter. Through professional and personal acquaintance with Hirschfeld, Martin not only gains employment but also finally receives surgery confirming his gender identity. *Life Nonetheless* highlights the important (and conflicting) role that sexological discourse and institutions played in allowing and disallowing queer livability.

In the section that follows, I investigate how the text represents sexual-scientific discourse as providing a meaningful framing for Martin's gender transition. This is similar to Schreber's presentation of medico-scientific discourse and examination as a frame that creates gendered knowledge. However, as I want to argue in this section, Martin's story outlines the possibility— whether real or imagined—of actively pursuing the permanent and legal recognition of his trans-invested self in ways that were not available to Schreber. As precarious hybrid of fictional and autobiographical account, the text points out that authorship can only be achieved by an act of translation from one medium to another, an act of *Umschreibung*, or transcription, that, as I will argue in this

---

69. The term "intersex" originated from the research of Berlin-based German-Jewish geneticist Richard B. Goldschmidt, who conducted butterfly experiment from the 1910s. See Ina Linge, "The Potency of the Butterfly: The Reception of Richard B. Goldschmidt's Animal Experiments in German Sexology around 1920," *History of Human Sciences* 34, no. 1 (February 2021): 40–70; Michael R. Dietrich, "Of Moths and Men: Theo Lang and the Persistence of Richard Goldschmidt's Theory of Homosexuality, 1916–1960," *History and Philosophy of the Life Sciences* 22, no. 2 (2000): 223–25, 229–30.

section, stands in close proximity to the *Umschreibung* of Martin's legally recognized sex.

2.1. Martin's Appropriation of Trans-investiture

Life Nonetheless begins with a passage in which Martin is presented as attempt-
ing to appropriate symbolic investiture in the realm of gender. Still recognized
as female and called Martina, the protagonist works as a nurse during World
War I. On his return, his brother, Henry, informs him that he is about to get
married. Up until this point in the narrative, Henry calls Martina "Mart" (LN
86). Henry, who has not failed to notice his "sister's" act of cross-dressing in
the clothes of their deceased brother, seems to recognize Martin's rejection of
his assigned female gender, but linguistically marks this not with the name
"Martin," which the latter prefers, but the shortened version "Mart." Martin is
thus positioned between genders, or in a pregendered condition. "Mart" is an
abbreviation of Martina that postpones the linguistic assignment of any gender.
Against Martin's will, a clear gender is withdrawn from Martin's name and the
problem of the change of gender is thus avoided, or at best postponed.

Upon the announcement of his brother's wedding, Martin makes a
request: he asks his brother to celebrate the wedding festivities on the day of
Martin's twenty-first birthday in order to celebrate both his brother's wedding and Martin's legal age of maturity, or *Mündigkeit* (already familiar from
Schreber's memoirs). On this day, Martin will receive his inheritance and
requests henceforth to be considered as dissolved of his previous life and his
position in the family as daughter. He announces this decision with the following words: "Celebrate with me, and I will celebrate with you. It is a
meaningful day for all of us. On this day I will be Martina once more, will be
your sister, for one last time" (LN 89). After the festivities, Martin's feelings
are explained as follows:

> Her first impulse was to change her outward appearance to emphasize her
> masculine side. Haircut and clothes were the first, most important undertak-
> ings. . . . [Her sister] Wilma was the second criterion. Wilma stopped short
> when she saw the strange, thin young man in front of her. Then, however,
> she threw her arms around him and laughed. "From now on I shall have a
> brother once more and will have to get used to 'Martin.'" (LN 93)

By having his brother's wedding ceremony coincide with his age of maturity,
the narrative recognizes the potential that both such rites of passage hold and

appropriates the investiture of maturity in the realm of gender, similar to Schreber's account. The intersection of the symbolic act of the wedding ceremony, which changes the civil status of his brother, and Martin's symbolic transgression of the boundary between adolescence and adulthood and the investiture of *Mündigkeit* offers Martin the possibility of transgressing another boundary, that between binary genders. By way of these symbolic festivities, Martin's gender transgression is legitimized within the family, even as he moves outside of the family, and he thereby considers himself trans-invested with a male gender.

Within the narrative, this trans-investiture—the performative, symbolic process whereby Martina is transformed into Martin—is supported by the assumption of a new name. The name functions as one of the symbolic operations by which a new social status can be assigned.[70] Before this act of investiture, the protagonist, despite feeling unhappy about his female name, is referred to as Martina, and female pronouns are used. Immediately after his moment of trans-investiture, Martina is transformed into Martin, and the text switches to male pronouns. Here it also becomes clear why the text switches between a first-person and third-person narration. While the first-person point of view enables the text to describe Martin's inner world, the third-person point of view enables a demarcation between Martin's social role as woman and his invested role as man.

The trans-investiture that Martin experiences at the moment of his gender change within the framework of his family is a transformative act that enables his transition from adolescent to adult, from sister to brother, from the social role of a woman to that of man. Taken literally, this act of trans-investiture is also an *Einkleidung*, a clothing of the subject in the robes and dress of a new status. Martin notes that his first impulse is to change his appearance so that he can now pass as a man. The new clothes support his trans-invested identity, and Martin is able to invest his inheritance into his new life as a man. Here we can again see that trans-investiture also depends on having access to economic means. It is Martin's financial independence as member of what appears to be a financially secure family that enables him to initiate his transition. Martin's access to such funds also coincides with his legal maturity, but the ability to make use of this *Mündigkeit* in turn marks him as belonging to a certain class. When one becomes *mündig*, one also reaches the legal age of *Selbstbestimmung*, or autonomy, as well as *Handlungsfähigkeit*, or agency. Yet one can only make use of autonomy and agency, become an autonomous agent, if one has

---

70. Santner, *My Own Private Germany*, xii.

the financial means to do so, and it is under these conditions only that Martin's age of maturity, or *Mündigkeit*, also enables him to become Martin.

Although Martin is transformed in the eyes of his family and in the written account of his life—in the narrative *she* becomes *he* at the very moment of transformation—Martin soon realizes that his self-declared trans-investiture is invalid in the documents of law and state. When Martin wants to take up residence in his previous flat in Berlin, he notes that he will be unable to do so because "provisionally, the male first name was still illegal" (LN 91). As a consequence, Martin is forced to move out of his flat because his landlady does not want to get sanctioned by the police.

A little while later, Martin introduces himself to Magnus Hirschfeld at the Institute of Sexology. Hirschfeld – as character in Amborn's account – cautions Martin that his new name lacks legal recognition. What Martin had staged as an official act of trans-investiture lacks legal backing, but it is also not exactly acknowledged as a transgression by the law. Although according to the change-of-name law of the Weimar Republic, it was punishable by law to deceive a police officer by concealing one's identity as listed on the official documents of identification, the wearing of clothes that did not match one's assigned gender was a legal gray area. The penal code of the Weimar Republic did not clearly punish such an act of cross-dressing, but those individuals who were recognized as transvestites by the police could be threatened with accusations of *groben Unfugs* (gross mischief) and *Erregung öffentlichen Ärgernisses* (indecent exposure).[71] Under such ambivalent circumstances, Martin's staging of trans-investiture can be considered to have an *extralegal* status. Whereas the illegal is written into the law, the extralegal might be something that is not even discussed in the law and thereby becomes an abandoned area within the law.[72]

Beyond his own experiences, Martin soon finds out about the dire consequences of such an act of trans-investiture that remains unrecognized by the law. Living in Berlin under the auspices of Hirschfeld's institute, Martin becomes enamored of Hanna, a fellow inhabitant. At the New Year's ball in the catacombs of the Friedrichstraße in Berlin, he is disappointed to find Hanna

---

71. Rainer Herrn, *Schnittmuster des Geschlechts: Transvestitismus und Transsexualität in der frühen Sexualwissenschaft* (Gießen: Psychosozial-Verlag, 2005), 66.

72. This extralegal status of trans-investiture can perhaps also help us understand why female homosexuality, although not explicitly declared unlawful by the German Criminal Code, was no less dangerous a position than male homosexuality. Indeed, any uncertainty about the lawfulness of one's actions might throw the subject into a constant sense of fright and alert. The random and erratic infliction of legal consequences might then result in a state of constant crisis.

inebriated and out of control. Martin is shocked when Hanna suddenly exposes her naked—and apparently male—body to everyone's gaze:

> The outer garment was thrown off, and the purple undergarment made of light silk willingly followed every movement. The hair fluttered wildly around the pale forehead. Now the music set in for the blaring finale, increasing the tempo to frenzy. The undergarment flew up and over, thrown over the head by two outstretched arms. A naked, male body took a few more steps, swaying here, there, uncertainly. Then he collapsed, covered by the bulging undergarment. (LN 154)

The passive sentence construction ("was thrown off") and the avoidance of proper name or pronoun as sentence subject postpones the assigning of gender until the final line. Here, after the "male body" appears, a male pronoun is finally used, but it remains ambiguous whether this describes the body (*der Körper*) or Hanna's gender as such. This ambiguity might indicate the narrator's frustration with a conflation of body and gender, the assumption that the sexed bodies determines gender above and beyond the individual's gender representation.

Martin acts as the naive spectator here, but rather than being seduced by Hanna's pastiche of a typical Weimar Berlin cabaret scene, Hanna's revelatory moment performs the logic of a bildungsroman. Martin develops as a person by way of this sentimental education. The narrative here aims at an *Aufklärung* similar to N. O. Body's text, which explicitly states the desire to educate the public. In *Life Nonetheless* this is confirmed when, in response to Hanna's collapse, Martin reads Hirschfeld's *Die Transvestiten* and suddenly feels differently about Hanna:

> After the shock of having seen Hanna as a man had been overcome, Martin calmed down. After all, he now recognized that the so-called abnormal can be expressed in a multitude of ways. As long as no other person was harmed, no one should complain about it. Instead, this multitude of expressions had to be respected. (LN 154)

Here the narrative emphasizes how sexological reading helps Martin to cultivate feelings of compassion for Hanna. When Hanna dies shortly after the cabaret scene, Martin reflects: "Today he thought differently about her, no longer with desire but with hot compassion" (LN 155). Martin's feelings supposedly change when he realizes that Hanna is not the "real" woman that he thought she was: he can no longer love her because loving her would put in question his own sexual identity. Similar to Schreber's stereotyping of normative female erotic desire as voluptuous and heterosexual, Martin has internalized masculine desire as heterosexual and body-normative. This internalized normative understanding of manhood and masculinity leads to his immediate rejection of Hannah as love interest, despite his previous infatuation. This episode is interesting also because Martin himself, raised as a girl but living as a man, would have been considered as deviating from the norm. Perhaps because his own sexual and gender identity is put into question, he cannot love Hanna, whose apparently ambiguous gender expression endangers Martin's heterosexual, male identity. At the same time, the strange position of the adjective "hot," which usually forms part of the phrase *heißes Begehren* (hot desire) but is here assigned to the somewhat awkward phrase "hot compassion" (*mit heißem Mitleid*) cast doubt onto Martin's sudden loss of desire.

Hanna's revelation could also be read as the expression of a desire, perhaps brought out by the ecstatic event and her intoxication, to voluntarily reveal herself and present herself to a spectatorship. This transgressive moment directly counters fears of being found out that otherwise dominate sexological and psychoanalytic life writings—think of Dori, who commits suicide out of fear that their fiancé might discover their secret. Notably, Hanna here does not come out in public, but in a queer space and to a queer audience. When Martin wants to stop Hanna, a bystander comments: "Leave her to it. The main attraction is yet to come!" (LN 154). Here the narrative once more reinforces the attraction that emanates from the concealment and revelation of the queer body that was discussed in Chapter 3.

When Hanna dies, Martin relates:

> "Name unknown" would now be written on the gravestone, because the documents and details held by the Institute did not correspond to reality. All research had been done in vain. And so a nameless person had gone from the world. One of many who lived, loved, fought. But a human being who was different from the others. One of the nameless ones. (LN 156)

To be "different from the others" refers to the unspeakable realm of gender or sexual otherness and to broader questions of alterity that were discussed in previous chapters. Not only does Hanna lack family relationships or any connection to others who can mourn her, she also does not have herself: her official identity is one that she clearly could not live with, but one that could not be legally changed. Despite building up a life as Hanna, making friends with

Martin *as* Hanna, her grave remains unnamed. The extralegal investiture of her name means that this cannot be transcribed onto the gravestone because it has no validity in the documents of law and state. Death revokes Hanna's trans-invested identity and turns her into a *Namenloser*, not a *Namenlose*, a word that contains the same ambiguity as the earlier instance of the pronoun "he" to describe both the body and gender. One wonders what clothes Hanna was buried in, and this passage suggests that it was not the dresses that Hanna had invested so much money and time in or the dresses in which she desired to present herself at the balls of the Berlin queer scene. Hanna's ecstatic dance, at the end of which her seemingly male body is revealed, reinforces the idea that Hanna's unlawfully invested female attire must be inhabited and that such inhabitation, such dwelling or *living* in, falls away after death. Without recognition as trans-invested woman, without an official trans-investiture, efforts of trans-investiture are here presented as linked to a person's active inhabitations of "woman" as a performative category that, after death and the discovery of the body, must always appear secondary. Schreber expressed similar worries when they felt compelled to inhabit the role of woman for fear of punishment. Elsewhere, Schreber expresses their expectation that "to the end of my days there will be strong indications of femaleness, but that I shall die as a man" (MNI 254).

Martin remains at the Institute of Sexology as one of its archivists. When working at the institute, Amborn's Hirschfeld tells Martin of another case of extralegal trans-investiture in order to explain to him the necessity for an official change of name and sex in the documents of law and state:

> The body of a young man was found in the Landwehr Canal. He had his personal documents with him, which gave the name Julian Egger. All seemed in perfect order. Legal investigations, however, revealed a case similar to yours, Martin. The usual inquiries that naturally followed revealed that "Julian" Egger did not exist, but that a person of the name "Juliana" did. Well, you can't put the poor soul on trial anymore. But who knows, maybe the uncertainty around the name, the fear of discovery, was the reason for the unfortunate deed?! (LN 101)

The unlivability of the name, the severance of the person from the name, and the lack of official trans-investiture lead to a very real death.

It becomes clear, then, why the institute's mission, "sacred to love and to sorrow," focuses on love as well as pain and sorrow, for both can only be guaranteed if life and death are recognizable and *real*. If medical assessments of bodies, such as in the case of Hanna, shortly after death, do not accept inhabitation, self-investiture, or chosen names as acceptable ways of determining who died, the institute appears to attempt a change in what is recognizable and how. Whereas the appropriation of trans-investiture provides a certain period of livability that allows Martin to leave his home and start a new life as a man, it becomes clear that an official trans-investiture is necessary in order to make one's gender function within society and the law.

2.2. Martin's Official Trans-investiture

Living as an extralegally invested man in Hirschfeld's institute and seeking to have his appropriated trans-investiture legally recognized through a change of legal status, Martin consults Dr. Kronfeld. Kronfeld (1884–1941) was a German-Jewish psychiatrist and cofounder of the Institute of Sexology, where he was working in the sexual forensic department.[73] In *Life Nonetheless*, a character named Kronfeld reminds Martin that in order to receive an official trans-investiture, a particular evaluation is necessary: "Well, Martin, we have already discussed that the legal change (*Umschreibung*) requires an examination" (LN 116). The *Umschreibung* in the documents of law and state depends on a reference from a qualified practitioner. Indeed, Kronfeld and others at the Institute of Sexology provided *Gerichtsgutachten*, court testimony provided by an expert to give evidence of a person's gender or sexual condition.[74] If, according to Santner's logic of investiture, social roles must be invested by official authority, Martin's attempts to legitimize his own gender transgression have no bearing on the recognition of his trans-invested status by the figures of law and authority until he receives an official *Umschreibung*.

As Rainer Herrn has shown, as early as 1908 or 1909, Hirschfeld supported some transvestites in receiving a *Transvestitenschein* from the police, a certificate, supported by a medical report, that allowed them to dress according to their lived gender.[75] However, regulations around a change of name were more difficult. In 1912, a transvestite was successfully registered as a "hermaphrodite," and, based on this change, a name change was sanctioned.[76] This was an exception to the rule, however, and overall it remained extremely dif-

---

73. On Kronfeld see Andreas Seeck, "Arthur Kronfeld (1886–1941)," in *Personenlexikon der Sexualforschung*, ed. Volkmar Sigusch and Günter Grau (Frankfurt am Main: Campus, 2009), 397–402.

74. See for example Rainer Herrn, *Der Liebe und dem Leid: Das Institut für Sexualwissenschaft 1919–1933* (Berlin: Suhrkamp, 1922), 267–84.

75. Herrn, *Schnittmuster des Geschlechts*, 126.

76. Herrn, *Schnittmuster des Geschlechts*, 126.

ficult for individuals to change their name in this way. In 1919, a new law was introduced that allowed Prussian citizens to legally change their surname, but changes to the first name were not introduced until 1920 and then only on a case-by-case basis.[77]

When Martin is informed that his *Umschreibung* requires a medical examination, he submits to it, but comments:

> Again and again having to put oneself on display, having one's body touched, having to answer to endless questions—how he hated it all! Couldn't human beings live as they pleased, whichever way pleases them, according to their nature? No, he wasn't allowed to do this. He was not even allowed to choose his clothes as he liked. Outwardly, he had to show where he belonged. Men on one side, women on the other. To this end, the state (*Vater Staat*) had enacted laws and hired civil servants who were paid and who had to do something, anything, to earn their money. (LN 117)

Both Martin and Schreber understand the necessity of a medical examination and the power such an examination might hold to confer trans-investiture, but Martin here also notes the violence of such an intervention, a violence that Schreber, as argued earlier, notes as the very condition of gender transgression. Martin here also shows a similar insight into the procedures of performative, symbolic investiture that Schreber experiences as a crisis. Martin understands the tautology of juridical power, which passes apparently arbitrary laws regarding gender and then reinforces them, seemingly for no particular reason. Notably, this juridical power is enacted by *Vater Staat*, the patriarchal state that embodies the sovereign and dictates on the binary order of gender identity. Martin, much like Schreber, here has an insight into the ways in which gender must perform itself according to sanctions and taboos of transgression.

In an essay about the diverse characters present at the historical Institute of Sexology, Rainer Herrn observes the meaning of the institute as—in Hirschfeld's words—"Forschungsstätte, . . . Lehrstelle, . . . Heilstätte und . . . Zufluchtsstätte"—research and teaching institution, a place of healing, a refuge.[78] In *Christopher and His Kind*, the narrator confirms its status as a refuge in particular:

---

77. Herrn, *Schnittmuster des Geschlechts*, 127.

78. Magnus Hirschfeld, "Das Institut für Sexualwissenschaft," *Jahrbuch für sexuelle Zwischenstufen* 19 (1919): 54, cited in Herrn, "Ge- und erlebte Vielfalt," 6.

I have a memory of Christopher looking down from a room in the Institute and watching two obvious plain-clothes detectives lurk under the trees which grow along the edge of the park. They hope that one of their wanted victims will be tempted to venture out of Hirschfeld's sanctuary for a sniff of fresh air. Then, according to the rules of the police-game, he can be grabbed and carried off to prison.[79]

The institute is a space outside the law, which would otherwise incriminate and incarcerate its visitors. But this function as safe space involves an aspect of complicity: the institute is a sanctuary that cannot be entered by enforcers of the law precisely because the enforcers of law have invested it with this status as sanctuary. Thus, its status as safe space is the direct result of recognition by the law. That this is the case is shown when the institute loses its status in 1933, when it is raided by National Socialist forces that no longer regard the institute as compatible with its laws. This means that the institute is somewhere without the law, protected from it, but only by virtue of being invested with this special status. In its efforts to assign official trans-investiture, the institute remains accountable to the powers of state and law: Martin, in order to achieve his *Umschreibung*, needs to have an examination, regardless of the fact that he despises this. How hospitable, we have to ask, is this treatment?

One reason for this complicity between the institute (and institution) and the law is the fact that the sexual sciences were still in the process of establishing themselves as a legitimate science. Similar to Freud's preoccupation with proving the method of psychoanalysis as legitimate in his writing of the Schreber case, sexologists had to prove that their scientific study of sex and the institutions built to support this were scientifically legitimate. Coinciding with the founding of the Institute of Sexology, Hirschfeld also used his private savings to start a foundation in his own name. Hirschfeld hoped that the foundation would support his efforts to achieve the honorary title of *Sanitätsrat*, which would serve a twofold purpose: it would give him official recognition by the Prussian state as well as tax breaks that would fund the future of the foundation and institute. Such recognition was important, as Hirschfeld hoped that the state might decide to cofund the institute or designate it as affiliate university institute.[80] These efforts were made with the explicit purpose to give credibility and authority to the institute and the discipline of sexology.

79. Isherwood, *Christopher and His Kind*, 22.

80. Rainer Herrn, "Outside in—inside Out: Topografie, Architektur und Funktionen des Instituts für Sexualwissenschaft zwischen Wahrnehmungen und Imaginationen," in *Metropolenzauber: Sexuelle Moderne und Urbaner Wahn*, ed. Gabriele Dietze and Dorothea Dornhof (Vienna: Böhlau, 2014), 41.

Nonetheless, the institute and its activities were met with suspicion. As part of Hirschfeld's efforts to maintain his foundation, evaluators were sent in 1920 to report on its activities. The resulting report saw evidence of Hirschfeld's lack of professionalism in the bourgeois décor of the rooms. The report presents these as providing a façade behind which Hirschfeld and his colleagues hide their dubious sexological practice and homosexual propaganda.[81] In providing a refuge for queer lives, the institute's mimicry of bourgeois normality and homeliness is precisely what marks it as suspicious. The institute consequently struggled to achieve the desired level of respectability. Similarly, the institute's attempt to normalize life inside its walls failed too. Martin notes this when he works for its archives: "And so Martin became a part of this world of abnormality and yet secretly yearned to be part of a normal world" (LN 103).[82]

In this private sanctity of medical relations, not only must the patient become a visitor, but the doctor, as host or provider of hospitality, must also become a friend or confidant. When Martin is invited to appear at the court of law to hear the results of his application to have his name legally changed, the text explains: "Dr. Hirschfeld was also invited as expert in this area" (LN 156). Martin addresses Hirschfeld as "Herr Doktor," and the narration refers to him as *Sanitätsrat* (medical consultant, LN 156, 157). After Martin receives official notice that his name change has been granted, the narrative continues: "When the door had closed behind them, he threw his arms around the *Sanitätsrat*'s neck. 'Oh Papa!'" (LN 158). Hirschfeld responds: "But Martin, I mean Toni, if anyone notices your strange behavior . . . people will talk. Be sensible, young man!" (LN 158). At the courts of law, Hirschfeld must appear as the carrier of his lawfully invested status as *Sanitätsrat* so that he may help Martin gain his official trans-investiture. But Martin's emotional slippage, addressing Hirschfeld not as sexological authority but as familial relation, again points out the difficult position the institute holds in trying to make unlivable life recognized in the documents of

81. Herrn, "Outside in—inside Out," 45. See also Herrn, *Der Liebe und dem Leid,* 88–102.

82. Herrn notes that those who visited the institute because they depended on its support nonetheless continued to feel critical about it. Lili Elbe, one of the early recipients of gender confirmation surgery, did not want to associate herself with sexual intermediates and understood her doctor's statement that she might be a homosexual as an insult. Christopher's first experience at Hirschfeld's institute is one of embarrassment as he finds out what "kind" of visitors it receives. The institute may function as a safe space, but it nonetheless continues to mark its visitors and residents as abnormal. The institute offers an exception from the persecution of those who are perceived to deviate from the gender and sexual norm, but it continues to be marked as an exception to a rule that is all the more powerful. See Herrn, "Ge-und erlebte Vielfalt."

law and state. In either case, the juridical power is once again personified as male: *Papa* replaces *Vater Staat* with a new patrimony. Within the space of the institute, life must appear livable precisely by an absence of markers that distinguish the institute from normal, bourgeois, everyday life. Martin's slippage points out the difficulties in keeping these two investitures separate and also highlights that what appears as livable and normal within the institute is queered outside: establishing familial relationship between inhabitants might work to normalize life within the space of the institute, but outside it runs the risk of casting Martin and Hirschfeld's relationship as homosexual.

When Martin applies to have his legal name changed and thus receive the lawful trans-investiture he had already appropriated, he is also informed that a certain procedure has to be adhered to:

> However, your official legal change (*Umschreibung*) depends on a number of conditions, which, in my estimation, should not form any obstacle. . . . [Y]ou must accept a first name that is provided by the court of law. The applicant is not free to choose this for him-or herself. Martin Marsell will be gone for good. . . . A name had to be found that could be used as a female as well as male name. For those reasons they found and decided on the name "Toni." (LN 113–14)

This regulation seems somewhat fantastical, but historical sources confirm that this was indeed common practice in such cases as Martin's. Hirschfeld reports that some transvestites opted for a gender-neutral name, such as Toni or Gert, or asked to be listed with their initial only.[83] In the self-described "transvestite" and lesbian magazines from the 1920s and early 1930s, the name Toni appears repeatedly. In the magazine *Die Freundin*, which was published from 1924 to 1933, a certain Toni Fricke writes about her application to have her name changed. An occasional contributor to the magazine's special section, "Der Transvestit," Fricke reports of her success when the Department of Justice (*Justizministerium*) agrees to change her name to the supposedly gender-neutral name Toni.[84]

---

83. Magnus Hirschfeld, *Sexualpathologie: Ein Lehrbuch für Ärzte und Studierende*, vol. 2, *Sexuelle Zwischenstufen: Das männliche Weib und der weibliche Mann* (Bonn: A. Marcus & E. Webers, 1918), 171 cited in Herrn, *Schnittmuster des Geschlechts*, 126–27. Thalmann and Herrn write that these gender-neutral names were part of an agreement between the lawyer of the Institute of Sexology, Walter Niemann, and the Prussian Minister of Justice from 1921. Thalmann and Herrn, "Fakten," p. 44.

84. Toni Fricke, "Einiges über das Problem der Namensänderung für Transvestiten," *Die Freundin* 9 (1925). No continuous pagination. Spinnboden Lesbenarchiv.

What does Martin gain from this name change? The name Martin was extralegally invested and thereby did not enable him to live life as the man that he found himself to be. As Toni, however, he can, thanks to lawful trans-investiture, leave Hirschfeld's institute and pursue a career as a *Krankenpfleger*, a male nurse, elsewhere. But what does it mean to be transcribed into the documents of state and law not as Martin but as Toni, a name that, in a certain sense, moves him back toward the boundary between male and female? Whereas Martin can be recognized by friends and colleagues as male, but only at the risk of having no legal recognition, Toni is a legally recognized name that enables him to find work, but only under the condition of continuing to mark him as deviating from the gender binary. By way of trans-investiture, his trans-identifying status is attached to his newly invested status. His subordination to the norm continues to be marked. Toni becomes a new variation on "Mart-," only this time lawfully so. Toni Fricke comments on her own name change with the following words: "Essentially I gained nothing."[85] Toni Fricke's experiences here once more reinforce the financial precarity that occurs when such trans-investiture is not legally recognized. She reports: "For several years now I have been living as a woman, and for as many years I have been fighting to make a living . . . Not because I would have attracted attention as a woman, but because my legal documents show me to be male."[86] The extralegal trans-investiture of the author prohibits her from finding employment and thereby banishes her to a life on the economic margins.

Both the status of the Institute and Toni's status as trans-invested man provide unsatisfactory forms of investiture. Similar to the procedure of trans-investiture, which marks a person as belonging to a certain gender while always also noting that this is an altered state, the institute can offer livability and normality only by remaining a space outside the normal order. To subject oneself to medical discourse and thus the law brings with it the hope to (re)gain a livable life that finds recognition through *Umschreibung* in the documents of state and law, but it continues to mark the queer or deviant subject as Other.

When Martin receives notice that his application to have his legal name changed has been granted, he receives two documents:

"One of the documents was the certificate confirming the legal change of name; the second is the certificate of citizenship. Since you received the legal change (*Umschreibung*) from a Prussian authority, you are now a

---

85. Fricke, "Einiges über das Problem."
86. Fricke, "Einiges über das Problem."

Prussian citizen. I imagine you agree with this?" Oh, what did it really
mean: Prussian, Swabian, Bavarian—Martin was indifferent. (LN 158)

Here Martin is uprooted for the second time. In order to become Martin, he
removes himself from his earlier life as sister; in order to become Toni, he
crosses not only the boundary toward legality, but also state borders. As Kathleen Canning suggests, citizenship must be understood not only in terms of
ethnicity and nationhood, but as a "social identity within civil societies."[87]
Martin, too, understands citizenship as a social identity. However, Martin has
already experienced how other social identities—most importantly in the realm
of gender—can be transgressed and how they are invested with meaning
beyond the individual's choice. Martin accepts this change in national identity,
seemingly because he does not mind it, but he hardly has a real choice if he
does not want to end like Hanna or Dori, whose extralegal trans-investiture was
withdrawn after death, or the case of Julian, whose lack of trans-investiture
may have led to his suicide. Martin is unable to question the official rites and
procedures of trans-investiture, because to do so would mean to deny himself
the social recognition that—albeit not without problems—offers a certain level
of livability. Trans-investiture is always dependent on the power mechanisms
of science and law, which can, by way of the performative, symbolic act of the
name change, invest the individual with a new gender, but always by continuing to mark the crossing of the gender binary. This is a compromise Martin
seems willing to make.

As in many cases of sexual-scientific life writings, the text is ambiguously
placed between autobiography and fiction. But even if we consider it to be
autobiography, the text is clearly the transcription of a construction of identity
by way of trans-investiture. The pseudonym hides the author and therefore
conceals the author's identity from the reader, who cannot (or is, at least, not
invited to) cross-check biographical details with the narrative. If Martin's success story seems unbelievable and too coherent at times, then this might be
because it did not happen as such. Perhaps the text itself is an *Umschreibung*,
a textual performance of trans-investiture that was denied to its author in precisely this form. If lawful trans-investiture is the transformative act of
Umschreibung in the documents of law and state, then the trans-investiture that

---

87. Kathleen Canning, "Claiming Citizenship: Suffrage and Subjectivity in Germany after the First World War," in *Weimar Publics / Weimar Subjects: Rethinking the Political Culture of Germany in the 1920s*, ed. Kathleen Canning, Kerstin Barndt, and Kristin McGuire
(New York: Berghahn Books, 2010), 117.

is performed on a textual level here can be seen as the transformative act of *Umschreibung* in the document of self. As I noted throughout the previous chapters of this study, it is precisely the literary aspects of life writing that makes possible such reflection and representation.

Within the narrative, the importance of writing such an account of oneself becomes apparent. Kronfeld tells Martin of the case of Max Richter:

> You are aware of the case of Max Richter and how he met his tragic end. In his days I stood up for him in the same way as I do for you now. His request to have his name changed had finally been granted. For years he behaved flawlessly and carried out his good job conscientiously and to great satisfaction. And then, suddenly . . . You just never know what is going on inside a person. As we can see from the notes he left behind, he suddenly could no longer bear to be considered a man, to act as such, and to assert himself. His shame was so great that he couldn't bring himself to ask for his name change to be reversed. That would have been possible. But no, he preferred to commit suicide. Poor guy! (LN 114–15)

Max Richter's case serves as an example to justify the decision to allow name changes only if the new name is considered gender neutral. Kronfeld's passage speaks of a fear of what is today sometimes referred to as "detransition" or "desistance," where a trans-identifying person transitions to the gender assigned at birth.[88] This expectation that gender identity has to be fixed and further transition avoided in order for gender to work also profoundly affected Schreber, whose periodic transformation means that Schreber's memoirs are often not taken seriously as a genuine expression of trans-identification and instead read as a symptom of mental ill health. But Kronfeld also points out another *Umschreibung* that takes place here: Max Richter's fate is known because he left an account—or transcript—of his life. Self-authorship frames the experiences of trans-investiture, whether lawful or not.

In Martin's narrative, diaries and accounts become an important way of showing or revealing his true self that appears more accurate, and more hospi-

---

88. Contemporary transgender health experts consider the language of "detransition" and "desistance" misleading as they do not adequately summarize the complexity of outcomes. Expectations of transition are also heavily based on permanence and confuse nonbinary experience of gender with forms of "detransition." See Ben Vincent, *Transgender Health: A Practitioner's Guide to Binary and Non-binary Trans Patient Care* (London: Jessica Kingsley, 2018), 121–24; Ben Vincent, *Non-binary Genders: Navigating Communities, Identities, and Healthcare* (Bristol: Policy Press, 2020), 104–5.

table, to Martin than the revelation of his naked body. After Martina leaves home, her sister Wilma finds the pages of what appears to be a diary. If she reads them, it is because "they were lying about open and ready to hand so that it was impossible to miss them. Apparently, Martina hadn't locked them away on purpose" (LN 47). Wilma assumes, and the narration suggests, that these pages were meant to serve as an account of Martin's life that he wanted to be read. This transcription of Martin's life makes Wilma understand Martin's unhappiness at being seen as a woman and so serves as an *Umschreibung* or trans-scription of his gender in the eyes of his sister. Such an account serves as a *mise en abyme* of the narrative itself. The text serves as a performative, trans(scriptive)-investiture. If to be transcribed into the documents of state and law is the achievement of lawful investiture, then on a textual level the narrative performs its own *Umschreibung*, but one that makes no compromises. Whereas lawful trans-investiture comes with uncomfortable levels of complicity with the law as well as medical sciences, textual *Umschreibung* acknowledges these difficulties as part of a struggle to achieve a livable life.

3. Conclusion

Both *Memoirs of My Nervous Illness* and *Life Nonetheless* show how life writing documents and thereby performatively establishes trans-investiture. Life writing documents attempts to effect trans-investiture through appropriation, for example when Martin, on the day of his twenty-first birthday and the day he reaches the legal age of maturity, begins to live as a man; or when Schreber inhabits the role of woman after having thus far resisted bodily transformation. Both examples of life writing also document the processes of official trans-investiture: Schreber understands that an official trans-investiture by way of a medical examination would give authority to their gender transformation and invest it with meaning. Martin makes use of the medico-scientific and legal frameworks that had emerged during the 1920s and early 1930s to recognize and invest gender-diverse life with meaning. He submits himself to medical examination and changes both name and citizenship in order to receive official trans-investiture from medico-scientific and legal authorities. Ultimately, neither Schreber's lack of official trans-investiture nor Martin's scientific and legal investiture as man effect the kind of livability that both protagonists desire. Over and above their experiences with appropriations of and official authorizations of trans-investiture, it is the written account of their trials, struggles, and partial successes communicated in narrative form that create the possibilities, whether real or imagined, for a livable life. Medical and legal practitioners certainly accomplish an *Umschreibung* in support of a legal trans-investiture in the documents of law and state—Schreber experiences such an *Umschreibung* from *entmündigt* to *mündig*, while Martin experiences an *Umschreibung* from female to male. Nonetheless, my analysis reveals that the documentation of the struggle for appropriated and official trans-investiture, as presented in queer life writings, opens up the possibility of a kind of *Umschreibung* that legitimizes name and gender in the documents of the self and legitimizes an experience of transition.

Such an *Umschreibung* in the documents of self, over and above legal and medical forms of recognition and care, enables the subject to express queer livability, whatever it may be. Schreber's narrative does not present their gender as permanently or definitively transitioned or fully formed, for example, but this does not mean that Schreber's appropriation of trans-investiture did not work for them under the given circumstances. There are many reasons why permanent transition was not possible for Schreber (they were married, of high social status, working as a judge, and perhaps did not want to lose these important parts of their life). Their trans-investiture is no less real for being periodic. Schreber's experience of trans-investiture, where gender must be enacted through a habitual and forced performance that requires repetition and fears sanction, shows the work that goes into keeping a trans-invested self alive.

In the final chapter of this study, I consider a narrative that presents a subject even less fully formed than Schreber. I will read the Wolf Man archive as a trans narrative of the most tentative kind. I investigate an archive of sexual-scientific life writing consisting of both written and verbal accounts in order to show the wider applicability of the arguments put forward in this study. In this investigation, I discuss the work of gender and weave together central aspects of this final chapter and all others: the endurance of transitioned gender over time in ways that are never fully complete; the important position of self-reflective writing in the creation of queer livability; the role of medical examination; the function of dressing and undressing; and the work of trans-investiture.

CHAPTER 5

Queer Livability and Sexual Subjectivity in the Wolf Man Archive

Like the Schreber case discussed in the previous chapter, the Wolf Man case was of central importance to the development of Sigmund Freud's psychoanalytic work. In this chapter, I go beyond Freud's case study to examine the larger Wolf Man archive, which contains both published and unpublished material including memoirs, transcripts of analytic encounters, and interviews spanning seven decades, from 1910 to 1980. I do so because this larger archive offers a greater insight into the Wolf Man's lifelong struggle to construct a livable sense of sexual subjectivity via memories of cross-dressing. As this chapter shows, the events and the self-constructions in the extensive Wolf Man archive reveal the central importance of dress, gaze, and narrative in negotiating and mediating queer livability.

I will present three interrelated readings of the Wolf Man archive that unsettle Freud's mastery of the case material. My first reading focuses on images of the veil, caul, and hood in the Wolf Man archive. Whereas Freud understands the veil as separating the Wolf Man from the world, my focus on queer livability emphasizes that the Wolf Man discovers the veil as gender accoutrement. Life writing enables the Wolf Man to experiment with manipulating the veil in order to achieve a sense of queer livability. My second reading reveals the importance of the Wolf Man's sister, Anna, as queer figure. Whereas Freud's reading is not concerned with Anna in any detail, my reading positions Anna as heir to the father's patriarchal throne as key in the Wolf Man's own negotiation of livability. My final reading explores the importance of vision, the gaze, and witnessing in the performance of selfhood in the context of the sexual-scientific encounter. In Freud's psychoanalytic theory, the gaze plays an important role in the primal scene and the central dream of the wolves in the Wolf Man case. In my reading, I shift the emphasis from moments of seeing to moments of being seen and being recognized as a gendered being. In doing so, my three interrelated readings go beyond Freud's case material to reveal the larger Wolf Man archive as an important source to understand how queer livability is negotiated and how sexual subjectivity is established in the context of early twentieth-century sexual sciences.

To what extent can the Wolf Man archive be considered queer in the context of my approach in this book? Like Schreber, discussed in the previous chapter, the Wolf Man never arrives at a point of gender transformation. And like Schreber, the Wolf Man continues to pass as a heterosexual male in the eyes of others. The Wolf Man never described himself in any explicit way as a "homosexual," "transvestite," or "cross-dresser," terms that were conceptually available to him during his lifetime.[1] His attempts to negotiate queer livability never congeal into a form of gendered or sexual identity. Rather, the functioning and dissolution of binary genders and the negotiation of gender via dress and masking, are key themes that run through the Wolf Man's writing and testimony. A hospitable approach to the Wolf Man archive welcomes ambiguity, ambivalence, and moments in which gender and sexual identity or embodiment cannot be neatly separated or temporally fixed. Here, I read the Wolf Man as a subject in the making. Such a hospitable reading reveals the Wolf Man's attempts to establish a form of queer livability of the most tentative kind.

Here I am guided by Marjorie Garber's chapter on the Wolf Man in her study *Vested Interests*, which uniquely argues that the Wolf Man archive can be read through the lens of cross-dressing and transvestism. Garber employs an expansive understanding of the terms "cross-dressing" and "transvestism" that includes but is far from limited to the "transsexual," the term most commonly used for self-identification at the time of Garber's writing. Rather than as an identity, Garber understands cross-dressing as the act of quite literally dressing in the clothes of a gender not assigned at birth (or at production: she also discusses, for example, Ken and Barbie dolls).[2] As will be seen, within the particular material of the Wolf Man archive, this use of the term "cross-dressing" as a mode rather than identity is appropriate. Furthermore, the term "cross-dressing" relies on a binary understanding of gender that can be crossed. Although this does not allow identifications beyond the binary, within the Wolf Man archive the gender binary and its crossing plays a significant role. In dif-

---

1. For the reasons outlined in this paragraph, I use pronouns he/him for the Wolf Man. Pankejeff claimed the pseudonym Wolf Man proudly and I therefore use the pseudonym when I refer to his writing and speaking since his encounter with Freud. When I refer to his past memories, I refer to Sergei.

2. Marjorie Garber, *Vested Interests: Cross-Dressing and Cultural Anxiety* (New York: Routledge, 1992), 3.

ferent contexts, the term "cross-dressing" can be problematic, as it could be seen to reduce trans-identification to dress only. This is not how I use it in this chapter. In the case of the Wolf Man, veiling, masking and dressing become methods that enable tentative experimentation with cross-gender masquerade in ways that do not lead to a sense of trans identity as such. By referring to "cross-dressing" in this chapter, I purposefully do not refer to a form of identity but signal the Wolf Man's gender method.

Garber is interested in transvestism as a primal scene, and even as a phenomenon that constitutes culture. In doing so, her work sets out to highlight the cultural significance of cross-dressing: responding to scholarly work that had not adequately recognized cross-dressing as culturally significant and as holding a primary function in the production of meaning, rather than as a result of it, her claim to look at the transvestite rather than through them offered an important shift in reading and viewing practices. In pursuing this goal, Garber reads the Wolf Man's analysis by Freud as a way to access transvestism as such a cultural primal scene.

What remains unclear in Garber's reading is how the Wolf Man himself perceived these instances of cross-dressing that occurred in his dream and waking life. Although Garber shows that the primal scene of transvestism offers an important theme in the Wolf Man's later life, her reading remains focused on investigating the "fascination with [transvestism]" and shies away from trying to understand how transvestism fit into the Wolf Man's emerging sense of sexual subjectivity.[3] In the decades since Garber's publication, scholars of transgender studies have pointed out this lacuna. In *Invisible Lives* Viviane Namaste argues that "what is missing from her [Garber's] research is a conceptualization of transvestite identity as a real, lived, viable experience."[4] By this, Namaste means that Garber "reduces the transvestite to a mere tropological figure, a textual and rhetorical device that points to the crisis of category and the category of crisis" and thereby "undermine[s] the possibility of 'transvestite' as a viable identity in and of itself."[5] As I explore in this chapter, the Wolf Man's moments of trans-identifications never culminate in a fully-fledged transvestite identity. Nonetheless, Namaste points out an important next step in scholarly explorations of trans-identifying lives: that these are not scenes, primal or otherwise, but viable subject positions. Transgender studies scholar

---

3. Garber, *Vested Interests*, 3.

4. Viviane K. Namaste, *Invisible Lives: The Erasure of Transsexual and Transgendered People* (Chicago: University of Chicago Press, 2000), 14.

5. Namaste, *Invisible Lives*, 14–15.

Susan Stryker, in her introduction to "The Transgender Issue" for *GLQ*, similarly writes that the guiding principle for transgender studies is

> predicated on an explicit recognition of transgendered people as active
> agents seeking to represent themselves through any number of strategies,
> rather than as passive objects of representation in a few dominant discourses. It is no longer sufficient (if indeed it ever was) to approach the
> topic as Marjorie Garber did in *Vested Interests*, where she proceeded
> solely "by looking at [transsexuals and transvestites], and the cultural
> gaze that both constructs and regards them," with absolutely no concern
> for transgender subjectivity.[6]

Instead, Stryker suggests that it is productive to tackle such topics as "subjectivity, agency, discursive placement, and strategies of self-representation."[7]
Here, I follow Stryker's call by exploring subjectivity in the context of the Wolf
Man archive to understand how the Wolf Man used strategies of self-
representation to negotiate queer livability.

Another criticism leveled at Garber, already indicated by Namaste's comments, is that Garber expects transvestism to offer a constructive troubling and
transgression of norms. Jay Prosser argues that for Garber

> the transgendered subject made visible a queerness that, to paraphrase
> Garber, threatened a crisis in gender and sexual identity categories. Crucial to the idealization of transgender as a queer transgressive force in this
> work is the consistent decoding of "trans" as incessant destabilizing
> movement between sexual and gender identities.[8]

As I argue in my introduction, sexuality studies' thematic exploration of
transgression sidelines important themes of safety, subjectivity, survival, self-
exploration, and livability.[9] In this chapter, I depart from Garber's work by
following Stryker's and Namaste's call to focus on moments of identification,
subjectivity, and interiority, with a specific focus on the Wolf Man's continuous

---

6. Susan Stryker, "The Transgender Issue: An Introduction," *GLQ* 4, no. 2 (April 1998):
148.

7. Stryker, "The Transgender Issue," 148.

8. Jay Prosser, *Second Skins: The Body Narratives of Transsexuality* (New York: Columbia University Press, 1998), 23.

9. See also Benjamin Kahan, *The Book of Minor Perverts: Sexology, Etiology, and the Emergences of Sexuality* (Chicago: University of Chicago Press, 2019), 21.

desire for self-expression through both writing and talking. In following Prosser and Namaste, the focus turns away from expectations of transgressed boundaries and instead toward the desire to make sense of trans-invested fragments of narrative. Nonetheless, in departing from Garber I also start with her groundbreaking work: as outlined at the beginning of this section, her chapter was the first to point out the relevance of transvestism and cross-dressing in the Wolf Man case. I follow Garber's reading to begin my analysis of the Wolf Man's trans-identification. Her reading opens up the case material to readings beyond Freud's singular focus on homosexuality in the Wolf Man case. In doing so, I show that the Wolf Man archive unsettles Freud's mastery of the case material.

Ultimately, my work in this chapter leads to an inquiry into the trans-invested self of the Wolf Man and thereby continues the discussion of trans-investiture that began in the previous chapter. In my continued approach via hospitable reading, I hold firm to what I have argued throughout the book: just because the Wolf Man never fully transitions in the eyes of others or makes his exploration of sexual subjectivity known, perhaps not even fully to himself, does not mean that his attempts are any less valid or worthy of scholarly attention than those narratives that present lasting and legally sanctioned transition, as for example N. O. Body's *A Man's Girlhood Years*, discussed in earlier chapters. The Wolf Man archive shows genuine attempts to explore the mode and method of trans-investiture, and this chapter is dedicated to tracing those attempts.

1. Masking and Veiling

"Wolf Man" was the pseudonym of Sergei Konstantinovitch Pankejeff (Freud's transliteration of his Russian name, Сергей Константинович Панкеев). He entered Freud's practice in 1910 at the age of twenty-three. Five years earlier, his only sister Anna had committed suicide by way of ingesting mercury.[10] Pankejeff was a wealthy Russian aristocrat who traveled to Vienna accompanied by his servant. At this time, Freud was still trying to establish psycho-

---

10. The reasons for Anna's suicide are not clear. Freud did not meet her but by way of her brother's account diagnosed her with dementia praecox (schizophrenia) and determined "neuropathic heredity in her family." Sigmund Freud, "From the History of an Infantile Neurosis (1918 [1914])," in *The Standard Edition of the Complete Psychological Works of Sigmund Freud*, trans. James Strachey, vol. 17, *1917–1919: An Infantile Neurosis and Other Works* (London: Hogarth, 1955), 21.

analysis as a reputable science, and Pankejeff's aristocratic status as well as his dream material—which earned Pankejeff the name Wolf Man, as he described a dream of several wolves sitting on a tree—offered a unique opportunity for Freud. From this dream material, Freud deducted the existence and importance of the primal scene in the child's development. This primal scene would become a central psychic event in the child's development and in Freud's psychoanalytic theory.

In 1914 the Wolf Man, with Freud's blessing, married his wife Therese and returned with her to Russia just at the outbreak of the October Revolution. He returned to Vienna in 1919, having lost his aristocratic wealth during the revolution, to enter a second analysis with Freud. A fact not often centrally acknowledged in scholarship on Freud's case studies is that his patient went on to become the patient of other (often female) analysts: the Wolf Man's analysis with Freud was followed by analysis with his American student Ruth Mack Brunswick, from 1926 to 1927. After his wife's suicide in 1938, the Wolf Man began a fourth analysis, with Brunswick in Paris, financed by the wealthy psychoanalyst Muriel Gardiner, but returned to Vienna before its completion. After the end of World War II the Wolf Man worked for an insurance company, but he understood his profession to be academic painter. Upon Gardiner's encouragement, the Wolf Man finally published his memoirs in 1971. Throughout his life he remained in psychoanalytic care. In 1977, the Wolf Man began suffering from dementia. He passed away in 1979, at the age of ninety-two.[11]

To trace the Wolf Man's desire to write and give an account of himself, I wish to consider what I call the Wolf Man archive. By archive I mean the collection of texts and transcripts that constitute the various self-accounts of the Wolf Man, both published and unpublished. This Wolf Man archive begins with Freud's case study "From the History of an Infantile Neurosis," most commonly referred to as the Wolf Man case. It was published in 1918 but written shortly after the completion of Freud's first analysis with the Wolf Man, which lasted from February 1910 to July 1914. My archive also contains the Wolf Man's memoirs, first published in English in 1971 under the title *The Wolf-Man by the Wolf-Man* and translated into German the following year as *Der Wolfsmann vom Wolfsmann*. These memoirs contain the Wolf Man's account of his life from 1905, beginning with the years leading up to his analysis with Freud, as well as his experiences of analysis itself. The last section of

---

11. For a detailed biographical summary of the Wolf Man's life, see Liliane Weissberg, "Patient and Painter: The Careers of Sergius Pankejeff," *American Imago* 69, no. 2 (Summer 2012): 163.

the Wolf Man's autobiographical account ends in the year 1938 with the death of his wife. The book also contains Freud's case study of the Wolf Man's analysis, as well as a foreword by Anna Freud; an introduction and conclusion by Muriel Gardiner, who knew the Wolf Man in Vienna; a psychoanalytic commentary on the Wolf Man's later analysis by Ruth Mack Brunswick; and a series of photographs of the Pankejeff family.[12]

A central component of this Wolf Man archive is the interview transcripts from the Sigmund Freud Collection at the Library of Congress. This collection is part of a larger body of materials collected by the Sigmund Freud Archives and its founder, the Austrian psychoanalyst Kurt R. Eissler. Eissler conducted a series of interviews in the 1950s with Freud's colleagues, associates, and patients, including the Wolf Man. The Wolf Man files contain transcripts of analytic conversations between Eissler and the Wolf Man that took place in Vienna in the summers of the years 1952, 1953, 1954, 1957, 1958, and 1960. Much of the material held at the Freud Collection was put under an embargo for decades following the interviews. The embargo on the conversation transcripts between Eissler and Pankejeff ran out in 2010; some of the material relating to other individuals will remain closed until the 2050s.[13] The transcripts of Eissler's interviews with the Wolf Man are hundreds of pages in length.[14] These transcripts tell of an analytic encounter between Eissler and the Wolf Man in which the latter reviews his analysis with Freud and his life following analysis with Freud, with topics ranging from the validity of the primal scene to insurance matters (Pankejeff worked as an insurance salesman), art, memories of his sister and his wife, and physical ailments.

Eissler's collection of material is an incredibly rich resource that presents testimonies, interviews, and analysis with Freud's inner circle and acquaintances. It is impossible to do justice to the full collection of files relating to Pankejeff in this chapter, and my research here is not the first to engage with these files. A recent article by W. Craig Tomlinson summarized the content of

---

12. On the relationship between the Wolf Man and Muriel Gardiner, see Erika Schmidt, "Muriel Gardiner and the Wolf Man: Preserving a Legacy," *American Imago* 76, no. 4 (Winter 2019): 513–31.

13. Interviews with Pankejeff from the dates July 25–30, 1952, July to August 1954, and July to August 1955 were opened in January 2010. Interviews from summer 1953, June 1957, July to August 1958, and July 1960 were opened in October 2016. I would like to thank the Manuscript Division library staff for providing this information.

14. W. Craig Tomlinson indicates that there may even be tapes of further sessions in the 1960s that have not yet been transcribed. W. Craig Tomlinson, "A Few More Thoughts on Sergei Pankejeff," *American Imago* 76, no. 4 (Winter 2019): 537.

Eissler's analysis with Pankejeff to relate it to key themes in Freud's case study.[15] Liliane Weissberg and John H. Baker examined the artworks produced by Pankejeff and held as part of the Sergei Pankejeff Papers at the Sigmund Freud Archives.[16] However, there have been no in-depth readings of the kind that trans scholars have called for, readings that focus on the ongoing and lasting performance of sexual subjectivity evident in these files. Rather than understandings the events, memories, and self-constructions presented in these transcripts as mere echoes of Freud's definitive case study, I use these transcripts to show how the repetition of certain themes across the Wolf Man's life—namely themes of masking, veiling, looking, and being looked at—reveal his lifelong struggle to achieve a livable life.

Taking such a historically comprehensive look at the Wolf Man's accounts beyond the historical period covered by the other texts in this book is predominantly guided by the content of the archive itself. The Wolf Man, like other sexual-scientific subjects, continued to give an account of himself at different periods of his life. Whereas other life writers discussed in this book did not leave behind an extensive archive that would allow us to trace the subject's development after the zenith of sexual science research in the early decades of the twentieth century, the Wolf Man archive makes such an exploration possible. It also allows an investigation into the question of what remains of sexual-scientific subjects once their main sexual-scientific interlocutors pass away.

In Freud's case of the Wolf Man, the figure of the wolf plays a central role, as it appears in the famous dream that forms its centerpiece. Its position within the case is carefully curated in order to draw the reader's attention to its climactic moment.[17] In a minutely crafted series of interpretations, Freud constructs the dream as a result of the child having witnessed the primal scene of parental coitus *a tergo* (although he suggests that the child perhaps watched the copula-

---

15. Tomlinson, "A Few More Thoughts."

16. Weissberg, "Patient and Painter"; John H. Baker, "Light and Darkness in Landscape Paintings by the Wolf Man," *American Imago* 76, no. 4 (Winter 2019): 485–512.

17. Discussing Freud's rhetorical mastery in handling the case of the Wolf Man, literary theorist Stanley Fish argues that Freud guides his readers' faith in the case material and the reader's gaze in such a way as to leave them no option but to be persuaded by his argument. He argues that "the centerpiece of the case, withheld from the reader for three chapters . . . appears as an already-interpreted object, even before the first word has been said about it, since we know in advance that whatever configuration emerges need only be reversed for its 'true' meaning to be revealed." Stanley Fish, *Doing What Comes Naturally: Change, Rhetoric, and the Practice of Theory in Literary and Legal Studies* (Oxford: Clarendon Press, 1989), 537.

tion between animals and transposed the scene).[18] For Freud, the wolf represents the child's Oedipal investment—first the wolf as feared father-figure, and then a first step in his research toward understanding castration and acquiring a fear of it.

The Wolf Man's dream of the wolves constitutes a nodal point in the narrative of Freud's case to which various tales of the wolf connect and around which themes of veiling and masking converge. According to Freud, the Wolf Man himself connected the wolves of the dream to the memory of his sister Anna, who had a habit of showing him a terrifying picture of a wolf standing on its hind legs, which had been the cause of much fear and anxiety. The Wolf Man believed that the picture illustrated the story of *Little Red Riding Hood* in a book of fairy tales.[19] In another instance, the analysand wondered whether the number of the wolves in the dream—six or seven—was taken from the story of *The Wolf and the Seven Young Goats*. Earlier in the case, Freud had intimated that the tale of the seven goats led the young child to ponder on the pregnant wolf: "Was the wolf a female creature, then, or could men have children in their bodies as well?"[20] In both readings of the case material, the figure of the wolf as "cross-dresser" is central. Garber notes that "what he [Freud] does not point out is that in both stories the wolf is a (grand)mother as well as a father-substitute, and that in both he is masquerading as a woman."[21] In this reading of the story, dressing up in the clothes traditionally associated with another gender is presented as a form of masquerade or concealment. The wolf of *The Wolf and the Seven Little Goats* seduces the goat-children in order to be admitted into their home by (seemingly) successfully passing as their mother. In *Little Red Riding Hood*, the wolf puts on the grandmother's nightgown and cap and thus lures the little girl into her grandmother's house.

However, what the fairy tale presents as a disguise, the (male) wolf dressed as mother, takes on the form of very real possibilities in young Sergei's mind: that the cloak reveals the wolf's womanhood and ability to birth children. Here the cloak already carries connotations of trans-investiture as a performative rite that allows an individual to transform into another gender. As the cloak or dress is wrapped around the wolf, young Sergei ponders not the possibility of concealment, but that the wolf experiences a form of transformation in body and gender. This tension between cross-dressing as deceit and as an

---

18. Freud, "History of an Infantile Neurosis," 57.
19. Freud, "History of an Infantile Neurosis," 30.
20. Freud, "History of an Infantile Neurosis," 25.
21. Garber, *Vested Interests*, 385.

innate expression of one's gendered being is key to discussions of transvestitism in the 1910s: the same year that the Wolf Man entered psychoanalysis with Freud, Hirschfeld published his *Die Transvestiten*. In it, he aims to link cross-dressing to an innate and inalterable drive, which bears no relation to deceitful masquerade.

Garber's discussion focuses on the wolf's fairy-tale counterpart, Red Riding Hood. Garber argues that "the Wolf-Man, despite his sobriquet, was himself the Red Riding Hood figure, the child with the "lucky hood.""[22] The "lucky hood" that Garber speaks of here is the caul—what Freud calls the "Glückshaube"[23]— that veiled the Wolf Man at birth and that, for him, was retrospectively interpreted as a sign of luck and special status. This veil that clouded or masked the young man's vision was the symptom that led him to seek out Freud's help: "His principal subject of complaint was that for him the world was hidden in a veil, or that he was cut off from the world by a veil."[24] It is this veil, too, that Freud seizes upon to cast the Wolf Man as a queer subject:

> The organ by which his identification with women, his passive homosexual attitude to men, was able to express itself was the anal zone. The disorders in the function of this zone had acquired the significance of feminine impulses of tenderness, and they retained it during the later illness as well.[25]

For Freud, the Wolf Man's neurosis is informed by his latent homosexual attachment to the father, and, in a move familiar to Freud's understanding of homosexuality, he equates his analysand's "identification with women" with a "homosexual attitude" and thereby conflates the categories of gender and sexuality, implying a link between homosexuality and trans-identification. Here and elsewhere, the material of psychoanalysis is resistant to the separation of gender and sexuality.

The caul, introduced in Freud's case as a *Glückshaube* and taken up by Garber as the "lucky hood," is described somewhat differently by the Wolf Man in the Eissler interviews: "I was born on December 24 and was born in a vest (*Hemd*), you know, the lucky vest (*Glückshemd*)."[26] The word *Hemd* is an ambig-

---

22. Garber, *Vested Interests*, 387–88.
23. Freud, "History of an Infantile Neurosis," 99.
24. Freud, "History of an Infantile Neurosis," 74–75.
25. Freud, "History of an Infantile Neurosis," 78.
26. Sergei Pankejeff, interview with Kurt R. Eissler, Sigmund Freud Papers: Interviews and Recollections, 1914–1998, Set A, 1914–1998, Interviews and Recollections, Pankejeff,

uously gendered item of clothing. It can be translated both as shirt and camisole, and thus confirms the transvestite character of the Wolf Man's veil, as indicated by Garber.[27] The Wolf Man here reveals the sartorial character of the caul or veil that effects the Wolf Man's cross-dressing and thereby also blurs the boundaries between body and dress—the caul, made of organic matter, merges with the *Hemd*, which dresses the child. Like the cross-dressing wolf he encountered in fairy tales, and whom he imagined to transform in body and gender, the caul or hood as *Hemd* foreshadows that what is at stake is not a simple masking, but a form of becoming and transformation in the realm of gender.

Freud explicitly links the caul with his patient's feeling that the world is hidden behind a veil: "Thus the caul was the veil which hid him from the world and hid the world from him."[28] This sentiment that the world is covered by a veil is the symptom that leads the Wolf Man to seek out Freud's help in the first place:

> His principal subject of complaint was that for him the world was hidden in a veil, or that he was cut off from the world by a veil. This veil was torn only at one moment—when, after an enema, the contents of the bowel left the intestinal canal; and he then felt well and normal again.[29]

The veil here appears as a forced separation that is placed between the Wolf Man and the world. But Freud's description of the veil lets us understand the veil as both desirable and undesirable, as a form of protection and of constraint. Freud presents two descriptions of the veil here that he seemingly conflates: "that for him the world was hidden in a veil, or that he was cut off from the world by a veil." According to the latter, the veil would serve as a kind of separation, the veil's implied opacity keeping the Wolf Man from interacting with it, or from observing and seeing what is beyond. The ability to see and be seen, the act of hiding and revealing oneself, is a process intricately linked to the Wolf Man's veil. The veil here functions as a partition, an enforced detachment that leaves Freud's patient cut off from the rest of the world, a condition that seems to be unlivable for the patient. But in the first part of the description— "that for him the world was hidden in a veil"—the world is draped in a veil that takes on a more comfort-giving characteristic. The world has access to a pro-

---

Sergius, 1952, July 25–26, 1952, Manuscript/Mixed Material (hereafter Sigmund Freud Papers). Translations of this material from the German are my own.

27. Garber likely did not have access to the Wolf Man files because the embargo had not expired by the time her monograph was published.

28. Freud, "History of an Infantile Neurosis," 100.

29. Freud, "History of an Infantile Neurosis," 74–75.

tection or comfort offered by a veil that young Sergei cannot access. He is excluded and desires to slip in under the veil, to be draped in the same veil, rather than to remove the veil entirely. Therefore, the careless rupture or tearing of the veil upon insertion of the enema takes on a more ambivalent character. While it can be taken as a sign that his condition improves, as Freud here seems to say, it can also be understood as a destructive act. Pursuing protection by the veil that has wrapped itself around the world, the desired veil is now ripped and destroyed. The patient's positive feelings, post-enema—"well and normal"—may then come as a result of having vented his frustration.

In its double meaning, the veil here strikingly recalls once more Butler's description of livable lives and the logic of framing discussed throughout this study. Both to be held and framed too tightly, and to find no framing and no protection, can form unlivable circumstances. Similarly, the Wolf Man's veil (or *Hemd*) at times seems to be too tight, obscuring his vision, separating him from the world, as well as too removed, wrapping the world in its protective embrace, but excluding the viewing subject. And it is significant that this veil first occurs as a symptom that leads Freud to discover the Wolf Man's supposed latent homosexuality. In this context, the veil's connection with livability is one that pertains to a question of sexuality and—following Freud's fluid understanding of both terms—gender. The veil then becomes the framing (and enacts the transformation) of his body and the indicator by which livability can be both secured and threatened for the queer subject. This returns us, once more, to the staging and framing of a livable queer life and the desire to speak about possibilities for livability. Freud describes the Wolf Man's account as a lament (*Klage*) that is finally answered (at least to some extent) by tearing the veil. In Freud's reading, the lament is solved through a physical act of defecation, but expressing his lament, addressing it to Freud, and being given the opportunity to give an account of himself is clearly another major contribution to the temporary resolution of his problem.[30] Speaking and writing can tear the veil and, at least momentarily, resolve the problem. But it requires ongoing intervention and action.

Freud, too, understands the veil, as caul or *Glückshaube*, as a condition of livability:

---

30. Although her analysis does not focus on the connection between the veil and gender in the way that my reading does, Anat Tzur Mahalel suggests that the Wolf Man's autobiographical writing complicates Freud's case study by playing with both lifting and replacing the veil, suggesting that "truth is better apprehended from beyond the veil." Anat Tzur Mahalel, "The Wolf Man's *Glückshaube*: Rereading Sergei Pankejeff's Memoir," *Journal of the American Psychoanalytic Association* 67, no. 5 (October 2019): 809.

Thus the caul was the veil which hid him from the world and hid the world from him. The complaint that he made was in reality a fulfilled wishful phantasy: it exhibited him as back once more in the womb, and was, in fact, a wishful phantasy of flight from the world. It can be translated as follows: "Life makes me so unhappy! I must get back into the womb!"[31]

Again, Freud's reading here highlights the ambiguous nature of the veil, which veils both the patient and the world. Whereas "hid[ing] him from the world" bears the connotations of a protective veil, "hid[ing] the world from him" is more akin to hiding or obscuring an object from someone's gaze. Freud explains this double meaning of the veil by arguing that his patient's lament— separation from the world by a veil—is really a fulfilled wishful fantasy of escaping from the world by a withdrawal back into his mother's womb. The return to the womb is a return to maternal protection and an inability to see or be exposed to the world. Notably, the caul covers the *face* of the newborn child. Such a defacement via the caul acts as a layer that protects the face from being looked at, or adds a veil that the onlooker perceives instead. The gendered veil, mask, or caul here functions as the object that allows the very possibility and agential negotiation of livability.

The dream of the wolves, as told to Freud, immediately brings onto the scene two wolf figures whose gender play is key to their role within each tale. In both cases, disguise via the cloak or hood as gender accoutrement enables and transforms both gender and the body. The case material offers a parallel between these imaginary forms of disguise and transformation, and the Wolf Man's own experience of the caul as veil or dress. For the Wolf Man, manipulating this veil ensures a sense of livability. Importantly, the veil's transformative power is not unidirectional. Whereas for both fairy-tale wolves the gender transformation takes place only once and is followed by a revelatory undoing, the Wolf Man experiments with putting on and taking off the sometimes protective, sometimes suffocating veil. As I show in the next section, these acts will build toward opportunities for trans-identification via the figure of the Wolf Man's sister, Anna.

2. Anna, the Real Son

My second reading of this chapter determines the important role of Anna in the Wolf Man's negotiation of queer livability. Unlike Freud, who dismissed Anna

---

31. Freud, "History of an Infantile Neurosis," 100.

as childhood rival without larger significance, I argue that Anna was the central queer figure in the Wolf Man's life. Anna's gender inversion and the siblings' cross-dressing activities, as I will show, reveal both Anna and the Wolf Man as queer figures, even while being part of the heteronormative family structure. Anna's trans-investiture, I will show, is a key memory that contributes to the Wolf Man's sense of sexual subjectivity in crisis and the ongoing and sustained "work" required to make queer life livable.

The centrality of Anna in the Wolf Man's history remains unacknowledged or at best dismissed in Freud's case.[32] George Dimock goes so far as to argue that the Wolf Man's memoirs constituted "a poignant struggle waged by Freud's most famous patient to reinstate, by way of his memoirs, his beloved sister at the center of his life story."[33] Juliet Mitchell suggests that "Freud's reason for not integrating the sister into the etiology of the Wolf Man's psychopathology is that this would make the power games of rivalrous siblings rather than the prohibition exemplified in the castration complex (and failure of the prohibition) determinate of psychic life."[34] The exclusion of the sister as a figure of identification is then a decision on Freud's part that secures his argument on the castration complex, a necessary step in his chain of argument that supports the construction of the primal scene, the central purpose of Freud's case here. In this section, however, I argue that Anna is central to the Wolf Man's sense of sexual subjectivity.

Anna is not the only woman whose significance has been neglected in the Wolf Man's psychoanalytic history. In 1926, following a suggestion made by Freud, whose illness prevented him from continuing analysis with the Wolf Man, the Wolf Man took up psychoanalysis with Freud's former student, Ruth Mack Brunswick. Brunswick's supplement to the analysis with the Wolf Man, which first appeared in the *Internationale Zeitschrift für Psychoanalyse* (*International Journal of Psychoanalysis*) in 1929 and is reprinted in the Wolf Man's memoirs, centers on a series of dreams that again allude to scenarios of cross-dressing. In one of these dreams, the Wolf Man's new female analyst appears dressed as a man. For Garber, whose chapter on the Wolf Man largely focuses on Brunswick's account, these dreams form "the point at which the latent dream thoughts of the case, the materials of transvestism, somewhat occluded in Freud's original discovery and retelling of the fairy tales behind the wolf-

---

32. George Dimock, "Anna and the Wolf-Man: Rewriting Freud's Case History," *Representations* 50 (Spring 1995): 53–75.

33. Dimock, "Anna and the Wolf-Man," 54.

34. Juliet Mitchell, *Mad Men and Medusas: Reclaiming Hysteria* (New York: Basic Books, 2000), 327.

dream, become manifest."[35] As such, these dreams bring to the foreground the material of cross-dressing already latent in his analysis with Freud. In front of a new analyst, the Wolf Man can finally give an account of himself that allows for themes of cross-dressing to arise more fully.

Brunswick reports that her patient dreams of "a woman wearing trousers and high boots, standing in a sleigh which she drives in a masterful manner, and declaiming in excellent Russian. The patient remarked that the trousers were a little humorous, and not, like a man's, entirely practical."[36] Garber comments that "the dream seems also a fantasy of the Wolf-Man as woman, in the driver's seat, restored to power."[37] Another "cross-dressing" dream recounts a scene in which "suddenly the patient's (woman) analyst appears, dressed like a page in a blue velvet knickerbocker suit and three-cornered hat. Despite her attire, which is boyish rather than masculine, she looks entirely female. The patient embraces her and takes her on his knee."[38] Brunswick interprets the female page as a "cross-dressed" dream-version of herself and understands the patient's erotic transference toward herself as female analyst as a heterosexual—and thereby, as Garber notes and questions—"normal" development.

The Wolf Man's female identification that arises in these dreams is directly linked to his sister's masculine behavior and display of cross-dressing. Garber reads these dreams in connection with a memory of cross-dressing taken from the Wolf Man's memoirs. Here the Wolf Man relates a memory of his sister Anna, who wants to attend a carnival event wearing a boy's costume:

> At carnival time Anna and I were invited to a children's fancy dress party, where Anna planned to appear in a boy's costume. I do not remember how old Anna was at the time; at any rate she was old enough for Mademoiselle to feel concerned about Anna's good reputation as a young girl. . . . My father thought there was no reason at all why Anna should not wear boy's clothes to the party. Mademoiselle, on the other hand, contended that it was not seemly for "*une jeune fille comme il faut.*"[39]

35. Garber, *Vested Interests*, 376–77.

36. Ruth Mack Brunswick, "A Supplement to Freud's 'History of an Infantile Neurosis' (1928)," in *The Wolf-Man by the Wolf-Man*, ed. Muriel Gardiner (New York: Basic Books, 1971), 284–85, cited in Garber, *Vested Interests*, 379.

37. Garber, *Vested Interests*, 379.

38. Brunswick, "Supplement to Freud's History," 294, cited in Garber, *Vested Interests*, 380.

39. Gardiner, *Wolf-Man by the Wolf-Man*, 17.

Depicting Anna as a boy is central to the Wolf Man's memories of his sister that weave through the entirety of the Wolf Man archive. During one of his first encounters with Eissler, the Wolf Man talks about the perceived gender inversion of both siblings: "In our childhood she [the sister] was really like a boy, impudent and cheeky and funny."[40] He further says: "By the way, I can remember that already during our childhood it was said that I should have been born a girl and my sister a boy, that our roles should have been switched."[41] A few years later, the Wolf Man also recounts to Eissler the same carnival scene that Garber refers to: "And then, now I know, at home back in the day we often had dances in the evening and there was a, a kind of fancy-dress ball. She wore a kind of men's outfit."[42]

The sister's act of cross-dressing and the gender inversion of the siblings occupied much of the Wolf Man's later life, not only in his encounter with Eissler, but also the writing of his memoirs (beginning in the late 1950s and culminating in their publication in 1971), where he again comments that during their childhood he and his sister were described as gender-inverted, she supposedly more boisterous and masculine, he more playful: "In our childhood it had been said that Anna should not have been born a girl but a boy. She had great will power and a strong sense of direction, and she always succeeded in evading the influence and authority of her governesses."[43] In his interview encounter with the journalist Karin Obholzer (conducted between January 1974 and September 1976 and published after his death in 1980), the Wolf Man asserts once more that Anna was never interested in dresses and should have become a man.[44]

In each description of Anna, Anna is seen as the real boy, more boisterous and determined than the brother. Growing up as the girl who is known to be the real boy, Anna's appearance at the fancy-dress party takes on the form of trans-investiture, the performative, symbolic investiture that allows an individual to transform into another gender. Just as Martin, discussed in the previous chapter, uses the moment of maturity or Mündigkeit to fully live as a man, Anna uses the symbolic moment of the fancy-dress party to transform into a boy, however temporary. Garber describes the time of carnival as a liminal time that

---

40. Pankejeff, Sigmund Freud Papers, July 25–26, 1952.

41. Pankejeff, Sigmund Freud Papers, July 25–26, 1952.

42. Pankejeff, Sigmund Freud Papers, July 28, 1954.

43. Gardiner, *Wolf-Man by the Wolf-Man*, 24.

44. The interviews with Obholzer were published—as requested by the Wolf Man himself—in 1980, a year after his death. Karin Obholzer, *Gespräche mit dem Wolfsmann: Eine Psychoanalyse und die Folgen* (Hamburg: Rowohlt, 1980), 108.

permits inversion and is associated with transvestism and homosexuality. Anna seizes on this symbolic moment to appear as a boy.

For the Wolf Man, Anna's cross-dressing as boy provides a direct parallel to the Wolf Man's own understanding of his gender role. Key to the Wolf Man's memories of his sister is the understanding that Anna's status as boy is the result of a role reversal between the two siblings, which ultimately casts the Wolf Man as girl. In the carnival scene above, the young Wolf Man's costume is not described. But in appearing as such at the party, the siblings' relationship is certainly queered: they either appear as "cross-dressed" couple—Anna as boy and Sergei as girl—or as same-sex pair—Anna as boy and Sergei as himself. The children's carnivalesque appearance calls to mind the *Homosexuellenbälle*, the fancy-dress balls of Hirschfeld's Berlin, which attracted not only "inverts" or "Uranians," but also self-described transvestites or cross-dressers. As shown in the previous chapter, these balls were another occasion that allowed the trying on and trying out of differently gendered performances. In any case, understanding Anna's cross-dressing as a role reversal between the two siblings allows the Wolf Man to explore his own positioning in relation to reversed binary gender roles.

Anna's act of cross-dressing puts her in the position of the father's heir, a position that the Wolf Man himself desires. Garber writes that Anna "is not punished for her desire to cross-dress; quite to the contrary, her plan is upheld by her father, and the real 'boy' of the family is supported by the patriarch in a striking show of 'male' solidarity."[45] But when the Wolf Man's father passes away at the age of forty-nine, the Wolf Man states: "What interested me above all was the inheritance, because, not from a material standpoint, less from a material standpoint, but more from an idealistic one. I wanted to be my father's heir, as it were. I felt his tutelage (*Bevormundung*), after all, which was a burden to me."[46] Here again, the concept of *Mündigkeit* and the unlivable circumstance of tutelage, discussed in the previous chapter, becomes important. To become the heir is to finally escape his father's tutelage and to become *mündig* in this way. But it is his sister who has already achieved this *Mündigkeit*: Anna as boy evades the governesses' authority, described in the German edition as her *Bevormundung*.[47] For Anna to be able to withdraw herself from the authority of the governess is a step toward becoming an autonomous, trans-invested,

45. Garber, *Vested Interests*, 382.
46. Pankejeff, Sigmund Freud Papers, July 28–30, 1952.
47. *Der Wolfsmann vom Wolfsmann*, ed. Muriel Gardiner (Frankfurt am Main: Fischer, 1972), 44.

and patriarchal figure, similar to the case of Martin and Schreber discussed in the previous chapter, where *Mündigkeit* was one of the vehicles by which trans-investiture was bestowed. This investiture of patriarchy, the desire to become the heir to the throne, is a central theme in the Wolf Man archive. Freud recalls that "some contemporary phantasies of quite another kind came up as well in the patient's memory . . . which represented the heir to the throne being shut up in a narrow room and beaten. . . . The heir to the throne was evidently he himself."[48] Freud assumes that the Wolf Man is the obvious heir to the throne. However, the material of the Wolf Man archive suggests that this lineage is far from clear.

The Wolf Man retells this memory in discussion with Eissler:

> This identification with that crown prince, and that story—there is also something in my father's story: the crown prince, who, back then, which was told back then, that he was locked into a closet, wasn't he?! Back then the story, Nicholas II—I don't know, there was a story. Someone had told a story.[49]

The son of the sovereign father who will become the heir to his patriarchal throne is the *Kronprinz*, the prince with the crown—or the caul. The crown of the prince as accoutrement to the act of patriarchal investiture recalls the lucky hood and the *Glückshemd*, the vestimentary investiture of the Wolf Man, given to him at birth, draped, redraped, and torn off repeatedly throughout his life. This crown or veil then becomes the condition under which he can obtain the investiture of patriarchy. However, it appears that Anna, the cross-dressed boy, is the real son and heir.

That the Wolf Man casts himself in the role of the crown prince after hearing a story about Nicholas II is an ominous sign of things to come. Emperor Nicholas II of Russia and his wife Alexandra Feodorovna had four daughters and one son, Alexei Nikolajewitsch Romanow, who, as first-born son, carried the title "tsarevich," or crown prince. As *Kronprinz* and *Thronfolger*, Alexei, much like the young Wolf Man, suffered from an unexplained disease. And, much like the Wolf Man, Alexei consulted not only Russian doctors, but also foreign specialists to diagnose his illness. Alexei suffered from hemophilia, a disease of the blood often referred to as the "royal disease," a sign that overdetermines him as the heir to his father's throne—not

---

48. Freud, "History of an Infantile Neurosis," 26.
49. Pankejeff, Sigmund Freud Papers, July 28, 1954.

only his blood is royal, but so is his illness. But he never inherited his father's throne, because in 1918 the heir and his family were shot as a result of the political upheaval of the Russian Revolution, which dismantled the tsarist autocracy.[50] If this was indeed the crown prince referred to during his childhood story—or, more likely, retrospectively projected as such—it is a foreboding omen of the Wolf Man's own life.

Throughout the Wolf Man archive, the patriarchal system is repeatedly invoked as a system of order known from his childhood. When he tells Eissler of the Pankejeff family's new manor, he describes it as "an island in Russia, as it were. So many centuries that it was behind the times. There were bears there and wolves. Life was still so patriarchal."[51] The wolf, a figure previously established as carrying the potential of cross-dressing, here appears as an animal that thrives in these patriarchal circumstances and that is firmly lodged in the Wolf Man's past.

The Wolf Man again mentions these patriarchal circumstances in another context. Together with a friend, the adolescent Wolf Man visits Kiev, where they are joined by two sex workers (*zwei Straßenmädchen*, literally two street girls).[52] Sergei, the wealthier of the two, pays for the services of both women. "The girl I had picked for myself, because I was covering the costs of their services, was the prettier of the two; he got the uglier one."[53] But the Wolf Man, in a move that makes his sexist treatment of the two women all the more apparent, becomes frightened about contracting a disease from the woman and abandons her. Later on he meets a farmer's girl (*Bauernmädel*), and his fears of contagion have all but disappeared: "I never thought of getting infected. I said to myself, in the countryside patriarchal circumstances still rule; there is no chance that such a young girl could be ill. In those days there was also an assumption that it is not dangerous in the countryside because the people are unspoiled."[54] As it happens, he contracts gonorrhea. The consequences of this disease will stay with him a lifetime: it is the same infection that will bring him to seek out Freud and that will lead to him becoming the heir to a psychoanalytic system that relies on the power invested by Freud the father. But this passage also shows the Wolf Man as the modernist subject who realizes that the patriarchal system, worshiped throughout childhood, reveals itself to be in crisis.

---

50. See Greg King and Penny Wilson, *The Fate of the Romanovs* (Hoboken, NJ: John Wiley, 2003).
51. Pankejeff, Sigmund Freud Papers, July 27, 1952.
52. Pankejeff, Sigmund Freud Papers, July 28–30, 1952.
53. Pankejeff, Sigmund Freud Papers, July 28–30, 1952.
54. Pankejeff, Sigmund Freud Papers, July 28–30, 1952.

His father's acceptance of Anna's gender inversion and his subsequent trust in Anna as the true *Kronprinz* were particularly painful for the Wolf Man. He admits to Eissler: "For example, I wished that he would talk to me about matters relating to the manor estate, that he would introduce me to the practical side of things, etc. But there was no word of that. About such matters he only spoke to my sister."[55] And then again:

> Regarding business matters, there was always talk that he would give her a share. It was as if I didn't exist. . . . Then there was that manor estate. It was my favorite estate, in Belarus, no?! . . . And then he—it was always said that this estate would go to my sister, and I would have the one, the estate, near Odessa, and the house, which actually fit better for a girl, so exactly the reverse.[56]

In a troubling twist of events, Sergei's sister was due to inherit precisely the manor house that Sergei had associated, in his youth, with the patriarchal circumstances he worshiped. In addition, his father talks about his business only to the sister. The status of the son, as cited above, is an *ideeller Standpunkt*, an idealistic or imagined position of power that is invested with the patriarchal authority of the father; that position is already taken by Anna.[57] For Anna to be construed as the real heir to the patriarchal throne also casts her as the recipient of the *Mündigkeit* that the Wolf Man so desperately yearned for in order to escape their father's tutelage. This circumstance would have provided an acutely painful experience for the Wolf Man.

Anna, as cross-dresser, is the real boy, the heir to the throne and the father's estate. The Wolf Man desires Anna's access to patriarchal power, but cannot attain it. But then Anna dies. As a consequence, he becomes the heir to the patriarchal throne. Garber writes:

> If in his retrospective imagination he translates this into a personal desire for masquerade, transvestism, and homosexual passivity or sodomy ("father has given permission to cross-dress and carnivalize"), it is because he identifies with, or has incorporated into himself, the persona of the now-dead Anna, whose suicide made him the father's favorite.[58]

---

55. Pankejeff, Sigmund Freud Papers, July 27, 1952.
56. Pankejeff, Sigmund Freud Papers, July 28, 1954.
57. Pankejeff, Sigmund Freud Papers, July 28–30, 1952.
58. Garber, *Vested Interests*, 382.

The Wolf Man's identification here is complex. In a role reversal with his sister, Anna becomes the heir to the patriarchal throne, and the Wolf Man feels the loss of this patriarchal power acutely. When Anna dies, he incorporates her trans-invested masculinity. This returns us to the first of the Wolf Man's two transvestite dreams that occurred during analysis with Brunswick. Here, as Garber points out, we encounter "a fantasy of the Wolf-Man as woman, in the driver's seat, restored to power and to a time before the Revolution—to, in fact, the Russia of his childhood."[59] Here, a reversal of binary gender roles becomes the condition under which patriarchal power, Mündigkeit and livability can be achieved. Even though the Wolf Man's identification with Anna eventually returns him to patriarchal power, he only achieves this by way of a series of trans identifications and role reversals.

In their psychoanalytic rereading of Freud's case of the Wolf Man, *The Wolf Man's Magic Word: A Cryptonymy*, Maria Torok and Nicolas Abraham similarly argue that the Wolf Man incorporated the sister into his "crypt," a psychic formation within the self that enshrines the dead sister. As a consequence, his sister's fluctuating gender expressions become integral to his own perception that he does not fit the requirements of the male heir. This does not mean that he identifies with his sister, in the sense that he perceives himself as a woman, but that dreams, memories and phantasies of switching gender in a binary model become part of his interior world, without ultimately culminating in any form of sexual *identity*.

Jacques Derrida, in his foreword to Torok and Abraham's work, describes this psychic crypt, into which the Wolf Man incorporates Anna, as a false or artificial unconscious, "lodged like a prosthesis, a graft in the heart of an organ, within the *divided self*."[60] The incorporation of the sister into his self then takes on further implications: his sister's gender-fluid expressions become a prosthetic addition to the Wolf Man's sexual subjectivity. Freud, despite failing to understand the Wolf Man's incorporation of his sister, nonetheless comments on the repression of his supposed homosexuality in a telling way: "The unconscious repressed homosexuality withdrew into his bowel. It was precisely this trait of hysteria which was of such great service in helping to clear up his later illness."[61] In the German original, the "trait of hysteria" is described as a *Stück*

---

59. Garber, *Vested Interests*, 379.

60. Jacques Derrida, "*Fors*: The Anglish Words of Nicolas Abraham and Maria Torok," trans. Barbara Johnson, in Maria Torok and Nicolas Abraham, *The Wolf Man's Magic Word: A Cryptonymy*, trans. Nicholas Rand (Minneapolis: University of Minnesota Press, 1986), xiii.

61. Freud, "History of an Infantile Neurosis," 113.

Hysterie, a "piece" or "item" of hysteria. This *Stück Hysterie* is reminiscent both of sexual body parts and of fabrics that may be used in order to produce gendered subjectivity. In the context of Anna as the real boy, these readings are intricately linked, as cross-dressing stands in for her identity as the real boy and heir to her father's throne. This *Stück* Anna then becomes the prosthetic piece lodged in the Wolf Man's crypt. It becomes a bodily and sartorial marker of the Wolf Man's trans-invested self. This prosthetic piece does not constitute a form of identity, but a prosthetic support of sexual interiority and subjectivity, of incorporating several forms of gendered expression into his psychic and bodily self.

Anna's trans-investiture is a key memory in the Wolf Man's life that forms a central component of his own sense of self. Anna's transgression in the realm of gender is understood by the Wolf Man as a role reversal between the two siblings. By incorporating her trans-invested self after her sudden death, the Wolf Man can become the patriarchal heir to his father's throne and achieve a sense of *Mündigkeit* that was previously denied. Here I do not mean to suggest that Anna's cross-dressing seduces the Wolf Man into appropriating Anna's behavior. Rather the opposite: as I argued in the first section of this chapter, the Wolf Man's early fantasies of cross-dressing via the fairy-tale wolf already bestowed on him an understanding of the potential livability of acts of covering up and uncovering under the veil or caul. Anna's cross-dressing models successful trans-investiture, which certainly caused complex feelings of jealousy in the Wolf Man. However, her death slides the Wolf Man into the position of Anna, and the memory of Anna becomes a prosthetic piece in the Wolf Man's trans-invested self. This series of gender transformations may not culminate in any form of identification on his part. But these memories and dreams of cross-dressing, both of himself and by his sister, queer the Wolf Man's attempt to establish a livable life in a patriarchal system. In his memory and dreams, the Wolf Man archive reveals cross-dressing—both enacted and imagined—as a powerful mechanism to achieve a livable life.

3. Mirror Rehearsal

Themes of vision, the gaze and witnessing play a key role not only in the psychoanalytic encounter, but also in what Freud considers one of the most important moments in the child's psychosocial development, the primal scene in which the child witnesses intercourse for the first time. Vision, the gaze, and witnessing are also important aspects of performances of cross-dressing in the

Wolf Man archive, and more broadly in the context of gender performativity and the ways in which we look at each other and recognize each other as gendered subjects. In the following section, I argue that vision, the gaze, and witnessing in the Wolf Man archive function as tools to express the Wolf Man's attempts to achieve a sense of queer livability and centrally shape his sense of sexual subjectivity.

In Garber's reading of the Wolf Man case, the primal scene of cross-dressing is intricately linked to scenarios of looking. Here Garber points toward another famous case of queer life writing, Radclyffe Hall's *Well of Loneliness*.[62] The protagonist Stephen Gordon recognizes their own identity as "invert" when reading Richard von Krafft-Ebing's *Psychopathia Sexualis*. This is reminiscent of Martin's discovery of "transvestism" when reading Hirschfeld's *Die Transvestiten* in *Und dennoch Ja zum Leben*, discussed in the previous chapter. Garber argues that "such scenes, such scenarios of looking, are part of the very structure of the recognition scene."[63] In Chapter 3, I discussed how Body and Dori play with the mechanism of scopophilia in order to frame the queer subject as desirable and livable. In this final section, I examine the importance of processes of looking in the Wolf Man archive, with particular emphasis on how queer livability arises from being looked at—and looking at oneself—in certain rehearsed ways.

The Wolf Man began consulting his second analyst, Ruth Mack Brunswick, because of a problem with his nose. His dermatologist, he claimed, had attempted to fix a minor problem and left him with what he perceived to be a hole in his nose. Brunswick notes that her patient's obsession with his botched nose job led to an obsessive compulsion to look at himself "in every shop window; he carried a pocket mirror . . . his fate depended on what it revealed or was about to reveal."[64] Both Garber and Brunswick note that the Wolf Man thus not only borrowed the mirror, but also the "feminine habit" of checking his reflection in the mirror from his wife, Therese, who had a certain habit of looking at herself in the mirror.[65] In dialogue with Eissler, the scene is narrated in the following way:

> P: Back in the day I sat all day and looked, with the mirror . . . I sat . . . had the mirror, and sat and looked.

---

62. Radclyffe Hall, *The Well of Loneliness* (London: Virago, 1982 [1928]).

63. Garber, *Vested Interests*, 389.

64. Brunswick, "Supplement to Freud's History," cited in Garber, *Vested Interests*, 377.

65. Brunswick, "Supplement to Freud's History," 281, cited in Garber, *Vested Interests*, 378.

E: . . . Nobody else, only Therese, knew, no one else noticed anything?

P: Nobody else! Nobody![66]

Although the gaze in this scene is aimed at his nose specifically, the repetition of the word "sat" three times emphasizes the physical performance required of this moment of self-contemplation. By way of the feminized gaze, gender is thus written onto the Wolf Man's entire body, sitting in front of the mirror. Similar to Schreber, who tries on and tries out his trans-invested self in front of the mirror in private, the Wolf Man's act of looking at himself in the mirror takes place as a secret or "closeted" performance of femininity.[67] I will return to Schreber later.

The Wolf Man's conversations with Kurt Eissler also show a further possible reading that reveals this scene as yet another expression of the Wolf Man's identification with his sister. Anna, the Wolf Man explains, attempted suicide by drinking mercury. When she began to feel ill, a doctor was called:

When the doctor came, she showed him the bottle and said that she had drunk that. And as it was reported to me after that, she wanted to live. She wanted to live, was devastated about what she had done, kept holding the mirror in her hand, because she had lost her teeth and she wanted to live. She wanted to live. And the doctor was totally calm, he said, he had pumped out her stomach, the danger is gone, she would live. But still, after two weeks she died of heart failure.[68]

It is easy to imagine that this horrific account of his sister's suicide remained a traumatic memory for the Wolf Man, who was himself repeatedly on the verge of suicide and had lost his wife Therese to suicide, as well as possibly his father.[69] During his first meeting with Eissler, the Wolf Man remem-

---

66. Sigmund Freud Papers, August 3–4, 1954.

67. Andrew J. Webber describes the Wolf Man case as a kind of "closet case," which hides as well as reveals queer lives. Webber takes this epistemological framework of the closet as a space for creative and yet constraining performances of self-fashioning from Eve Sedgwick. See Andrew J. Webber, "Psychoanalysis, Homosexuality and Modernism," in *The Cambridge Companion to Gay and Lesbian Writing*, ed. Hugh Stevens (Cambridge: Cambridge University Press, 2011), 39; Eve Kosofsky Sedgwick, *Epistemology of the Closet* (Berkeley: University of California Press, 2008).

68. Pankejeff, Sigmund Freud Papers, July 28–30, 1952.

69. Schmidt, "Muriel Gardiner," 516.

bers how, after another serious case of depression, he had suggested to his mother that they should suicide together. The account of Anna's desire to die and struggle to live, then, offers a parallel to the Wolf Man's struggles for livability. And his compulsive checking of his wife's pocket mirror might then also be a reenactment of his sister's demise.

In the last moments of her life, Anna looks at herself in the mirror and presents a sense of insecurity that seems uncharacteristic for her otherwise assertive self. The Wolf Man, reflecting back on their childhood during the Eissler interviews, notes that, in her later years, Anna "neglected her appearance and dress, dressed in very simple clothes, and imagined that she would never find a husband who would marry her out of love, and not because of her money."[70] This is because, the Wolf Man reflects, "For her in the end, beauty was the best and most important thing in life, beauty that she thought was lacking herself."[71] What inhibits Anna in the end is precisely what Mademoiselle had predicted when she cross-dressed as a boy for carnival: that she risks losing the ability to become *une jeune fille comme il faut*, a proper girl who meets the expectations of womanhood.[72] Indeed, the Wolf Man spells this out for us: "She wanted to be a woman and couldn't be."[73] Here, the patriarchal investiture of Anna as the heir to the father's throne is thwarted by simultaneous expectations of womanhood, which Anna cannot meet. This is reminiscent of another scene in which the sister's desire to become a maid is thwarted. During his childhood years, the gardener and his two children, a son of Sergei's age and a daughter, lived on the grounds of the Pankejeff property. At the age of six, Anna ran away to a nearby town with the daughter of the gardener in order to be hired as a maid, or *Dienstmädchen*.[74] Yet Anna's desire to be a "Dienst*mädchen*" is thwarted because, as Eissler uncovers, "what the sister *wanted* to be and was *never able* to be" was "a maid."[75] Anna's loss of teeth and face before her death is symbolic of her life as a woman. The horrific loss of her teeth in the weeks leading up to her death only confirms the loss of youth and beauty that made this incompatibility painfully clear.

When the Wolf Man looks into his pocket mirror, he sees both his sister's demise and his own despair about his nose reflected back at him:

---

70. Pankejeff, Sigmund Freud Papers, July 27, 1952.

71. Pankejeff, Sigmund Freud Papers, July 27, 1952.

72. Gardiner, *Wolf-Man by the Wolf-Man*, 17.

73. Pankejeff, Sigmund Freud Papers, July 28, 1954.

74. Pankejeff, Sigmund Freud Papers, July 28, 1954; Obholzer, *Gespräche mit dem Wolfsmann*, 110.

75. Pankejeff, Sigmund Freud Papers, July 28, 1954.

All of a sudden I really do develop a pimple on my nose. . . . It seems to me that I am ugly, that my companions laugh at me. Then a second ailment arises. My oil glands swell. . . . And so I have this red nose . . . which I powder in such a way, right, that nobody will notice a thing, but I constantly have to powder my nose again.[76]

The loss of teeth and the porosity of the nose again speak of a defacement. Similar to his later problems with his nose, when no one apart from Therese was allowed to know that this problem existed, it is a matter of urgency here that nobody finds out about the hole in the Wolf Man's nose. Hiding his face under a thin layer of powder, the threat of exposure is imminent and forever present. The mirror reflects back at him images of his wife and his sister Anna, and the threat of the slippage of the mask or the face that might reveal these overlaying images.

The Wolf Man's mirror scenes—looking at his nose in private with only his wife present, and his fear of showing his nose in public—are reminiscent of Schreber's gender rehearsal in their private chambers, discussed in the previous chapter. Indeed, Schreber alone might rival the Wolf Man's status as Freud's heir and most celebrated patient. In 1908, after all attempts at consulting a local expert had failed, the Wolf Man traveled abroad to consult a series of specialists. Of the specialists he consulted abroad, he notes, his father was convinced of the validity of Kraepelin's work.[77] Emil Kraepelin (1856–1926) was a German psychiatrist who had, in the late 1870s, studied neuropathology in Leipzig under Paul Flechsig, who, in turn, treated Daniel Paul Schreber, discussed in the previous chapter. Schreber and the Wolf Man are thus not only psychoanalytic siblings, but also the offspring of the same lineage of psychiatrists. And it is precisely the Wolf Man's lineage, via Kraepelin, that establishes him as psychoanalytic heir. Kraepelin disagreed with Freud's theories on infantile sexuality. "In the light of his struggles," Whitney Davis argues, "the Wolf Man appeared, we can safely assume, as a possible living confirmation of Freud's most closely defended intellectual commitment," that of infantile sexuality.[78] Consequently, the Wolf Man case became a cornerstone in Freud's psychoanalytic project.

Schreber's performance requires a mirror, a performative repetition and

---

76. Pankejeff, Sigmund Freud Papers, July 25–26, 1952.

77. Pankejeff, Sigmund Freud Papers, July 28–30, 1952.

78. Whitney Davis, *Dreaming the Dream of the Wolves: Homosexuality, Interpretation, and Freud's "Wolf Man"* (Bloomington: Indiana University Press, 1995), 30.

rehearsal of this gendered act that could be viewed, if not by others, certainly by themselves: "I venture to assert flatly that anybody who sees me standing in front of a mirror with the upper part of my body naked would get the undoubted *impression of a female trunk*—especially when the illusion is strengthened by some feminine adornments."[79] Schreber's transformation only works if it is acted out and if this acting out is being witnessed. But simultaneously, when it is seen, it must be presented as such, not chanced upon. It is not the "[naked] upper part of my body" that convinces onlookers that Schreber's body is that of a woman, but importantly the *reflection* of this body in the mirror, the staged image reflected back at Schreber.

The Wolf Man archive presents a desire similar to that of Schreber, to reveal oneself at one's own will and the simultaneous fear of being revealed by events outside one's power. Thinking through Anna's desire to become a maid, Eissler argues that he finds a counterpart to his sister's desire in the figure of the red-headed son of the gardener, who was perceived by Sergei to be a clown and envied as such. As Eissler summarizes, what Sergei envied was "that he is a redhead, and he will be the clown, can be . . . just like in the circus . . . and that you have the tendency to it, to be a clown, to imitate people, and . . . to make fun of people, . . . make people laugh."[80] Sergei wants to hide his sadness behind the mask of the clown which provides a facade of laughter and humor. Eissler summarizes the parallel between the siblings as follows: "The sister said I would be able to live if I were allowed to be a maid! You're saying, really, I could live if I were a clown. If I could take life lightly."[81] This parallel suggests that the taking on of a new identity on the part of Anna is mirrored in the desire to take on the part of the clown, so that the taking on of the mask of the clown goes beyond a simple play-acting. Indeed, another passage confirms this. As a child, the Wolf Man had a special talent for mimicking people around him:

> In my childhood I exhibited special skills, e.g., e.g. [*sic*] mimicking, right, acquaintances who visited us. I copied their voices, their movements, etc. At first, my father said I would become a famous actor, but it was, as I later found out, more of a talent of imitation, not acting.[82]

The Wolf Man, as he understands himself, is not an actor. He does not perform a role but by mimicking seemingly becomes another person. The

---

79. Daniel Paul Schreber, *Memoirs of My Nervous Illness*, trans. Ida MacAlpine and Richard Hunter (New York: New York Review Books, 2000), 248.

80. Eissler, Sigmund Freud Papers, July 28, 1954.

81. Eissler, Sigmund Freud Papers, July 28, 1954.

82. Pankejeff, Sigmund Freud Papers, July 25–26, 1952.

copying of voices here is also reminiscent of a passage in Schreber's *Memoirs*. Anguished by the mysterious and relentless voices that assault Schreber throughout their psychotic state, they realize that the only way to drown them out is "to confuse these birds by deliberately throwing in similar sounding words."[83] Schreber copies in order to drown them out, an act that points toward the logic of performativity, a kind of forceful repetition that cannot be avoided. To put on the mask of the clown, then, bears resemblance to the taking on of the veil. Yet Eissler recognizes him as an amateur imitator:

> Wolf Man often interrupts with amusing stories. He is evidently proud of knowing such funny stories and tells them with great joy. It is not what one would call a natural sense of humor; it is a case of purposeful indulgence in stories that portray a real or apparent opponent in a contemptuous way.[84]

His clown's mask—another kind of veil—remains a mask, but a mask that here becomes visible. Eissler understands that the Wolf Man's humor is not genuine. The mask refuses to merge with the Wolf Man's face. As with Anna's failed identity as a maid, the Wolf Man fails to become the clown; he does not pass, because the mask refuses to merge with his face. For the Wolf Man, however, this merging of mask and face seems to be the condition of livability.

The unlivable threat of being discovered as the bearer of a mask or veil, of having one's gaze revealed, is written into the very dream of the primal scene. Freud connects the opening of the veil with the experience of the dream of this primal scene: "The tearing of the veil was analogous to the opening of his eyes and to the opening of the window."[85] That this tearing of the veil, too, is closely related to the scenario of looking becomes clear in the primal dream:

> The wolves sat quite still and without making any movement on the branches of the tree, to the right and left of the trunk, and looked at me. It seemed as though they had riveted their whole attention upon me.—I think this was my first anxiety-dream. I was three, four, or at most five years old at the time. From then until my eleventh or twelfth year I was always afraid of *seeing* something terrible in my dreams.[86]

---

83. Schreber, *Memoirs of My Nervous Illness*, 193.
84. Eissler, Sigmund Freud Papers, July 25–26, 1952.
85. Freud, "History of an Infantile Neurosis," 101.
86. Freud, "History of an Infantile Neurosis," 29.

This dream expresses several variations on the act of seeing. The child's assumption that the wolves are looking back at him—in the German original "Es *sah so aus*, als ob sie ihre ganze Aufmerksamkeit auf mich gerichtet hätten," "it looked as if their entire attention was on me"—confirms the gaze of the child, who looks at the wolves, but by way of this gaze also picks up on another act of looking, that of the wolves themselves and an exchange of looks. I see and I am seen. Such an exchange of looks can carry sexual undertones, for example when looking and being looked at becomes part of sexual arousal in the context of scopophilia or exhibitionism, as discussed in Chapter 3. But here the child feels terror, not arousal. His terror at the thought of witnessing the same scene again can then be translated as: I do not want to be seen. And the action that reveals both wolf and boy to each other's gaze is the veil: "*Suddenly the window opened of its own accord, and I was terrified to see that some white wolves were sitting on the big walnut tree in front of the window.*"[87] The window, which previously functioned as a separation between outside and inside, opens up and reveals the wolves to little Sergei, but also Sergei to the gaze of the wolves. The "something terrible" that the boy fears seems to refer not only to the presence of the terrifying wolves, but specifically to the fact that they are looking straight at him, that their attention is on him, that the windows (and curtains or veils) have been removed so that the wolves can now see him. It is their seeing presence and their gaze upon him that terrifies him.

During one of his first encounters with the Wolf Man, Eissler reports, the latter stood "confidently in front of the mirror and talk[ed] about how good he looks."[88] The same mirror made a previous appearance during the very first encounter between Eissler and the Wolf Man. Eissler narrates:

> Later, when he showed me around his bedroom, he stood in front of the mirror and said: "This is where my wife stood and said, 'I am turning old and ugly.' But she wasn't ugly. She was a great beauty, a Reich German (*Reichsdeutsche*)." P had a portrait of her above the two beds that stood next to one another. He also had a photograph. . . . The picture of his sister hangs above the mirror in front of which he made this comment.[89]

In a striking collage of images, the Wolf Man, his sister, and his wife all come together. The Wolf Man is placed in front of the mirror, taking the posi-

---

87. Freud, "History of an Infantile Neurosis," 29.
88. Eissler, Sigmund Freud Papers, July 27, 1952.
89. Eissler, Sigmund Freud Papers, July 25–26, 1952.

tion of his wife, whose portrait and photograph is, we can assume, reflected in the mirror. At the same time, the Wolf Man faces the portrait of his sister above the mirror. Similar to his performance in front of his wife's mirror that I recounted earlier, this scene has a certain theatrical character as the Wolf Man curates his own mirror reflection in a way that shows him fully in control. Here he shows himself in the way he wants to be seen.

The images of sister and wife here function, to use a phrase I introduced in the second chapter of this study, as *prosthetic* devices that support the Wolf Man's gendered construction. And indeed, throughout this chapter we have seen how the Wolf Man's gender construction relies on the material of cross-dressing—masks and veils—and a series of trans-identifications with his sister. Yet the mirrored chamber threatens to become a house of mirrors with reflections that are maddeningly complex and difficult to take control over—both by the Wolf Man and by his readership. A venue for clowning around, his private chambers become a circus in which the Wolf Man is himself a divided creature, both clown and wild animal from the forests of his patriarchal childhood.

The scene of the Wolf Man in front of the mirror also shows the importance of visibility, and the dangers that come with it. To be seen by the right person at the right time, to open the doors of his private chambers just at the right time, is where the Wolf Man can become an agent in the construction of his own identity. The Wolf Man's passing in this moment is achieved by an act of witness—in this instance by Eissler, but on other occasions by other analysts and, after the publication of his memoirs, by many more. Erika Schmidt argues that "this [analytic] community functioned as something of a holding environment, and the Wolf Man took pride in his identity as Freud's most famous patient."[90] Certainly, analysis provided a framework of support for the Wolf Man, even after his main interlocutors, Freud and Brunswick, had passed away. This is a framework of support that was not available to his trans-invested sister, who left no archive before her early death. Unlike Anna, the Wolf Man manages to make his voice heard. Nonetheless, the psychoanalytic framework, tied as it was to the mechanism of homosexuality, was unable to fully recognize the Wolf Man's memories of trans-investiture.

Eissler's comments on the Wolf Man's behavior and thoughts throughout also bring to the foreground the collaborative aspect of the Wolf Man's closet performance. Eissler asks the questions and offers commentary, continually blurring the boundary between life narrative, psychoanalytic encounter, and biographical interview. In this hybrid form, the interviews or analytic sessions

---

90. Schmidt, "Muriel Gardiner," 514.

allow the Wolf Man to repeat—and perform—his life story, again and again, and to maintain a connection to psychoanalysis at a time when it had matured into a much more powerful and widespread discourse than when the Wolf Man began his analysis with Freud in 1910. The Wolf Man's archive thereby shows the importance of a readership or witness who can recognize and therefore make more livable one's sexual subjectivity. Spectatorship and the act of witness are fundamental preconditions of the investiture of gender. The Wolf Man's presentation of acts of gendered performance and of masking, dressing up, and clowning around are a kind of dress rehearsal inside the mirrored chambers that prepares Pankejeff for his role as trans-invested Wolf Man, a role that, after the loss of his father's estate and the fall of the Russian Empire, seemingly also invests him with the power to become the heir to Freud's psychoanalytic throne as one of the most famous psychoanalytic personae. And the Wolf Man's conversation with Eissler supports his investiture as psychoanalytic heir, a role that had, by then, only increased in significance. This status as famous son in turn leads to another kind of visibility in the corpus of psychoanalytic writings. The material yielded by the Wolf Man's case continues to be of interest to a large readership, and the Wolf Man lives on, not in his civic identity, but as the psychoanalytic persona of the Wolf Man. As in the previous chapters of this study, we can see how sexological and psychoanalytic discourses serve as a vehicle for the presentation of livable queer identities, but that above and beyond this it is giving an account of oneself that provides the possibilities, whether real or imagined, for a livable life. In that sense, I question Freud's mastery of the case material to acknowledge the Wolf Man's own attempts to master his own narrative. By way of rehearsing, again and again, the Wolf Man's trans-invested performance, the Wolf Man archive ultimately presents a textual performance of the logic of trans-investiture and reveals the requirements, but also the limitations, of achieving a livable queer life.

Conclusion

As the focus of the final chapter in this book, the Wolf Man material offers an opportunity to bring together the themes discussed in each chapter. The Wolf Man's ongoing process of giving an account of himself in written and verbal form presents a strong desire to address himself in front of a reader or listener in order to gain a sense of livability. This is particularly important as the Wolf Man's livability was constantly at stake: throughout his life, the Wolf Man experienced distressing periods of mental ill health that were deemed so urgent by the analyst Muriel Gardiner that she secured the necessary travel permits to allow him to leave Vienna in 1938 to seek therapy with Ruth Mack Brunswick in Paris and London, only shortly after the Nazis had arrived in Austria.[91] He sought analytic help time and again. In a fashion familiar to scholarship about other texts discussed in this study, scholars have tried to analyze the gaps and convergences between fact and fiction, between biography and storytelling, in the Wolf Man materials.[92] Whereas some of these scholars have argued that the Wolf Man appeals to a particular genre of writing, including the detective novel, or that the patient's writing and speaking evidenced the healing power of the talking cure, I argued, as I have done in Chapter 1 and throughout this book, that giving an account of oneself is a fundamental process of achieving a sense of livability—both real and imagined.

A hospitable approach to the Wolf Man archive foregrounded ambiguity and ambivalence. Here gender and sexual identity or embodiment cannot be neatly separated or temporarily fixed. A hospitable reading can offer an openness toward this lack of resolve and indeed understand such a lack as the very mechanism of livability, while also recognizing that the unsettled nature of sexual subjectivity in the Wolf Man case can be felt as acutely painful. In this chapter, I have resisted a presentist reclaiming of the Wolf Man "for" queer or trans history. As becomes clear from my analysis in this chapter, the Wolf Man does not understand himself as a cross-dresser or a queer figure in any other sense. However, he does engender memories and dreams where gender is queered in order to establish a sense of livability. In that sense, his archive can reveal the power of imagining and enacting cross-dressing as a way of achieving livability.

In Chapter 2 I discussed the prosthetic function of both sexual-scientific discourse and the life writing that arises in this context. The central role taken up by the Wolf Man case in Freud's oeuvre shows the prosthetic power of the Wolf Man's narrative. In this final chapter, I demonstrated that the psychoanalytic method of the talking cure becomes an important form of prosthetic support for the Wolf Man's sense of self that gives the Wolf Man a method for communication but also thwarts his attempts to understand himself outside of the framework provided by Freud's psychoanalytic theory. Freud's mastery of

---

91. Schmidt, "Muriel Gardiner," 516.

92. See, for example, Peter Brooks, "Fictions of the Wolfman: Freud and Narrative Understanding," *Diacritics* 9, no. 1 (Spring 1979): 71–81; Celeste Loughman, "Voices of the Wolf Man: The Wolf Man as Autobiographer," *Psychoanalytic Review* 71, no. 2 (Summer 1984): 211–25; David Hadar, "The Wolf Man's Novel," *American Imago* 69, no. 4 (Winter 2012): 559–78.

the Wolf Man case and the powerful framing provided by the psychoanalytic method is one that I investigated as well as disrupted in this chapter.

Such examinations of discursive framing are closely linked to my discussion in Chapter 3, where I investigated how framing (through clothes and dress, but also photographical and epistemological framing) negotiates and mediates queer livability in sexual-scientific life writing. Just as Chapter 3 discussed various forms of bodily framing and veiling, the relationship between body and clothes is central to the Wolf Man's trans-identifications as he remembers both memories and dreams of cross-dressing. As in Dori's and Schreber's cases, discussed in Chapters 3 and 4, the Wolf Man's trans-invested self engenders acts of looking and being looked at in order to support his queer livability. What makes the Wolf Man a particularly interesting case is his desire to experiment with and act out his trans-invested subjectivity, even beyond the act of life writing.

How does his trans-invested sense of subjectivity endure over time, and what work is required for this to work? The Wolf Man archive goes beyond the early decades of the twentieth century and endures even as the nature of sexual-scientific research changes. The sources I investigate in this chapter go beyond Freud's case study and consider the Wolf Man's memoirs as well as transcripts of his conversation with Eissler. Rather than tracing this change and the disruption in sexual-scientific practices in the 1920s and 1930s during the rise of National Socialism, in this chapter I trace the sexual-scientific narrative of the Wolf Man as it endures even after his sexual-scientific interlocutors pass. In doing so, I emphasize again in this final chapter that this book is about those who produce writing and testimony in order to explore their sense of sexual subjectivity and establish a livable life, whether real or imagined.

Conclusion

In this book I have argued that we have much to learn from a closer engagement with sexual-scientific life writing, a form of writing that constructs a
sense of sexual subjectivity in the context of early twentieth-century sexual
sciences. As sexual-scientific life writings, the texts discussed in this study
share a number of key traits: writers focus on experiences of sexual and erotic
desire, they reflect on their own bodies and how they are perceived by others,
and they account for processes of becoming or being a gender different from
the one assigned at birth. For these reasons, they proved to be of such interest
to sexologists and psychoanalysts, who were exploring the origin and development of sex, gender and sexuality. While sexual-scientific readings of both
memoirs and case studies focus on their relevance for a diagnosis, my book has
shown that these narratives give insight into a broader awareness of sexual
subjectivity that goes beyond sexual-scientific theories and diagnoses. Taken
together, they outline the possibilities of a livable queer life—whether real or
imagined—that is made possible via life writing.

My aim in this study was to give prominence to the voices of sexual-
scientific life writers. In doing so, I do not claim that queer and trans people
in the first decades of the twentieth century were only able to achieve a livable life by referencing sexual-scientific discourses or engaging directly with
sexual scientists. Instead, I argued that, where encounters between queer and
trans individuals and sexual scientists took place, sexual-scientific life writing evidences the important work and effort that queer and trans writers put
into making sexual-scientific discourse work for them. I argued that such
voices emerge within an entangled network formed by sexual-scientific discourses and individuals whose lives intersect with them, whether such individuals are in direct relationship with sexual-scientific practitioners as
patients, or known to practitioners via their writing, or drawing on sexual-
scientific discourse without the practitioners' knowledge. If we understand
sexual-scientific discourse and its interlocutors as constituting an entangled

and mutually influential network of sexual knowledge production, we can see that sexual-scientific life writings offer creative and constructive modes for exploring sexual subjectivity that take on meaning within this network of knowledge production. Across all five chapters, it thus becomes clear that sexological and psychoanalytic life writings perform an invaluable role in the creation and critique of sexual knowledge.

The foregrounding of sexual-scientific life writing in this study led to various conceptual gains. At the heart of my analysis was the question about how queer livability is achieved in sexual-scientific life writing. Here, I developed a theory of livability based on the work of Judith Butler, where livability is a balancing act between categories of recognition that frame life in livable ways, and categories that constrain and suffocate the subjects thus framed. My study showed that sexual-scientific life writings do not necessarily aim for a programmatic transgression or confusion of sexual, gendered or normative boundaries. For many sexual-scientific life writers, such transgression risks losing opportunities of recognition that form part of a livable life. Nor do they attempt to normalize queer life by, for example, strictly subordinating it to a binary system of gender, because such a subordination to restrictive norms would pose unlivable constraints. Instead, what is at stake in sexological and psychoanalytic life writings is an attempt, at the level of narrative, to negotiate a livable life by finding an amenable, legal, medico-scientific, sartorial and identificatory framework for expressing a sense of livable sexual subjectivity. Such livable framing can be achieved in unexpected ways. Performing as *Probier-Mamsell* (or model) in the department store, Dori is offered an opportunity to try on and try out a performance of gender via costume, work, and play. This gendered performance is, in this instance, clearly marked as artificial and provokes the laughter of Dori's customers. Yet, by providing a stage for Dori's queer masquerade and recognizing it as a valuable contribution to the commercial activity, the department store offers an opportunity to test the balance between a loss of recognition and the pressure of normative constraints.

By turning away from examining "fully formed subjects" and instead looking at subjects that reflect on what it means to become a socially-recognized man, as in the case of Body, or subjects that experience bodily becoming as periodic, as in the case of Schreber, I aimed to reveal the work that goes into becoming a livable subject. In navigating the various constraints of a livable framing of queer life, sexual-scientific life writing shows the various creative and agential ways in which life writers have created possibilities for queer livability. One operative mechanism by which sexological and psychoanalytic life writings negotiate a livable gender identity is the process of trans-investiture. Trans-investiture relies on the discursive and legal transcription, or *Umschreibung*, of the new gender status in the documents of law and state. Significantly, however, sexological and psychoanalytic life writings show that such a legal *Umschreibung* is often unattainable and that its constraining conditions are perceived as unlivable. Instead, the narratives discussed aim to achieve a trans-invested, livable life by conducting a textual performance of trans-investiture, similar to the more everyday behavioral performance of gender, and thereby effect their own *Umschreibung* on the level of narrative. This *Umschreibung* is also a direct response to the normative and unlivable constraints put on the queer or trans subject as it is challenged to hold itself accountable in the documents of law and state. By performing a textual *Umschreibung*, sexual-scientific life writing reaffirms frameworks of recognition without being subjected to unlivable constraints. This once again evidences the power of life writing in constructing the possibility of a life worth living.

Such trans-investiture also speaks of a transformative vesting of the self in gendered items of clothing in order to express sexual subjectivity. Indeed, dressing up, veiling and concealing—as variations on acts of self-framing—were themes throughout all chapters of this study. The autobiographical claim to authenticity communicated by sexological and psychoanalytic life writings (discussed in Chapter 1) can, in itself, be understood as a kind of masking or framing on the level of genre. The queer or trans body, too, was shown to appear in these life writings in a mediated way, mediated by contextual framing and linguistic interpellation. Thus, Schreber's gender transformation relies on the bands and chains that frame and hold their body, but also emphasize the restraints of womanhood. These permutations of the theme of veiling and masking show that concealment and masquerade must not be understood in any crude way as a deceitful or secretive hiding of an interior life. Instead, such masquerade functions as a mode of becoming and an integral part of the self that is coming into focus. Indeed the distinctions between face and mask, body and dress, as well as life and narrative are put into question. Embodiment, here, can take place only under the condition of masquerade, and the mask or veil thus taken on is fashioned into a kind of bodily prosthesis that supports the effect of trans-investiture. Dressing up, veiling and masking in these narratives functions as an opportunity to try out possibilities for a livable life. Life writing acts as a space in which the framing of a livable life can be tested out.

Part of this rehearsal of gender identity and transformation is the exhibition of the queer self to a spectator or readership. Within the narratives, such exhibition takes place in the form of various visualization processes. Body reveals his male self as the veil of womanhood is withdrawn. In the cases of

Schreber and the Wolf Man, the mirror visualizes and reflects back a trans-invested subject. In these examples of sexual-scientific life writings, it is precisely by way of narrating such instances of revelation and display that livability is negotiated. The narrative itself becomes the composite queer body that is offered to a reader or spectatorship in order to gain recognition. As such, both spectatorship and the act of witness are fundamental aspects of the investiture of gender. Sexual-scientific life writings thus take on the nature of confessional speech-writing, most evident in the conversation between Kurt Eissler and the Wolf Man, which could be understood as both biographical interview and analytic encounter. Sexological and psychoanalytic exhibition, questioning and confession are thereby reclaimed through self-authorship in the form of life writing. Indeed, life writing can be understood both as the process of writing about a life lived, and as the act of writing this life into existence in the moment of composition.

In sexological and psychoanalytic life writings, then, the links between body, identity and desire are rethought and reshaped to create the possibilities of a livable queer life. Here, sexological and psychoanalytic life writers are not objective observers, but active participants in the creation and critique of sexual knowledge. This dynamic understanding of a livable life, which relies on a function of self-authorship, was made possible by the methodological approach of hospitable reading. A hospitable approach to sexual-scientific life writing recognizes the textual strategies employed in these texts as valid expressions of an emerging sense of sexual subjectivity in the early decades of the twentieth century. Developed to respond to the claim of authenticity of life writings, this approach also enabled a hospitable reading on another level. By recognizing the agency and relative autonomy of sexological and psychoanalytic self-authorship, these life writings once again show that they are not secondary to sexual-scientific authority, but are generative forces in the production of sexual knowledge.

A hospitable approach to sexual-scientific life writing also recognizes the *Mündigkeit* (maturity) or autonomous agency of these texts. *Mündigkeit* describes the moment at which a person becomes of age, but this *Mündigkeit* can, as was the case with Schreber, be withdrawn if a person is not deemed to be able to look after their own affairs. Kant offers *Mündigkeit* as key to Enlightenment thought, by defining its opposite, *Unmündigkeit* (immaturity) as "the incapacity to use one's intelligence without the guidance of another."[1] In Kant's

---

1. Immanuel Kant, "What Is Enlightenment?," in *Sources of the Western Tradition*, ed. Marvin Perry, 3rd ed., vol. 2 (Boston: Houghton Mifflin, 1995), 56–57.

understanding of the term, the sovereign self knows itself and can think independently of figures of authority. On the one hand, sexual-scientific life writers aim at becoming autonomous subjects in this way. We are reminded of Schreber's rebellion at his *Entmündigung*, which took away his autonomous agency, and Martin's *Mündigkeit*, which enabled him to finally live as a man, as well as Anna Pankejeff's refusal of the *Bevormundung* (patronage) of figures of authority and power. On the other hand, sexual-scientific life writing presents a more modernist understandings of *Mündigkeit* as arising from a scrutinization of the self that is always still emerging, that is not necessarily fully formed, and that establishes a livable life with reference to medico-scientific discourse and requiring medico-scientific approval. Taken together, both understandings of *Mündigkeit* present an overwhelming sense of wanting to be taken seriously, at one's word. This does not mean that a hospitable approach should demand sexual-scientific life writers to be *mündig*, to fully know themselves or to be fully formed. Instead, a hospitable approach recognizes the struggle for *Mündigkeit* and the textual and narrative methods employed to achieve this.

My study investigates the period of sexual modernity from around 1900 to the 1930s. But it also, and necessarily, goes beyond this timeframe. This is because a rehearsal of trans-invested life is a performative effort, which has to be repeated again and again. This is shown by the expanse and extent of the Wolf Man archive. Although the Wolf Man's analysis with Sigmund Freud took place in 1910, his archive of life writing extends into the late 1970s until his death. In the same way as some sexual-scientific life writers continue to give testimony in order to test the boundaries of a livable life, my methodological approach to sexual-scientific life writing via hospitable reading revealed the importance of a continued response to the texts' call for recognition. Such a response might happen after the facts and implicate us, as contemporary readers today, in recognizing possibilities for queer livability presented in sexual-scientific life writing. This call for recognition in sexual-scientific life writing shows the enduring importance of recognizing queer and trans lives expressed in life writing. By continuing to read these texts, by foregrounding the voices of sexual-scientific life writers, and by acknowledging the creativity and agency invested in sexual-scientific life writing, readers can recognize and thereby contribute to making queer livability, whether real or imagined, possible. As contemporary readers of these texts, whether we are literary scholars, historians, or scientists, and whether we identify with the sexual subjectivities presented in this textual archive or not, hospitable reading asks for a respect of historical distance. By introducing this distance, we are encouraged to postpone judgment. If we dismiss sexual-scientific life writing for being complicit with medico-scientific theories, we miss out on revealing the literary and textual strategies they present. If we assume that they symbiotically emerged alongside sexual-scientific theories, we sideline the very real pain and suffering caused by medical intervention and scientific authority.

My hope is that the work presented in this book can speak to contemporary readers and scholars in several ways. The methodology of hospitable reading and the various conceptual tools that I developed in this monograph will provide a solid ground on which to further investigate the historical archive of sexual-scientific life writing as well as historical trans narratives. As the discussions of sexual-scientific life writing across five chapters have shown, there is no single unifying narrative of gender diversity or historical trans identification. Lived experiences of gender transition might be narrated as livable or unlivable, they might be permanent or periodic, and they might make use of sexological terminology or reject it. I hope that future research will be able to investigate further the different and differential positioning of queer and trans individuals in the context of early twentieth century sexual knowledge production. How do class and wealth, for example, affect access to sexual-scientific knowledge differently? How do individuals outside of the urban centers of Berlin and Vienna create a sense of community and belonging? Within a medico-scientific context that scrutinizes the body and its abilities, how do disabled writers relate to sexual knowledge production? How did people of color and marginalized ethnic groups conceptualize their gendered and sexual identities in relation to German sexual sciences and its entanglement with racial theories? Beyond the German-speaking world, how did queer life writers make use of linguistic, national and institutional frameworks of sexual knowledge production? Research on the creation of sexual knowledge outside of urban centers, on global sexology, and on the intersection between sexual and racial theories is thriving and I hope that my research can offer tools and methodologies to give prominence to autobiographical voices and life writing in these important discussions. In doing so, I hope that future research can highlight the diversity and intersectional identities of queer and trans authors.

The ethical positioning offered in *Queer Livability: German Sexual Sciences and Life Writing* and the theoretical concepts developed to understand sexual-scientific life writing can also inform our gaze on queer and trans historical sources more broadly. It enables a deeper engagement with sexual knowledge production beyond the purely medical. In this way, it contributes to recent scholarship on historical sexology that looks beyond its closely delimited medico-scientific realm and investigates how the sexual sciences engage in trans-disciplinary exchange with literature, the arts and cultural production.[2] This approach also counter-acts the diagnostic gaze and instead focuses on the self-presentation of the writing self. Such an approach stands in dialogue with research on "visual sexology" and the study of visual culture and medical photography within an ethical framework.[3] Here, I see my literary analysis speaking to and informing the study of visual sexology, where it can contribute to an awareness of agency and the gaze to answer important questions about our responsibility as scholars of historical life writing and historical sexology to recognize subjectivity, voice and agency. As a result, the ethical approach I developed to focus on world-making and the imagining of a livable life in textual form can also be applied to other forms of self-representation, self-reflection or creative engagement with sexual subjectivity. In these ways, my book has the potential to not only shift our perspective on the sources examined within its chapters, but to change some of the larger ways in which we approach the history and literature of sexuality and gender.

Beyond its relevance to further studies in the history of sexuality, this book contributes tools and methodologies for the study of life writing more broadly. Its ethical approach and broad understanding of life writing will be useful to the study of texts whose literary merit is not recognized or underval-

---

2. Laura Marcus and Ankhi Mukherjee, eds., *A Concise Companion to Psychoanalysis, Literature, and Culture* (Oxford: Wiley Blackwell, 2014); Heike Bauer, *English Literary Sexology: Translations of Inversion, 1860–1930* (Basingstoke: Palgrave Macmillan, 2009); Robert Deam Tobin, *Peripheral Desires: The German Discovery of Sex* (Philadelphia: University of Pennsylvania Press, 2015); Kate Fisher and Jana Funke, "British Sexual Science beyond the Medical: Cross-Disciplinary, Cross-Historical, and Cross-Cultural Translations," in *Sexology and Translation: Cultural and Scientific Encounters across the Modern World*, ed. Heike Bauer (Philadelphia: Temple University Press, 2015).

3. On visual sexology, see Heike Bauer, Melina Pappademos, Katie Sutton, and Jennifer Tucker, eds., "The Visual Archive of Sexology," special issue, *Radical History Review* 142, no. 1 (January 2022); Katie Sutton, "Sexology's Photographic Turn: Visualizing Trans Identity in Interwar Germany," *Journal of the History of Sexuality* 27, no. 3 (September 2018): 442–79; Jennifer Evans and Elissa Mailänder, "Cross-Dressing, Male Intimacy and the Violence of Transgression in Third Reich Photography," *German History* 38, no. 2 (June 2020): 25–43; Katharina Sykora, "Umkleidekabinen des Geschlechts: Sexualmedizinische Fotografie im frühen 20. Jahrhundert," *Fotogeschichte: Beiträge zur Geschichte und Ästhetik der Fotografie* 24, no. 92 (March 2004): : 15–30; Kathrin Peters, "Anatomy Is Sublime: The Photographic Activity of Wilhelm von Gloeden and Magnus Hirschfeld," in *Not Straight from Germany: Sexual Publics and Sexual Citizenship since Magnus Hirschfeld*, ed. Michael Thomas Taylor, Annette F. Timm, and Rainer Herrn (Ann Arbor: University of Michigan Press, 2017).

ued. Wherever a writer is reduced to a singular subject position—the patient, the prisoner, the historical transvestite—their writing is often understood as a trivial form of documentation or testimony without literary effect. However, my study shows that a hospitable reading of sexual-scientific life writing can reveal creative textual strategies, knowledge about the formation of sexual subjectivity and agency in negotiation of power relations. Reading other forms of neglected life writing, other texts that are not considered aesthetically demanding, can reveal similar insights into the lives of "those who are socially and culturally immaterial."[4] My hope is that further analyses of marginalized or trivialized life writing can benefit from the theoretical tools developed in this study to recognize the value—both ethical and aesthetic—of life writing beyond the canon.

Although my readings in these chapters focus on a historically specific period, where concepts of sexual and gender diversity emerged and were shaped, we would do well to extent the same hospitable reading to contemporary queer and specifically trans narratives. In *The Transgender Issue*, Shon Faye writes that there is a pressure on trans and nonbinary people to always write autobiographically, to produce a confession of their lived, gendered and sexual experiences.[5] What Faye makes visible here is at once the inhospitable demands on trans writers to explain their very existence in the most intimate detail, as well as the reductive way in which much trans autobiographies are then read as confession only. Evan Vipond similarly recognizes the normative expectations of what trans lives can and should look like via the repeated expectation of coming-of-age or coming-out narratives.[6] A hospitable approach to contemporary trans autobiography and life writing will engage in an analysis of what livability might mean in a contemporary and otherwise situated context. It will also focus on the uses of genre, textual or narrative strategies, and the ways in which authors inhabit, shape and adapt genre or narrative conventions to create a livable narrative. In this way, the capacious category of life writing, which I have proposed in this study, can remain open to diverse forms of writing and diverse genres and forms of expression in order to highlight the remarkable creativity and knowledge that these narratives conjure.

---

4. Sarah Colvin, "Leaning In: Why and How I Still Study the German," *German Life and Letters*, 69, no. 1 (January 2016): 136. Sarah Colvin has made use of the concept of hospitable reading to inform her ethical and aesthetic approach to life writing by prisoners.

5. Shon Faye, *The Transgender Issue: An Argument for Justice* (London: Allen Lane / Penguin, 2021), 15.

6. Evan Vipond, "Becoming Culturally (Un)intelligible: Exploring the Terrain of Trans Life Writing," *a/b: Auto/Biography Studies* 34, no. 1 (December 2019): 28–32.

Since the early twentieth century, new labels and terms to describe sexual and gender diversity emerged, often based on the very concepts coined by sexual scientists and sexual-scientific life writers. More of these labels will continue to emerge and gain meaning and significance. Sexual-scientific life writing and its engagement with concepts and theories as they develop can offer a model for our understanding of sex, gender and sexuality today: they highlight how processes of self-reflection, self-representation and a call for recognition are vital to gaining an understanding of our gendered selves. They offer a model for understanding how our own sexual subjectivity emerges out of institutional and discursive frameworks in the twenty-first century. While the texts studied in this book have focused largely on medico-scientific frameworks of sex, gender and sexuality, they can also offer a model for thinking about other discursive and institutional frames, such as social media, educational institutions and sexual rights politics today. In light of continued attacks on LGBTQ+ rights, livelihoods and livability today, my reading of sexual-scientific life writing can show the vital importance of practices of attentive and hospitable listening and reading. Finally, sexual-scientific life writing insists on complex modes of identification, on subjects as always still emerging, on ambiguity, ambivalence, and moments in which gender and sexual identity or embodiment cannot be neatly separated or temporally fixed. This complexity of sexual-scientific life writing shows that they cannot be reduced to either stories of complicity between patient and practitioner, nor to stories of boundless transgression. Instead, the texts and textual archives studied in *Queer Livability: German Sexual Sciences and Life Writing* reveal the literary, epistemological and embodied work that goes into creating the possibilities of queer livability.

Bibliography

ARCHIVAL SOURCES

Kinsey Institute Library and Archive, Indiana University
    Magnus Hirschfeld Collection (accessed via Alexander Street Press/ProQuest)
Library of Congress, Washington D.C.
    Sigmund Freud Collection
Schwules Museum Archive and Library, Berlin
    Sammlung zum Institut für Sexualwissenschaft und Magnus Hirschfeld
Spinnboden Lesbenarchiv, Berlin

PRIMARY SOURCES

Amborn, Erich. *Und dennoch Ja zum Leben*. Schaffhausen: Verlag Meier, 1981.
Baer, K. M. "Über den Mädchenhandel." *Zeitschrift für Sexualwissenschaft* 1, no. 9 (1908): 513–28.
Baer, M. "Mädchenhandel." *Arena* 3, no. 5 (August 1908): 549–55.
Baer, M. *Der internationale Mädchenhandel*. In *Großstadt-Dokumente* 37. Berlin: Hermann Seemann Nachfolger, 1908.
Body, N. O. *Aus eines Mannes Mädchenjahren*, edited by Hermann Simon. Berlin: Edition Hentrich, 1993.
Body, N. O. *Aus eines Mannes Mädchenjahren*, edited by Hermann Simon. Berlin: Hentrich & Hentrich, 2022.
Brugman, Til. "Warenhaus der Liebe." In *Das vertippte Zebra: Lyrik und Prosa*, edited by Marion Brandt, 72–81. Berlin: Hoho, 1995.
Brunswick, Ruth Mack. "A Supplement to Freud's 'History of an Infantile Neurosis' (1928)." In *The Wolf-Man by The Wolf-Man*, edited by Muriel Gardiner, 263–307. New York: Basic Books, 1971.
Deutsch, Helene. *The Psychology of Women: A Psychoanalytic Interpretation*. Vol. 1. New York: Grune & Stratton, 1944.
Duc, Aimée. *Sind es Frauen? Roman über das dritte Geschlecht*. Berlin: Gabriele Meixner, 1976.

Elbe, Lili. *Ein Mensch wechselt sein Geschlecht: Eine Lebensbeichte*, edited by Niels Hoyer. Dresden: Carl Reissner, 1932.

Faye, Shon. *The Transgender Issue: An Argument for Justice*. London: Allen Lane / Penguin, 2021.

Freud, Sigmund. "From the History of an Infantile Neurosis (1918 [1914])." In *The Standard Edition of the Complete Psychological Works of Sigmund Freud*, translated by James Strachey, vol. 17, *1917–1919: An Infantile Neurosis and Other Works*, 1–122. London: Hogarth, 1955.

Freud, Sigmund. "Psycho-analytic Notes on an Autobiographical Account of a Case of Paranoia (Dementia Paranoides)." In *The Standard Edition of the Complete Psychological Works of Sigmund Freud*, translated by James Strachey, vol. 12, *1911–1913: The Case of Schreber, Papers on Technique and Other Works*, 1–82. London: Hogarth, 1958.

Freud, Sigmund. "Studies on Hysteria (1893–1895)." In *The Standard Edition of the Complete Psychological Works of Sigmund Freud*, translated by James Strachey, vol. 2, *1893–1895*. London: Hogarth, 1955.

Freud, Sigmund. *Three Essays on the Theory of Sexuality*. In *The Standard Edition of the Complete Psychological Works of Sigmund Freud*, translated by James Strachey, vol. 7, *1901–1905: A Case of Hysteria, Three Essays on Sexuality and Other Works*, 123–246. London: Hogarth, 1953.

Fricke, Toni. "Einiges über das Problem der Namensänderung für Transvestiten." *Die Freundin* 9 (1925): no continuous pagination. Spinnboden Lesbenarchiv, Berlin.

Gardiner, Muriel, ed. *The Wolf-Man by the Wolf-Man*. New York: Basic Books, 1971.

Gardiner, Muriel, ed. *Der Wolfsmann vom Wolfsmann*. Frankfurt am Main: Fischer, 1972.

Grune, Karl, and Paul Legband, dirs. *Aus eines Mannes Mädchenjahren*, 1919; considered lost.

Hall, Radclyffe. *The Well of Loneliness*. London: Virago, 1982 [1928].

Highsmith, Patricia. *The Price of Salt*. New York: Coward-McCann, 1952.

Hirschfeld, Magnus. *Berlins drittes Geschlecht*. In *Großstadt-Dokumente* 3. Berlin: Hermann Seemann Nachfolger, 1904.

Hirschfeld, Magnus. "Das Ergebnis der statistischen Untersuchungen über den Prozentsatz der Homosexuellen." *Jahrbuch für sexuelle Zwischenstufen* 6 (1904): 109–78.

Hirschfeld, Magnus. "Das Institut für Sexualwissenschaft." *Jahrbuch für sexuelle Zwischenstufen* 19 (1919): 51–61.

Hirschfeld, Magnus. *Die Homosexualität des Mannes und des Weibes*. Berlin: Louis Marcus Verlagsbuchhandlung, 1914.

Hirschfeld, Magnus. *Die Transvestiten: Eine Untersuchung über den erotischen Verkleidungstrieb*. Berlin: Alfred Pulvermacher, 1910.

Hirschfeld, Magnus. "Leonardo da Vinci." *Jahrbuch für sexuelle Zwischenstufen* 10 (1909–10): 421–26.

Hirschfeld, Magnus. *Psychobiologischer Fragebogen: Herausgegeben mit seinen Mitarbeitern*. Magnus Hirschfeld Collection, Kinsey Institute for Research in Sex, Gender, and Reproduction, 1930. Distributed by Alexander Street Press. https://search.alexanderstreet.com/view/work/bibliographic_entity%7Cbibliographic_details%7C2054290

Hirschfeld, Magnus. *Psychobiologischer Fragebogen.* Magnus Hirschfeld Collection, Kinsey Institute for Research in Sex, Gender, and Reproduction, 1949. Distributed by Alexander Street Press. https://search.alexanderstreet.com/view/work/bibliograp hic_entity%7Cbibliographic_details%7C2054280

Hirschfeld, Magnus. *Sexualpathologie: Ein Lehrbuch für Ärzte und Studierende.* Vol. 1, *Geschlechtliche Entwicklungsstörungen mit besonderer Berücksichtigung der Onanie.* Bonn: A. Marcus & E. Webers, 1917.

Hirschfeld, Magnus. *Sexualpathologie: Ein Lehrbuch für Ärzte und Studierende.* Vol. 2, *Sexuelle Zwischenstufen: Das männliche Weib und der weibliche Mann.* Bonn: A. Marcus & E. Webers, 1918.

Hirschfeld, Magnus. *Sexualpathologie: Ein Lehrbuch für Ärzte und Studierende.* Vol. 3, *Störungen im Sexualstoffwechsel mit besonderer Berücksichtigung der Impotenz.* Bonn: A. Marcus & E. Webers, 1920.

Hirschfeld. Magnus. *Titus-Perlen: Wissenschaftliches Sexual-Hormon-Präparat nach Vorschrift von Sanitätsrat Dr. Magnus Hirschfeld unter ständiger klinischer Kontrolle des Instituts für Sexualwissenschaft.* Berlin: Berlin-Pankow Titus Chemischpharm. Fabrik, 1931[?]. In Promonta (no. 21), Sammlung zum Institut für Sexualwissenschaft und Magnus Hirschfeld, Schwules Museum Archive and Library, Berlin.

Hirschfeld, Magnus. "Zur Methodik der Sexualwissenschaft." *Zeitschrift für Sexualwissenschaft* 1, no. 12 (1908): 45–705.

Homann, Walter. *Tagebuch einer männlichen Braut.* Hamburg: Männerschwarm Verlag, 2010.

Isherwood, Christopher. *Christopher and His Kind.* London: Eyre Methuen, 1977. Spinnboden Lesbenarchiv, Berlin.

Isherwood, Christopher. *Mr Norris Changes Trains.* London: Hogarth Press, 1952.

Killmer, E. "'Er' und 'sie' kaufen ein." *Die Freundin* 6, no. 16 (1930): no pagination. Spinnboden Lesbenarchiv, Berlin.

Kraepelin, Emil. *Clinical Psychiatry: A Textbook for Students and Physicians, Abstracted and Adapted from the 6th German Edition of Kraepelin's "Lehrbuch der Psychiatrie".* Edited by Allen Ross Diefendorf. New York: Macmillan, 1904.

Krafft-Ebing, Richard von. *Psychopathia Sexualis: Mit besonderer Berücksichtigung der conträren Sexualempfindung: Eine klinisch-forensische Studie.* 5th ed. Stuttgart: Verlag von Ferdinand Enke, 1890.

Krafft-Ebing, Richard von. *Psychopathia Sexualis, with special reference to Contrary Sexual Instinct: A Medico-Legal Study, Authorized Translation of the Seventh Enlarged and Revised German Edition.* Translated by Charles Gilbert Chaddock. Philadelphia: F. A. Davis, 1894.

Liebetreu, O. *Urningsliebe: Aus den Erlebnissen einer gleichgeschlechtlich Liebenden.* Leipzig: Fickers, 1930.

May, Joe, dir. *Asphalt.* 1929; London: Eureka, 2005. DVD.

Messter, Oskar, dir. *Aus eines Mannes Mädchenzeit,* 1913; Deutsche Kinemathek.

Nordau, Max. *Entartung.* 2 vols. Berlin: C. Duncker, 1893.

Obholzer, Karin. *Gespräche mit dem Wolfsmann: Eine Psychoanalyse und die Folgen.* Hamburg: Rowohlt, 1980.

Ostwald, Hans. "In der Passage." *Das neue Magazin* 14 (October 1904): 438–42.

Panizza, Oskar. *"Der operirte Jud'."* In *Der Korsettenfritz: Gesammelte Erzählungen,* edited by Bernd Mattheus. Munich: Matthes & Seitz, 1981.

Pheby, Alex. *Playthings*. Norwich: Galley Beggar Press, 2015.
Reichsschrifttumskammer. *Liste des schädlichen und unerwünschten Schrifttums*. Berlin: Reichsdruckerei, 1935.
Schreber, Daniel Paul. *Denkwürdigkeiten eines Nervenkranken*. Berlin: Kadmos, [1903] 2003.
Schreber, Daniel Paul. *Memoirs of My Nervous Illness*. Translated by Ida MacAlpine and Richard Hunter. London: William Dawson, 1955.
Schreber, Daniel Paul. *Memoirs of My Nervous Illness*. Translated by Ida MacAlpine and Richard A. Hunter. Cambridge, MA: Harvard University Press, 1988.
Schreber, Daniel Paul. *Memoirs of My Nervous Illness*. Translated and edited by Ida MacAlpine and Richard A. Hunter. New York: New York Review Books, 2000.
Staatliche Landesfachstelle für Volksbüchereiwesen Sachsen. "Richtlinien für die Bestandsprüfung in den Volksbüchereien Sachsens." *Die Bücherei: Zeitschrift der Reichsstelle für das Volksbüchereiwesen* 2, no. 6 (1935): 279–80.
Steindamm, Johannes. *Beiträge zur Warenhausfrage*. Berlin: E. Ebering, 1904.
Thiele, Adolf. "Kann Homosexualität strafbar sein?" *Sozialistische Monatshefte* 24 (December 1909): 1560–67.

SECONDARY SOURCES

Abraham, Nicolas, and Maria Torok. *The Wolf Man's Magic Word: A Cryptonymy*. Translated by Nicholas Rand. Minneapolis: University of Minnesota Press, 1986.
Adamson, Jane. "Against Tidiness: Literature and/versus Moral Philosophy." In *Renegotiating Ethics in Literature, Philosophy and Theory*, edited by Jane Adamson, Richard Freadman, and David Parker, 84–110. Cambridge: Cambridge University Press, 1998.
AG Queer Studies, ed. *Verqueerte Verhältnisse: Intersektionale, ökonomiekritische und strategische Interventionen*. Berlin: Männerschwarm Verlag, 2009.
Ahmed, Sara. "Orientations: Toward a Queer Phenomenology." *GLQ* 12, no. 4 (2006): 543–74. https://doi.org/10.1215/10642684-2006-002
Allamand, Carole. "The Autobiographical Pact, Forty-Five Years Later." *European Journal of Life Writing* 7 (2018): CP51–CP56. https://doi.org/10.5463/ejlw.7.258
Althusser, Louis. "Ideology and Ideological State Apparatuses." In *Lenin and Philosophy and Other Essays*, translated by Ben Brewster, 127–36. New York: Monthly Review Press, 1972.
Armstrong, Aurelia. "Agency Reconfigured: Narrative Continuities and Connective Transformations." *Contretemps* 3 (July 2002): 42–53.
Attridge, Derek. *Reading and Responsibility: Deconstruction's Traces*. Edinburgh: Edinburgh University Press, 2010.
Baker, John H. "Light and Darkness in Landscape Paintings by the Wolf Man." *American Imago* 76, no. 4 (Winter 2019): 485–512. https://doi.org/10.1353/aim.2019.0037
Bauer, Heike. *English Literary Sexology: Translations of Inversion, 1860–1930*. Basingstoke: Palgrave Macmillan, 2009.
Bauer, Heike. *The Hirschfeld Archives: Violence, Death, and Modern Queer Culture*. Philadelphia: Temple University Press, 2017.

Bauer, Heike, Melina Pappademos, Katie Sutton, and Jennifer Tucker, eds. "The Visual Archive of Sexology." Special issue, *Radical History Review* 142, no. 1 (January 2022).

Benjamin, Walter. "Critique of Violence." In *Selected Writings*, vol. 1, *1913–1926*, edited by Michael W. Jennings, 236–52. Cambridge, MA: Belknap Press of Harvard University Press, 1996.

Bode, Frauke. "Paratext." In *Handbook of Autobiography/Autofiction*, vol. 1, *Theory and Concepts*, edited by Martina Wagner-Egelhaaf, 364–71. Berlin: de Gruyter, 2018.

Booth, Wayne. *The Company We Keep: An Ethics of Fiction*. Berkeley: University of California Press, 1988.

Borch-Jacobsen, Mikkel, and Sonu Shamdasani. *The Freud Files: An Inquiry into the History of Psychoanalysis*. Cambridge: Cambridge University Press, 2011.

Bourdieu, Pierre. *Language and Symbolic Power*. Translated by Gino Raymond and Matthew Adamson. Cambridge, MA: Harvard University Press, 1991.

Braun, Christina von. "'Der Jude' und 'das Weib': Zwei Stereotypen des 'Anderen' in der Moderne." In *Deutsch-jüdische Geschichte im 19. und 20. Jahrhundert*, edited by Ludger Heid and Joachim H. Knoll, 289–322. Bonn: Burg, 1992.

Breger, Louis. "Daniel Paul Schreber: From Male into Female." *Journal of the American Academy of Psychoanalysis* 6, no. 2 (April 1978): 123–56. https://doi.org/10.15 21/jaap.1.1978.6.2.123

Briesen, Detlef. *Warenhaus, Massenkonsum und Sozialmoral*. Frankfurt am Main: Campus Verlag, 2001.

Brooks, Peter. "Fictions of the Wolfman: Freud and Narrative Understanding." *Diacritics* 9, no. 1 (Spring 1979): 71–81. https://doi.org/10.2307/464701

Brown, Dennis. *The Modernist Self in Twentieth-Century English Literature: A Study in Self-Fragmentation*. London: Palgrave Macmillan, 1989.

Bull, Sarah. "More Than a Case of Mistaken Identity: Adult Entertainment and the Making of Early Sexology." *History of Human Sciences* 34, no. 1 (February 2021): 10–39. https://doi.org/10.1177/0952695120903954

Butler, Judith. *Bodies That Matter: On the Discursive Limits of "Sex"*. New York: Routledge, 1993.

Butler, Judith. *Excitable Speech: A Politics of the Performative*. London: Routledge, 1997.

Butler, Judith. *Frames of War: When Is Life Grievable?* London: Verso, 2009.

Butler, Judith. *Gender Trouble: Feminism and the Subversion of Identity*. New York: Routledge, 1990.

Butler, Judith. *Giving an Account of Oneself*. New York: Fordham University Press, 2005.

Butler, Judith. "Performative Acts and Gender Constitution: An Essay in Phenomenology and Feminist Theory." *Theatre Journal* 40, no. 4 (1988): 519–31. https://doi.org /10.2307/3207893

Butler, Judith. *Precarious Life*. London: Verso, 2000.

Butler, Judith. *Undoing Gender*. London: Routledge, 2004.

Canetti, Elias. *Crowds and Power*. Translated by Carol Stewart. New York: Continuum, 1981.

Canning, Kathleen. "Claiming Citizenship: Suffrage and Subjectivity in Germany after the First World War." In *Weimar Publics / Weimar Subjects: Rethinking the Political Culture of Germany in the 1920s*, edited by Kathleen Canning, Kerstin Barndt, and Kristin McGuire, 116–37. New York: Berghahn Books, 2010.

Colvin, Sarah. "Leaning In: Why and How I Still Study the German." *German Life and Letters* 69, no. 1 (January 2016): 123–41. https://doi.org/10.1111/glal.12111

Connor, Steven. "The Modern Auditory I." In *Rewriting the Self: Histories from the Renaissance to the Present*, edited by Roy Porter, 203–23. London: Routledge, 1997.

Crozier, Ivan. "Introduction: Havelock Ellis, John Addington Symonds and the Construction of Sexual Inversion." In *Sexual Inversion: A Critical Edition*, edited by Ivan Crozier, 1–95. Basingstoke: Palgrave Macmillan, 2008.

Crozier, Ivan. "Pillow Talk: Credibility, Trust and the Sexological Case History." *History of Science* 46, no. 4 (December 2008): 375–404. https://doi.org/10.1177/00732 7530804600401

Cryle, Peter, and Elizabeth Stephens. *Normality: A Critical Genealogy*. Chicago: University of Chicago Press, 2017.

Damousi, Joy, Birgit Lang, and Katie Sutton, eds., *Case Studies and the Dissemination of Knowledge*, Abingdon: Routledge, 2015.

Davidson, Arnold. *The Emergence of Sexuality: Historical Epistemology and the Formation of Concepts*. Cambridge, MA: Harvard University Press, 2001.

Davis, Colin. "Derrida's Haunted Subjects." In *Haunted Subjects: Deconstruction, Psychoanalysis and the Return of the Dead*, 128–50. Basingstoke: Palgrave Macmillan, 2007.

Davis, Colin. "Speaking with the Dead: De Man, Levinas, Agamben." In *Haunted Subjects: Deconstruction, Psychoanalysis and the Return of the Dead*, 111–27. Basingstoke: Palgrave Macmillan, 2007.

Davis, Whitney. *Dreaming the Dream of the Wolves: Homosexuality, Interpretation, and Freud's "Wolf Man"*. Bloomington: Indiana University Press, 1995.

Deleuze, Gilles, and Félix Guattari. *Anti-Oedipus: Capitalism and Schizophrenia*. Translated by Robert Hurley, Mark Seem, and Helen R. Lane. London: Continuum, 2004.

Derrida, Jacques. "*Fors*: The Anglish Words of Nicolas Abraham and Maria Torok." Translated by Barbara Johnson. In Nicolas Abraham and Maria Torok, *The Wolf Man's Magic Word: A Cryptonymy*, translated by Nicholas Rand, xi–xlviii. Minneapolis: University of Minnesota Press, 1986.

Derrida, Jacques. *Of Hospitality: Anne Dufourmantelle Invites Jacques Derrida to Respond*. Translated by Rachel Bowlby. Stanford: Stanford University Press, 2000.

Deutsch, Helene. *Confrontations with Myself: An Epilogue*. New York: Norton, 1973.

Dietrich, Michael R. "Of Moths and Men: Theo Lang and the Persistence of Richard Goldschmidt's Theory of Homosexuality, 1916–1960." *History and Philosophy of the Life Sciences* 22, no. 2 (2000): 219–47. http://www.jstor.org/stable/23332244

Dimock, George. "Anna and the Wolf-Man: Rewriting Freud's Case History." *Representations*, no. 50 (Spring 1995): 53–75. https://www.jstor.org/stable/2928725

Doan, Laura. *Disturbing Practices: History, Sexuality, and Women's Experience of Modern War*. Chicago: University of Chicago Press, 2013.

Dobler, Jens. "Nachwort." In Walter Homann, *Tagebuch einer männlichen Braut*, 154–75. Hamburg: Männerschwarm, 2010.

Dolezal, Luna. "Disability as Malleability: The Prosthetic Metaphor, Merleau-Ponty and the Case of Aimee Mullins." In *Medial Bodies between Fiction and Faction: Reinventing Corporeality*, edited by Denise Butnaru, 123–45. Bielefeld: Transcript, 2020.

Dolezal, Luna. "The Metaphors of Commercial Surrogacy: Rethinking the Materiality of Hospitality through Pregnant Embodiment." In *New Feminist Perspectives on Embodiment*, edited by Clara Fischer and Luna Dolezal, 221–44. London: Palgrave Macmillan, 2018.

Eakin, Paul John. "Foreword." In *On Autobiography*, translated by Katherine Leary, edited by Paul John Eakin, vii–xxviii. Minneapolis: University of Minnesota Press, 1989.

Emmanuel, Levinas. *Entre Nous: Thinking-of-the-Other*. Translated by Michael B. Smith and Barbara Harshav. New York: Columbia University Press, 1998.

Evans, Jennifer, and Elissa Mailänder. "Cross-Dressing, Male Intimacy and the Violence of Transgression in Third Reich Photography." *German History* 38, no. 2 (June 2020): 25–43. https://doi.org/10.1093/gerhis/ghaa031

Felski, Rita. *The Gender of Modernity*. Cambridge, MA: Harvard University Press, 1995.

Fish, Stanley. *Doing What Comes Naturally: Change, Rhetoric, and the Practice of Theory in Literary and Legal Studies*. Oxford: Clarendon Press, 1989.

Fisher, Kate, and Jana Funke. "British Sexual Science beyond the Medical: Cross-Disciplinary, Cross-Historical, and Cross-Cultural Translations." In *Sexology and Translation: Cultural and Scientific Encounters across the Modern World*, edited by Heike Bauer, 95–114. Philadelphia: Temple University Press, 2015.

Foote, Stephanie. "Afterword: Ann Aldrich and Lesbian Writing in the Fifties." In Ann Aldrich, *We Walk Alone*, edited by Marijane Meaker, 169–92. New York: First Feminist Press, 2006.

Forrester, John. *Dispatches from the Freud Wars: Psychoanalysis and Its Passions*. Cambridge, MA: Harvard University Press, 1997.

Forrester, John. "If P, Then What? Thinking in Cases." *History of Human Sciences* 9, no. 3 (August 1996): 1–25. https://doi.org/10.1177/095269519600900301

Foucault, Michel. "About the Beginnings of the Hermeneutics of the Self: Two Lectures at Dartmouth." *Political Theory* 21, no. 2 (May 1993): 198–227. https://www-jstor-org.uoelibrary.idm.oclc.org/stable/191814

Foucault, Michel. *The History of Sexuality*. Vol. 1, *The Will to Knowledge*. Translated by Robert Hurley. London: Penguin, 1998.

Foucault, Michel. *Politics, Philosophy, Culture: Interviews and Other Writings, 1977–1984*. Edited by Lawrence D. Kritzman. New York: Routledge, 1988.

Foucault, Michel. "What Is an Author?" In *Modernity and Its Discontents*, edited by James L. Marsh, John D. Caputo, and Merold Westphal, 299–314. New York: Fordham University Press, 1992 [1969].

Foucault, Michel. *Herculine Barbin: Being the Recently Discovered Memoirs of a Nineteenth Century French Hermaphrodite*. Translated by Richard McDougall. New York City: Pantheon, 1980.

Frankland, Graham. *Freud's Literary Culture*. Cambridge: Cambridge University Press, 2006.

Freadman, Richard. "Ethics, Autobiography and the Will: Stephen Spender's *World within World*." In *The Ethics in Literature*, edited by Andrew Hadfield, Dominic Rainsford, and Tim Woods, 17–37. London: Macmillan, 1999.

Fuechtner, Veronika. *Berlin Psychoanalytic: Psychoanalysis and Culture in Weimar Republic Germany and Beyond*. Berkeley: University of California Press, 2011.

Funke, Jana. "The Case of Karl M.[artha] Baer: Narrating 'Uncertain' Sex." In *Sex, Gender and Time in Fiction and Culture*, edited by Ben Davies and Jana Funke, 132–53. London: Palgrave Macmillan, 2011.

Garber, Marjorie. *Vested Interests: Cross-Dressing and Cultural Anxiety*. New York: Routledge, 1992.

Gay, Peter. *Modernism: The Lure of Heresy*. London: Norton, 2008.

Geller, Jay. "Freud, Blüher, and the *Secessio Inversa*: *Männerbünde*, Homosexuality, and Freud's Theory of Cultural Formation." In *Queer Theory and the Jewish Question*, edited by Daniel Boyarin, Daniel Itzkovitz, and Ann Pellegrini, 90–120. New York: Columbia University Press, 2003.

Genette, Gérard. *Paratexts: Threshold of Interpretation*. Translated by Jane E. Lewin. Cambridge: Cambridge University Press, 1997.

Genette, Gérard, and Marie Maclean. "Introduction to the Paratext." *New Literary History* 22, no. 2 (Spring 1991): 261–72. https://www.jstor.org/stable/469037

Gilman, Sander L. *Freud, Race, and Gender*. Princeton, NJ: Princeton University Press, 1993.

Gilman, Sander L. "Jews and Mental Illness: Medical Metaphors, Anti-Semitism, and the Jewish Response." *Journal of the History of the Behavioral Sciences* 20, no. 2 (April 1984): 150–59. https://doi.org/10.1002/1520-6696(198404)20:2%3C150::A ID-JHBS2300200204%3E3.0.CO;2-0

Gilman, Sander L. *The Jew's Body*. London: Routledge, 1991.

Gilman, Sander L. "Whose Body Is It, Anyway? Hermaphrodites, Gays, and Jews in N. O. Body's Germany." In N. O. Body, *Memoirs of a Man's Maiden Years*, translated by Deborah Simon, vii–xxiv. Philadelphia: University of Pennsylvania Press, 2006.

Gilman, Sander L., Jutta Birmele, Jay Geller, and Valerie D. Greenberg, eds. *Reading Freud's Reading*. London: New York University, 1994.

Gilmore, Leigh. "Learning from Fakes: Memoir, Confessional Ethics, and the Limits of Genre." In *Contemporary Trauma Narratives: Liminality and the Ethics of Form*, edited by Susana Onega and Jean-Michel Ganteau, 21–35. Abingdon: Routledge, 2014.

Günther, Dagmar. "'And Now for Something Completely Different': Prolegomena zur Autobiographie als Quelle der Geschichtswissenschaft." *Historische Zeitschrift* 272, no. 1 (2001): 25–61. https://doi.org/10.1524/hzhz.2001.272.jg.25

Hacking, Ian. "The Looping Effects of Human Kinds." In *Causal Cognition: A Multidisciplinary Debate*, edited by Dan Sperber, David Premack, and Ann James Premack, 351–94. Oxford: Oxford University Press, 1995.

Hadar, David. "The Wolf Man's Novel." *American Imago* 69, no. 4 (Winter 2012): 559–78. https://www.jstor.org/stable/26305037

Haeberle, Erwin J. Introduction to Magnus Hirschfeld, *Die Homosexualität des Mannes und des Weibes*, v–xxv. Berlin: de Gruyter, 1984.

Haraway, Donna. "A Cyborg Manifesto: Science, Technology, and Socialist-Feminism in the Late 20th Century." In *The International Handbook of Virtual Learning Environments*, edited by Joel Weiss, Jason Nolan, Jeremy Hunsinger, and Peter Trifonas, 117–58. New York: Springer, 2006.

Haraway, Donna. "Situated Knowledges: The Science Question in Feminism and the Privilege of Partial Perspective." *Feminist Studies* 14, no. 3 (Fall 1988): 575–99. https://doi.org/10.2307/3178066

Haraway, Donna. *Staying with the Trouble: Making Kin in the Chthulucene*. Durham, NC: Duke University Press, 2016.

Heaney, Emma. *The New Woman: Literary Modernism, Queer Theory, and the Trans Feminine Allegory*. Evanston, IL: Northwestern University Press, 2017.

Herrn, Rainer. *Der Liebe und dem Leid: Das Institut für Sexualwissenschaft 1919–1933*. Berlin: Suhrkamp 2022.

Herrn, Rainer. "Ge- und erlebte Vielfalt—Sexuelle Zwischenstufen im Institut für Sexualwissenschaft." *Sexuologie* 20, nos. 1–2 (2013): 6–14.

Herrn, Rainer. "Outside in—inside Out: Topografie, Architektur und Funktionen des Instituts für Sexualwissenschaft zwischen Wahrnehmungen und Imaginationen." In *Metropolenzauber: Sexuelle Moderne und urbaner Wahn*, edited by Gabriele Dietze and Dorothea Dornhof, 25–56. Vienna: Böhlau, 2014.

Herrn, Rainer. *Schnittmuster des Geschlechts: Transvestitismus und Transsexualität in der frühen Sexualwissenschaft*. Gießen: Psychosozial-Verlag, 2005.

Herrn, Rainer. "Wie die Traumdeutung durch die Türritze einer geschlossenen Anstalt sickert: Zum Umgang mit der Psychoanalyse an der Psychiatrischen und Nervenklinik der Charité." In *"Heroische Therapien": Die deutsche Psychiatrie im internationalen Vergleich*, edited by Hans-Walter Schmuhl and Volker Roelcke, 69–99. Göttingen: Wallstein, 2013.

Herrn, Rainer, Michael Thomas Taylor, and Annette F. Timm. "Magnus Hirschfeld's Institute for Sexual Science: A Visual Sourcebook." In *Not Straight from Germany: Sexual Publics and Sexual Citizenship since Magnus Hirschfeld*, edited by Michael Thomas Taylor, Annette F. Timm, and Rainer Herrn, 37–79. Ann Arbor: University of Michigan Press, 2017.

Hill, Darryl B. "Sexuality and Gender in Hirschfeld's *Die Transvestiten*: A Case of the 'Elusive Evidence of the Ordinary.'" *Journal of the History of Sexuality* 14, no. 3 (July 2005): 316–32. https://doi.org/10.1353/sex.2006.0023

Hochschild, Arlie Russell. *The Managed Heart: Commercialization of Human Feeling*. Berkeley: University of California Press, 2012 [1983].

Horvat, Ana, Orly Lael Netzer, Sarah McRae, and Julie Rak. "Unfixing the Prefix in Life-Writing Studies: Trans, Transmedia, Transnational." *Auto/biography Studies* 34, no. 1 (May 2019): 1–17. https://doi.org/10.1080/08989575.2019.1548084

Hulverscheidt, Marion. "Zu den medizinhistorischen Aspekten der Lebensgeschichte von Karl Martha Baer oder What a doctor could tell about Nobody." In N. O. Body, *Aus eines Mannes Mädchenjahren*, edited by Hermann Simon, 167–99. Berlin: Hentrich & Hentrich, 2022.

International Holocaust Remembrance Alliance. "Memo on Spelling Antisemitism." Accessed March 24, 2021. https://www.holocaustremembrance.com/antisemitism/spelling-antisemitism

Iskin, Ruth E. *The Poster: Art, Advertising, Design, and Collecting, 1860–1900s.* Hanover, NH: Dartmouth College Press, 2014.

Jacobs, Joela. "Speaking the Non-human: Plants, Animals, and Marginalized humans in Literary Grotesques from Oskar Panizza to Franz Kafka." PhD diss., University of Chicago, 2014.

Jazbinsek, Dietmar. "Der internationale Mädchenhandel: Biographie eines sozialen Problems." WZB Discussion Paper, No. FS II 02-501, Wissenschaftszentrum Berlin für Sozialforschung (2002).

Jazbinsek, Dietmar, and Ralf Thies. "Großstadt-Dokumente: Metropolenforschung im Berlin der Jahrhundertwende." *Schriftenreihe der Forschungsgruppe Metropolenforschung des Forschungsschwerpunkts Technik-Arbeit-Umwelt am Wissenschaftszentrum für Sozialforschung* 98 (1997).

Kahan, Benjamin. *The Book of Minor Perverts: Sexology, Etiology, and the Emergences of Sexuality.* Chicago: University of Chicago Press, 2019.

Kahan, Benjamin. "What Is Sexual Modernity?" Print Plus platform of *Modernism/Modernity* 1, no. 3 (October 2016). https://doi.org/10.26597/mod.0015

Kant, Immanuel. "What Is Enlightenment?" In *Sources of the Western Tradition*, 3rd ed, vol. 2, edited by Marvin Perry et al., 56–57. Boston: Houghton Mifflin, 1995.

Kemp, Jonathan. *The Penetrated Male.* New York: punctum books, 2013.

Kennedy, Hubert. "Karl Heinrich Ulrichs: First Theorist of Homosexuality." In *Science and Homosexualities*, edited by Vernon Rosario, 26–45. New York: Routledge, 1997.

King, Greg, and Penny Wilson. *The Fate of the Romanovs.* Hoboken, NJ: John Wiley, 2003.

Kofman, Sarah. *Freud and Fiction.* Cambridge: Polity Press, 1991.

Kolkenbrock, Marie. *Stereotype and Destiny in Arthur Schnitzler's Prose: Five Psycho-Sociological Readings.* London: Bloomsbury, 2018.

Kraß, Andreas, ed. *Queer denken: Gegen die Ordnung der Sexualität.* Frankfurt am Main: Suhrkamp, 2003.

Kraß, Andreas, ed. *Queer Studies in Deutschland: Interdisziplinäre Beiträge zur kritischen Heteronormativitätsforschung.* Berlin: Frankfurter Kulturwissenschaftliche Beiträge, 2009.

Lacan, Jacques. *The Seminar of Jacques Lacan.* Vol. 3, *The Psychoses.* Translated by Russell Grigg, edited by Jacques-Alain Miller. New York: Norton, 1993.

Lang, Birgit. "The Shifting Case of Masochism: Leopold von Sacher-Masoch's *Venus im Pelz* (1870)." In *A History of the Case Study: Sexology, Psychoanalysis, Literature*, edited by Birgit Lang, Joy Damousi, and Alison Lewis, 19–54. Manchester: Manchester University Press, 2017.

Lang, Birgit, Joy Damousi, and Alison Lewis, eds. *A History of the Case Study: Sexology, Psychoanalysis, Literature.* Manchester: Manchester University Press, 2017.

Lang, Birgit, and Katie Sutton. "The Aesthetics of Sexual Ethics: *Geschlecht und Gesellschaft* and Middle-Class Sexual Modernity in *Fin-de-Siècle* Germany."

Oxford German Studies 44, no. 2 (June 2015): 177–98. https://doi.org/10.1179/007
8719115Z.00000000083

Lang, Birgit, and Katie Sutton. "The Queer Cases of Psychoanalysis: Rethinking the Scientific Study of Homosexuality, 1890s–1920s." *German History* 34, no. 3 (September 2016): 419–44. https://doi.org/10.1093/gerhis/ghw038

Lauretis, Teresa de. "Habit Changes. Response." In *Feminism Meets Queer Theory*, edited by Elizabeth Weed and Naomi Schor, 315–34. Bloomington: Indiana University Press, 1997.

Lejeune, Philippe. "The Autobiographical Pact." In *On Autobiography*, translated by Katherine Leary, edited by Paul John Eakin, 3–30. Minneapolis: University of Minnesota Press, 1989.

Leng, Kirsten. "Anna Rüling, Michel Foucault, and the 'Tactical Polyvalence' of the Female Homosexual." In *After the History of Sexuality: German Genealogies with and beyond Foucault*, edited by Scott Spector, Helmut Puff, and Dagmar Herzog, 95–108. Oxford: Berghahn Books, 2012.

Lerner, Paul. *The Consuming Temple: Jews, Department Stores, and the Consumer Revolution in Germany, 1880—1940*. Ithaca, NY: Cornell University Press, 2015.

Linge, Ina. "Sexology, Popular Science and Queer History in Anders als die Andern (Different from the Others)." *Gender and History* 30, no. 3 (2018): 595–610. https://doi.org/10.1111/1468-0424.12381

Linge, Ina. "The Potency of the Butterfly: The Reception of Richard B. Goldschmidt's Animal Experiments in German Sexology around 1920." *History of Human Sciences* 34, no. 1 (February 2021): 40–70. https://doi.org/10.1177/095269511989
0545

Linton, Anne E. *Unmaking Sex: The Gender Outlaws of Nineteenth-Century France*. Cambridge: Cambridge University Press, 2022.

Looby, Christopher. "The Literariness of Sexuality: Or, How to Do the (Literary) History of (American) Sexuality." *American Literary History* 25, no. 4 (Winter 2013): 841–54. https://doi.org/10.1093/alh/ajt040

Lothane, Zvi. *In Defense of Schreber: Soul Murder and Psychiatry*. Hillsdale, NJ: Analytic Press, 1992.

Loughman, Celeste. "Voices of the Wolf Man: The Wolf Man as Autobiographer." *Psychoanalytic Review* 71, no. 2 (Summer 1984): 211–25.

Love, Heather. "Close but Not Deep: Literary Ethics and the Descriptive Turn." *New Literary History* 41, no. 2 (Spring 2010): 371–91. https://doi.org/10.1353/nlh.2010
.0007

Love, Heather. "Doing Being Deviant: Deviance Studies, Description, and the Queer Ordinary." *differences* 26, no. 1 (May 2015): 74–95. https://doi.org/10.1215/104073
91-2880609

Love, Heather. *Feeling Backward: Loss and the Politics of Queer History*. Cambridge, MA: Harvard University Press, 2007.

MagShamhráin, Rachel. "The Ambivalence of the Department Store Kleptomaniac: On the Juridico-Medical Treatment of Cases of Middle-Class Female Theft around 1900." In *The Berlin Department Store: History and Discourse*, edited by Godela Weiss-Sussex and Ulrike Zitzlsperger, 63–91. Frankfurt am Main: Peter Lang, 2013.

Mahalel, Anat Tzur. "The Wolf Man's Glückshaube: Rereading Sergei Pankejeff's Memoir." *Journal of the American Psychoanalytic Association* 67, no. 5 (October 2019): 789–814. https://doi.org/10.1177/0003065119885880

Mak, Geertje. *Doubting Sex: Inscriptions, Bodies and Selves in Nineteenth-Century Hermaphrodite Case Histories*. Manchester: Manchester University Press, 2012.

Man, Paul de. "Autobiography as De-facement." *MLN* 94, no. 5 (December 1979): 919–30. https://www.jstor.org/stable/2906560

Mancini, Elena. *Magnus Hirschfeld and the Quest for Sexual Freedom: A History of the First International Sexual Freedom Movement*. New York: Palgrave Macmillan, 2010.

Manion, Jen. *Female Husbands: A Trans History*. Cambridge: University of Cambridge Press, 2020.

Marcus, Laura, and Ankhi Mukherjee, eds. *A Concise Companion to Psychoanalysis, Literature, and Culture*. Oxford: Wiley Blackwell, 2014.

Marhoefer, Laurie. *Racism and the Making of Gay Rights: A Sexologist, His Student, and the Empire of Queer Love*. London: University of Toronto Press, 2022.

Martin, Biddy. "Extraordinary Homosexuals and the Fear of Being Ordinary." *differences* 6, nos. 2–3 (Summer–Fall 1994): 100–125. https://doi.org/10.1215/10407391-6-2-3-100

Matysik, Tracie. "Beyond Freedom: A Return to Subjectivity in the History of Sexuality." In *After the History of Sexuality: German Genealogies with and beyond Foucault*, edited by Scott Spector, Helmut Puff, and Dagmar Herzog, 185–201. Oxford: Berghahn Books, 2012.

McNay, Lois. *Gender and Agency: Reconfiguring the Subject in Feminist and Social Theory*. Cambridge: Polity Press, 2000.

Meyerowitz, Joanne. "Thinking Sex with an Androgyne." *GLQ* 17, no. 1 (2010): 97–105. muse.jhu.edu/article/409154

Miller, J. Hillis. "The Critic as Host." *Critical Inquiry* 3, no. 3 (Spring 1977): 439–47. https://www.jstor.org/stable/1342933

Mitchell, David T., and Sharon L. Snyder. *Narrative Prosthesis: Disability and the Dependencies of Discourse*. Ann Arbor: Michigan University Press, 2000.

Mitchell, David T., and Sharon Snyder L. "Narrative Prosthesis." In *The Disability Studies Reader*, 4th ed., edited by Lennard J. Davis, 222–35. London: Routledge, 2013.

Mitchell, Juliet. *Mad Men and Medusas: Reclaiming Hysteria*. New York: Basic Books, 2000.

Morton, Timothy. *Ecology without Nature: Rethinking Environmental Aesthetics*. Cambridge, MA: Harvard University Press, 2007.

Mosse, George L. *Nationalism and Sexuality: Middle-Class Morality and Sexual Norms in Modern Europe*. Madison: University of Wisconsin Press, 1988.

Mottier, Véronique. "Sexuality and Sexology: Michel Foucault." In *Politics of Sexuality: Identity, Gender, Citizenship*, edited by Terrell Carver and Véronique Mottier, 113–23. London: Routledge, 1998.

Müller, Klaus. *Aber in meinem Herzen sprach eine Stimme so laut: Homosexuelle Autobiographien und medizinische Pathographien im neunzehnten Jahrhundert*. Berlin: Rosa Winkel, 1991.

Namaste, Viviane K. *Invisible Lives: The Erasure of Transsexual and Transgendered People*. Chicago: University of Chicago Press, 2000.

Niederland, William. *The Schreber Case: Psychoanalytic Profile of a Paranoid Personality*. Hillsdale, NJ: Analytic Press, 1984.

Nolte, Karen. *Gelebte Hysterie: Erfahrung, Eigensinn und psychiatrische Diskurse im Anstaltsalltag um 1900*. Frankfurt am Main: Campus, 2003.

Nussbaum, Martha. "Exactly and Responsibly: A Defense of Ethical Criticism." *Philosophy and Literature* 22, no. 2 (October 1998): 343–65. https://doi.org/10.1353/phl.1998.0047

Nussbaum, Martha. *Love's Knowledge: Essays on Philosophy and Literature*. Oxford: Oxford University Press, 1990.

O'Donnell, Mike, ed. *Structure and Agency*. London: Sage, 2010.

Oosterhuis, Harry. "Sexual Modernity in the Works of Richard von Krafft-Ebing and Albert Moll." *Medical History* 56, no. 2 (2012): 133–55. https://doi.org/10.1017/mdh.2011.30

Oosterhuis, Harry. *Stepchildren of Nature: Krafft-Ebing, Psychiatry, and the Making of Sexual Identity*. Chicago: University of Chicago Press, 2000.

Peters, Kathrin. "Anatomy Is Sublime: The Photographic Activity of Wilhelm von Gloeden and Magnus Hirschfeld." In *Not Straight from Germany: Sexual Publics and Sexual Citizenship since Magnus Hirschfeld*, edited by Michael Thomas Taylor, Annette F. Timm, and Rainer Herrn, 170–90. Ann Arbor: University of Michigan Press, 2017.

Peters, Kathrin. *Rätselbilder des Geschlechts: Körperwissen und Medialität um 1900*. Kempten: Diaphanes, 2010.

Pick, Daniel. "Stories of the Eye." In *Rewriting the Self: Histories from the Renaissance to the Present*, edited by Roy Porter, 186–99. London: Routledge, 1997.

Plett, Konstanze. "N. O. Body im Recht." In N. O. Body, *Aus eines Mannes Mädchenjahren*, edited by Hermann Simon, 201-218. Berlin: Hentrich & Hentrich, 2022.

Plötz, Kirsten. *Einsame Freundinnen: Lesbisches Leben während der zwanziger Jahre in der Provinz*. Hamburg: MännerschwarmSkript, 1999.

Porter, Roy. "The Patient's View: Doing the History of Medicine from Below." *Theory and Society* 14, no. 2 (1985): 175–98.

Posner, Richard A. "Against Ethical Criticism." *Philosophy and Literature* 21, no. 1 (April 1997): 1–27. https://doi.org/10.1353/phl.1997.0010

Pretsell, Douglas. "The Evolution of the Questionnaire in German Sexual Science: A Methodological Narrative." *History of Science* 58, no. 3 (2020): 326–49.

Pretzel, Andreas. *NS-Opfer unter Vorbehalt: Homosexuelle Männer in Berlin nach 1945*. Münster: LIT Verlag, 2002.

Prickett, David James. "Magnus Hirschfeld and the Photographic (Re)invention of the 'Third Sex.'" In *Visual Culture in Twentieth-Century Germany: Text as Spectacle*, edited by Gail Finney, 177–99. Bloomington: Indiana University Press, 2006.

Prosser, Jay. *Second Skins: The Body Narratives of Transsexuality*. New York: Columbia University Press, 1998.

Riley, Denise. *The Words of Selves: Identification Solidarity Irony*. Stanford: Stanford University Press, 2000.

Roazen, Paul. *Helene Deutsch: A Psychoanalyst's Life*. London: Routledge, 2019 [1985].

Rose, Nikolas. "Assembling the Modern Self." In *Rewriting the Self: Histories from the Renaissance to the Present*, edited by Roy Porter, 224–48. London: Routledge, 1997.

Rowe, Dorothy. *Representing Berlin: Sexuality and the City in Imperial and Weimar Germany*. Aldershot: Ashgate, 2003.

Rubin, Gayle. "Geologies of Queer Studies: It's Déjà Vu All over Again." In *Deviations: A Gayle Rubin Reader*, 347–56. Durham, NC: Duke University Press, 2011.

Runte, Annette. *Biographische Operationen: Diskurse der Transsexualität*. Munich: W. Fink, 1996.

Salamon, Gayle. *Assuming A Body: Transgender and Rhetorics of Materiality*. New York: Columbia University Press, 2010.

Sandford, Stella. "From *Geschlechtstrieb* to *Sexualtrieb*: The Originality of Freud's Conception of Sexuality." In *The Oxford Handbook of Philosophy and Psychoanalysis*, edited by Richard G.T. Gipps and Michael Lacewing. Oxford: Oxford University Press, 2019.

Santner, Eric L. *My Own Private Germany: Daniel Paul Schreber's Secret History of Modernity*. Princeton, NJ: Princeton University Press, 1996.

Schader, Heike. *Virile, Vamps und wilde Veilchen: Sexualität, Begehren und Erotik in den Zeitschriften homosexueller Frauen im Berlin der 1920er Jahre*. Sulzbach/Taunus: Helmer, 2004.

Schaffner, Anna Katharina. *Modernism and Perversion: Sexual Deviance in Sexology and Literature, 1850–1930*. Basingstoke: Palgrave Macmillan, 2012.

Schatzman, Morton. *Soul Murder: Persecution in the Family*. New York: Random House, 1973.

Schmidt, Erika. "Muriel Gardiner and the Wolf Man: Preserving a Legacy." *American Imago* 76, no. 4 (Winter 2019): 513–31. https://doi.org/10.1353/aim.2019.0038

Schmidt, Nina. *The Wounded Self: Writing Illness in Twenty-First-Century German Literature*. Rochester, NY: Camden House, 2018.

Schuder, Werner, ed. *Kürschners Deutscher Literatur-Kalender* 95. Berlin: de Gruyter, 1984.

Scott, Joan. "The Evidence of Experience." *Critical Inquiry* 17, no. 4 (Summer 1991): 773–97. https://www.jstor.org/stable/1343743

Scott, Maria C. *Empathy and the Strangeness of Fiction: Readings in French Realism*. Edinburgh: Edinburgh University Press, 2020.

Sedgwick, Eve Kosofsky. *Epistemology of the Closet*. Berkeley: University of California Press, 2008.

Seeck, Andreas. "Arthur Kronfeld (1886–1941)." In *Personenlexikon der Sexualforschung*, edited by Volkmar Sigusch and Günter Grau. 397–402. Frankfurt am Main: Campus, 2009.

Shildrick, Margrit. *Dangerous Discourses of Disability, Subjectivity and Sexuality*. Basingstoke: Palgrave Macmillan, 2009.

Sigusch, Volkmar. *Geschichte der Sexualwissenschaft*. Frankfurt am Main: Campus-Verlag, 2008.

Simon, Hermann. "N. O. Body – Karl M. Baer." In N. O. Body, *Aus eines Mannes Mädchenjahren*, edited by Hermann Simon, 131–62. Berlin: Hentrich & Hentrich, 2022.

Simon, Hermann. "Wer war N. O. Body?" In N. O. Body, *Aus eines Mannes Mädchen-jahren*, 167–246. Berlin: Edition Hentrich, 1993.

Simon, Hermann. Preface to N. O. Body, *Aus eines Mannes Mädchenjahren*, no continuous pagination. Berlin: Edition Hentrich, 1993 [1907].

Smith, Jill Suzanne. *Berlin Coquette: Prostitution and the New German Woman, 1890–1933*. Ithaca, NY: Cornell University Press, 2013.

Sobchack, Vivian. "A Leg to Stand On: Prosthetics, Metaphor, and Materiality." In *The Prosthetic Impulse: From a Posthuman Present to a Biocultural Future*, edited by Marquard Smith and Joanne Morra, 17–41. Cambridge, MA: MIT Press, 2006.

Spector, Scott. *Violent Sensations: Sex, Crime and Utopia in Vienna and Berlin, 1860–1914*. Chicago: University of Chicago Press, 2016.

Still, Judith. *Derrida and Hospitality: Theory and Practice*. Edinburgh: Edinburgh University Press, 2010.

Stryker, Susan L.. "The Transgender Issue: An Introduction." *GLQ* 4, no. 2 (April 1998): 145–58. https://doi.org/10.1215/10642684-4-2-145

Stryker, Susan L., and Paisley Currah. "General Editors' Introduction." *TSQ* 2, no. 4 (November 2015): 539–43. https://doi.org/10.1215/23289252-3151466

Sulloway, Frank J. "Reassessing Freud's Case Histories: The Social Construction of Psychoanalysis." *Isis* 82, no. 2 (June 1991): 245–75. http://www.jstor.org/stable/234821

Sutton, Katie. *Sex between Body and Mind: Psychoanalysis and Sexology in the German-Speaking World, 1890s–1930s*. Ann Arbor: University of Michigan Press, 2019.

Sutton, Katie. "Sexological Cases and the Prehistory of Transgender Identity Politics in Interwar Germany." In *Case Studies and the Dissemination of Knowledge*, edited by Joy Damousi, Birgit Lang, and Katie Sutton, 85–103. Abingdon: Routledge, 2015.

Sutton, Katie. "Sexology's Photographic Turn: Visualizing Trans Identity in Interwar Germany." *Journal of the History of Sexuality* 27, no. 3 (September 2018): 442–79. https://doi.org/10.7560/JHS27305

Sutton, Katie. "'We Too Deserve a Place in the Sun': The Politics of Transvestite Identity in Weimar Germany." *German Studies Review* 35, no. 2 (May 2012): 335–54. muse.jhu.edu/article/478043

Sykora, Katharina. "Umkleidekabinen des Geschlechts: Sexualmedizinische Fotografie im frühen 20. Jahrhundert." *Fotogeschichte: Beiträge zur Geschichte und Ästhetik der Fotografie* 24, no. 92 (March 2004): 15–30.

Tamagne, Florence. *A History of Homosexuality in Europe*. Vol. 1. New York: Algora, 2004.

Thalmann, Rolf, Rainer Herrn. "Fakten und Überlegungen zur Identität des Buchautors Erich Amborn: *Und dennoch Ja zum Leben*." In *Mitteilungen der Magnus-Hirschfeld-Gesellschaft* 53 (2015): 43-49.

Thorson, Helga. "Masking/Unmasking Identity in Early Twentieth-Century Germany: The Importance of N. O. Body." *Women in German Yearbook: Feminist Studies in German Literature and Culture* 25, no. 1 (2009): 149–73. muse.jhu.edu/article/363361

Tobin, Robert Deam. *Peripheral Desires: The German Discovery of Sex*. Philadelphia: University of Pennsylvania Press, 2015.

Tomlinson, W. Craig. "A Few More Thoughts on Sergei Pankejeff." *American Imago* 76, no. 4 (Winter 2019): 533–42. https://doi.org/10.1353/aim.2019.0039

Vincent, Ben. *Non-binary Genders: Navigating Communities, Identities, and Healthcare.* Bristol: Policy Press, 2020.

Vincent, Ben. *Transgender Health: A Practitioner's Guide to Binary and Non-binary Trans Patient Care.* London: Jessica Kingsley, 2018.

Vipond, Evan. "Becoming Culturally (Un)intelligible: Exploring the Terrain of Trans Life Writing." *a/b: Auto/Biography Studies* 34, no. 1 (December 2019): 19–43. https://doi.org/10.1080/08989575.2019.1542813

Wagner-Egelhaaf, Martina. *Autobiographie.* Stuttgart: Metzler, 2000.

Wagner-Egelhaaf, Martina. "Einleitung: Was Ist Auto(r)fiktion?" In *Auto(r)fiktion: Literarische Verfahren der Selbstkonstruktion*, edited by Martina Wagner-Egelhaaf, 7–21. Bielefeld: Aisthesis, 2013.

Walter, Tilmann. "Das frühe homosexuelle Selbst zwischen Autobiographie und medizinischem Kommentar." *Forum Qualitative Sozialforschung* 6, no. 1 (2005): 1–24.

Warner, Michael. "Publics and Counterpublics." *Public Culture* 14, no. 1 (Winter 2002): 49–90. https://doi.org/10.1215/08992363-14-1-49

Webber, Andrew J. "The Case Study." In *A Concise Companion to Psychoanalysis, Literature, and Culture*, edited by Laura Marcus and Ankhi Mukherjee, 34–48. Oxford: Wiley Blackwell, 2014.

Webber, Andrew J. "Psychoanalysis, Homosexuality and Modernism." In *The Cambridge Companion to Gay and Lesbian Writing*, edited by Hugh Stevens, 34–49. Cambridge: Cambridge University Press, 2011.

Weber, Philippe. *Der Trieb zum Erzählen: Sexualpathologie und Homosexualität, 1852–1914.* Bielefeld: Transcript, 2008.

Webster, Brenda S. "Helene Deutsch: A New Look." *Signs* 10, no. 3 (Spring 1985): 553–71. https://doi.org/10.1086/494160

Weissberg, Liliane. "Patient and Painter: The Careers of Sergius Pankejeff." *American Imago* 69, no. 2 (Summer 2012): 163–84. https://www-jstor-org.uoelibrary.idm.oclc.org/stable/26305016

Weiss-Sussex, Godela. "Confronting Stereotypes: Department Store Novels by German-Jewish Authors, 1916–1925." In *Tales of Commerce and Imagination: Department Stores and Modernity in Film and Literature*, edited by Godela Weiss-Sussex and Ulrike Zitzlsperger, 89–106. Oxford: Peter Lang, 2015.

Wiegman, Robyn, and Elizabeth A. Wilson. "Introduction: Antinormativity's Queer Conventions." *differences* 26, no. 1 (May 2015): 1–25. https://doi.org/10.1215/10407391-2880582

Wilden, Anthony. *System and Structure: Essays in Communication and Exchange.* London: Routledge, 2001 [1972].

Williams, Linda. *Hard Core: Power, Pleasure, and the "Frenzy of the Visible".* Berkeley: University of California Press, 1999.

Williams, Linda. "Porn Studies: Proliferating Pornographies On/Scene: An Introduction." In *Porn Studies*, edited by Linda Williams, 1–24. Durham, NC: Duke University Press, 2004.

Williams, Linda. *Screening Sex.* Durham, NC: Duke University Press, 2008.

Williams, Raymond. "The Magic System." *New Left Review* 1, no. 4 (July–August 1960): 27–32.

Wolff, Charlotte. *Magnus Hirschfeld: A Portrait of a Pioneer in Sexology*. London: Quartet Books, 1986.

Woods, Angela. *The Sublime Object of Psychiatry: Schizophrenia in Clinical and Cultural Theory*. Oxford: Oxford University Press, 2011.

Woods, Roger. "Introduction: The Purposes and Problems of German Life Writing in the Twentieth Century." In *German Life Writing in the Twentieth Century*, edited by Birgit Dahlke, Dennis Tate, and Roger Woods, 1–24. Rochester: Camden House, 2010.

Index

Printed and bound by CPI Group (UK) Ltd, Croydon, CR0 4YY

13/04/2025

14656534-0003